July 1988
Bob Guion

LAST DAYS OF THE THIRD REICH
The Collapse of Nazi Germany, May 1945

Below: one of the most famous
pictures of the fighting for Berlin.
Men of the Red Army storm
across the square in front of the
Reichstag building, 1 May 1945.

JAMES LUCAS

LAST DAYS OF
THE THIRD REICH

The Collapse of Nazi Germany, May 1945

Foreword by the Rt Hon Sir Bernard Braine, DL, MP

WILLIAM MORROW AND COMPANY, INC. *New York*

ILLUSTRATION ACKNOWLEDGMENTS
All Imperial War Museum except the following:
private copyright, 127 (top); US Army Signal Corps, page 99,
111, 157 (bottom), 161 (bottom), 166, 179, 200, 210, 211, 213,
225 (bottom), 226.

Designed by David Gibbons;
maps and diagrams by Anthony A. Evans.

First published in 1986 in the U.K. by Book Club Associates by arrangement with
Arms and Armour Press Limited as *Last Days of the Reich*

Library of Congress Cataloging-in-Publication Data

Lucas, James Sidney.
    Last days of the Third Reich.

    Bibliography: p.
    Includes index.
    1. World War, 1939–1945.   2. World War, 1939–1945—
Germany.   3. Germany—History—1933–1945.   I. Title.
D755.7.L83   1986   943.086   86-16392
ISBN 0-688-06638-0

Printed in the United States of America

2 3 4 5 6 7 8 9 10

CONTENTS

FOREWORD
by the Rt Hon Sir Bernard Braine, DL, MP

This is a book that had to be written. It is concerned not only with the military collapse of Nazi Germany in the spring of 1945, gripping though that story is, and about which a great deal has already been written, but with the unremitting horror and suffering for the defeated in the weeks that followed the end of hostilities, about which the full story has never been told. For the victors the war was over, but for the losers the agony and the killing went on.

James Lucas is an acknowledged authority on the achievements of the German Army in the Second World War. As a soldier himself, he writes vividly about men in battle. One can almost hear the roar of artillery, the chattering of machine-guns, the clatter of tanks, and feel the tension and awfulness of armed conflict. But in this book he also describes how, when the mighty German military machine finally crumbled, broke and surrendered, almost seventy million bewildered and terrified human beings were left 'hopeless, friendless, despoiled and outcast'. It has been a miracle, and indeed a great tribute to the resilience of the German people, that out of the sea of misery Mr Lucas depicts there was to rise a modern democratic state, which in our time has become a model of how free men and women can live together and in peace with their neighbours.

There were of course, others who had been sucked into the maelstrom of war, backed the wrong side, and then found themselves trapped in the collapse. It was to the eternal shame of the victors that in accordance with the Yalta Agreement hundreds of thousands of hapless Soviet citizens who hated Stalin more than Hitler, and Russian exiles who were not Soviet citizens at all, and Yugoslavs who had entered into the war in the first place on the allied side, were forcibly handed over to the Red Army or to Tito's partisans. Those who were not instantly murdered in droves were consigned to the hell of Stalin's prison camps. The fate of those sent back to Tito's Yugoslavia was in some cases even worse.

Years later some of us in Britain determined that the world should know what had happened, and resolved to erect a monument both to the memory of the Victims of Yalta and as a reminder to the rest of us of how thin is the skin of civilisation and how necessary it is for free men and women to protest against inhumanity whenever and wherever it occurs. A public appeal for funds was launched, and on 6 March 1982 I presided at a moving unveiling ceremony in South Kensington. Survivors of the deportations were present, a Russian choir sang, many wept openly. Unknown to me, James Lucas was present. Later he told me that there and then he resolved one day to tell the story of the sufferings, not only of non-Germans, but of the German people themselves, many of whom were driven from their homes, separated from their loved ones, reviled, tortured and killed. This book is the outcome.

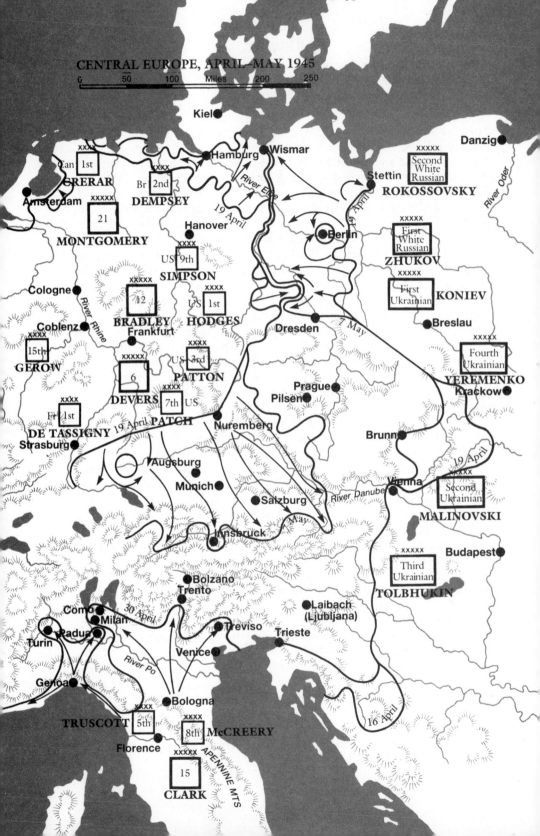

CENTRAL EUROPE, APRIL–MAY 1945

0   50   100   Miles   200   250

PREFACE

This book is the product of memories and of a promise made more than forty years ago. At that time, as a soldier of Eighth Army who had come up out of Italy into Austria, I was stationed near the Wörthersee, the great lake in the province of Carinthia. Now that the war in Europe was over I hoped to enjoy a long and happy period as a member of the army of Occupation, but those first few months in southern Austria were not happy ones and the memories of what I saw there never leave me.

The fields along the Wörthersee were packed with a mass of people in primitive encampments. These hopeless thousands, I discovered, were from a number of European racial groups. These were predominantly Germans, the so-called Volksdeutsche or racial Germans, a term which distinguished them from the Reichsdeutsche or Germans living in Germany proper. The Volksdeutsche in Carinthia had fled from Jugoslavia together with the Slovene and Croat peoples who had abandoned their homelands to avoid persecution by Tito's government. There were also people from other nations in these encampments: Magyars, Cossacks and White Russians. The camps in which they existed were unguarded. Of course they were. Where could those unfortunates go without money, documents, ration cards or employment? Above the camps hung a misama of misery, hopelessness and despair stemming from an awareness of the fate that awaited them all. For the Croats and Slovenes, the Cossacks and the Russians this would be deportation followed by imprisonment or execution at the hands of their racial and political enemies. For the Magyars and the Volksdeutsche, the future held little more than a lifetime spent in camps for displaced persons and refugees.

One of the Germans who had fled Jugoslavia was a girl, Hilde, who, accompanied by her sister had left the family farm near Marburg to reach safety in Carinthia. Before the sisters were allowed to cross the border into Austria Hilde had been subjected to rape by a succession of frontier guards.

Saddened by the suffering and misery that was evident on every side, I promised Hilde that one day I would write of what the common people had endured when their world came to an end as it did when Hitler's Germany was defeated in May 1945. This, then, is the purpose of the book; to tell the story of Europe during the month of Allied victory, from the viewpoint of the ordinary men and women.

The memories of those who survived weeks of battle, and forcible expulsion from their homes highlight the impersonal descriptions of the fighting. The period covered is a short one: from May Day when the Red Army captured Berlin through to 9 May, when the document of capitulation brought the war to its official end. Those two dates, however, are not rigid cut-off points. In order to set the scene it is necessary to detail events which occurred before 1 May and to take the narrative past 9 May, because fighting continued in some areas for more than a week after the official cease-fire.

The text is laid out by Fronts; East, South and West, and each Front is then divided into sectors. Thus the Eastern Front, which crossed a vast area, includes chapters on Kurland, Berlin, Prague and Austria. The southern Front describes events in the Jugoslav and Italian sectors while the Western Front concentrates chiefly upon the fighting around Hamburg and the north of Germany, and Bavaria in the south.

This, then, is the story of quite ordinary people over whom there swept a destructive war and who have not forgotten those events and happenings even though they are four decades removed in time. But the book does not consist entirely of the reminiscences of Germans. The war that touched them touched people of other nations and their stories are also included.

When one corresponds with or interviews people about events which occurred within a single, short time-span, it is inevitable that many of them will have had a common experience. To avoid repetition of that shared experience, personal accounts have in some cases been amalgamated into a single narrative.

The Associations, Institutions and Libraries in a number of national archives such as the Public Record Office, the Institut für Zeitgeschichte, the Heeresgeschichtliches Museum and the Imperial War Museum were very valuable sources of information. To the officers of all those archives I am deeply grateful and in particular to my colleagues in the Imperial War Museum, Terry Charman of the Department of Printed Books, the staff of the Department of Documents and to Rose Gerrard of the Department of Photographs for her expert advice on photographic sources. To all the former soldiers of the German, American and British armies who collaborated go my special thanks as they do to the staff of Arms and Armour Press and to my agents, Sheila Watson and Mandy Little. But it is to my dear wife Traude and to our daughter, Barbara, to whom go my chief thanks for without their unfailing support and help my books could not be written.

INTRODUCTION

Armageddon is a battlefield. The religious believe that upon Armageddon's Field the Forces of Good will contend with those of evil for control of the world. The religious further believe that the battle will result in a victory for Almighty God and out of that battle will come everlasting peace, harmony and happiness.

At the end of the war in Europe in May 1945, it was widely believed that Armageddon had been fought and won on that continent. Those who believed that were not just seekers after signs and wonders, nor even those who had deep religious beliefs. Millions of very ordinary people who may never have heard of the word Armageddon nevertheless believed firmly that in Germany's southern hills and on her northern heaths, evil had been overthrown, that the forces of good had triumphed and that the future promised glorious things.

Hitler's Nazi system was first imposed upon Germany. He then shackled it onto most of Europe and finally sought to inflict it upon the entire world. In the minds of millions it was the most terrible evil that had ever confronted the human race. Even before the Nazis gained power in January 1933, a campaign was being waged against them, expressing that accusation, in the Press, on radio, in films and on the stage. Every medium was used to spread the word that Naziism was an evil creed and the campaign grew more strident and, by repetition, more deeply implanted as Europe edged closer towards war. The outbreak of a second war in just over twenty years, raised the intensity of the campaign to full power and it went into overdrive towards the end of hostilities.

The early victories which grossly expanded Hitler's satanic Empire were followed by reverses on every battle front, a procession of defeats which rolled on and on until by the end of April 1945, the Allies had overrun almost all the Reich territory and were thrusting towards the capital, Berlin, in which city lurked Satan, personified in Adolf Hitler. As the Allied armies swept across Germany there was proof of the evil and corrupt nature of Nazi rule. One concentration camp after another was captured, in some of which the scenes of horror were too much to bear even for battle-hardened soldiers. Each passing day brought new evidence of Nazi brutality and callousness towards those who were considered to be enemies, either for racial, political or social reasons. Sometimes these were not opponents at all, but those who as a result of mental illness or congenital deformity were considered undesirables and who were, therefore, 'liquidated'. The details of this catalogue of shocking misdeeds and bestial horrors rationalized the hate programme which had begun before 1933. In May 1945, after six years of bitter struggle, the evil had been defeated and with optimism in their hearts the peoples of the world looked beyond the great battlefield of Armageddon towards that eternity of peace, prosperity and joy which was the foretold outcome.

Those who thus raised their eyes and their hopes from the scenes of carnage and destruction could not see the German survivors upon whose homeland the battle had been fought as anything other than children of Darkness and possessed of demons. This attitude *vis-à-vis* the German people resulted from a decade of propaganda, and echoes of that attitude persist today. In the minds of many people the terms German and Nazi are still synonymous and inseparable.

This book is less concerned with Allied attitudes than in German people's memories of those events which, more than four decades ago, overwhelmed them. For the Germans the year 1945 was the one in which the heavens fell. The orderly world which they had known was smashed in a fury of battle. The power and pride which they had shared as comrades in the Third Reich were swept away, and the privileges to which, as conquerors, they had become accustomed, were torn from them. On the field of Armageddon, which was Germany in 1945, the fighting ended leaving nearly seventy million people hopeless, friendless, despoiled and outcast. The men, most of whom were prisoners of war, could now be exploited by the Allied victors for slave labour. The women were considered as prostitutes or legitimate victims of vicious sexual aggression. German laws were taken from the people and replaced by military decree under which any overheard criticism that things might have been better in the time of the Third Reich, resulted in prison sentences of unimaginable ferocity. German boys, some as young as twelve were given sentences of life imprisonment by American military courts for carrying out guerrilla warfare. In the Russian zone of occupation summary executions of those partisan 'Wehrwolves' was the norm. All over Germany persecution and tryanny held sway. There were mass evictions set against backgrounds of frightful terror, but these reprisals were being meted out to the Germans – to the children of Satan who were of no account.

The battle of Armageddon had lasted for nearly six years and during its course there had been military operations of great complexity and vast movement. There had been thousandfold examples of outstanding heroism and craven cowardice alike. In the first week of May a stuttering of surrenders led up to that great ceremony of capitulation in Berlin on the 8th. Scrawled signatures on pieces of paper brought the war to an end. Under the terms of the surrender, the fighting was to end at midnight on 9 May 1945, but unofficially fighting continued for many days more as small pockets of German soldiers, serving on what had been the Eastern and Southern Fronts, strove to reach a Fatherland that no longer existed, but which was under the control of the occupying Powers: Russia, America, France and Great Britain.

The official end to hostilities may have halted the marching of the combatant armies, but there were other armies, made up of masses of men, women and children, which crossed and recrossed Germany during those first weeks. The lucky ones were going home. Those western Europeans who had laboured in the factories of Hitler's Third Reich were on the road back to their homelands. Almost spontaneously, they had formed themselves, into national contingents and had set out in disciplined and happy groups. Other marchers were ex-prisoners of war; soldiers from the Western Allied nations who had been liberated after being marched and counter-marched by their captors across the length and breadth of Germany. Now they were marching towards areas in the West from which they would be flown home. All over Europe formations of German soldiers, sailors and airmen were on the march to surrender themselves to uncertain fates in prison camps. Many were convinced, as a result of their own government's propaganda, that as POWs they would slave for decades in the cotton fields of America, in the coal-mines of the United Kingdom or on farms in colonial France. The same propaganda convinced others who were taken by the Red Army that they would never see Germany again. They had prepared themselves, mentally, to be worked to death in the Soviet Union's concentration camps or to be murdered immediately after surrender, for many German soldiers anticipated nothing less than summary execution.

This is not the last beat in the cadence of marching that sounded in Germany in those May days. Together with the surrendering German formations were men of other races who had deserted their own countries to serve with the German Army. For them the outlook was hopeless. They were traitors and could expect only to be treated as such by the governments to whom they were returned. Only a little less harsh was the imprisonment inflicted upon millions of ordinary Russian soldiers and civilians who had been taken prisoner by the Germans. Almost without exception they were sentenced to decades of imprisonment for, in the view of the Soviet authorities, dereliction of duty. According to Communist ethics the soldiers should have fallen in battle and the civilians should have served with the partisans. That these people (and they numbered in excess of two millions) had survived was proof of their guilt. Those who returned to the Soviet Union from German Stalager or from forced labour received no welcome as did the returning soldiers and slave workers of the Western nations, and many of those being returned to the Soviet Union from Germany could measure their life-spans in days or weeks.

The greatest single national group of those who were on the march were the Volksdeutsche – Germans from colonies all over Europe.* Peasants, who had lived as German minorities all over Europe, were driven out of lands which their families had farmed for centuries. There had been a time when the Volksdeutsche lived in harmony with Slavs, Magyars and Roumanians. Now the people of those countries in which they had once settled were driving them out and plundering them, ravaging the women and killing the men who resisted.

---

*Volksdeutsch were members of extensive German communities in other European nations, such as Roumania, Hungary, Czechoslovakia, Jugoslavia, etc., as distinct from Reichsdeutsch, who were German nationals born and living within German territory before the war.

The guns fell silent in Europe on 9 May and their thunder was replaced by weeping as the victims of the war considered the losses, the suffering and the agony that they had experienced during nearly six years of armed conflict. Many of those who wept then weep still; for lost homelands, for those who will never come home again. Misery is the legacy of war and today we are the inheritors of that awful legacy. The prophesied eternity of peace and harmony did not materialize.

In modern history no nation had been reviled as was the Germany of Adolf Hitler and as a result of that campaign of hatred prominent men in civilized countries produced plans to remove from Germany all her factories and to reduce her population in numbers so that it would become a manageable workforce of peasants. Amid the general demand for vengeance were wiser heads with clearer vision who realized that no nation could be held in subjugation for ever and who had begun to plan the reconstruction of German society along democratic lines. They appreciated that there would have to be a military occupation to begin with, but when the time was ripe civilian power would be reinstated. Germany was divided into four zones: French, American, British and Russian. In their separate zones the Powers introduced their own particular standards. The British TUC plan to reshape German Trades Unions along modern lines was so brilliantly successful that it was adopted throughout the whole of western Germany. Parliamentary democracy returned with local elections, and freedom of the Press was introduced by the British Section of the Control Commission for Germany. The US plans considered the eventual reconstruction of German industry and the Soviets introduced State control and workers' militias. Each Zone was a mirror of the nation which occupied it.

The organization of the zones was no *ad hoc* administration, but the implementing of a plan which had been laid out and rehearsed even before the Western Allies had landed in Normandy on D-Day. Immediately behind the armies of the West as they overran the territory and captured the cities of Germany, came officers of the Control Commission with lists and plans to restore and to rebuild. These teams of men and women, most of them fluent in the language of the people whom they were to administer, took up the broken pieces of German life and reassembled them. It was no easy task, but it was one that was undertaken with energy and ability. The Soviets brought in their own teams. These were led by German communists many of whom had been members of parliament in the Reichstag before 1933. With them came those Germans who had accepted that they could continue their careers under a Red Star as effectively as they had under the swastika. The *emigrés* and the opportunists returned with the Red Army, setting up in the Soviet Zone of Germany the sort of government which they had failed to impose upon the German people in 1918.

What is recounted here is a tragedy; the defeat and partition of Germany. It is a tragedy because it furnishes examples of the inhumanity of man to man, both as a matter of personal revenge and as part of an instrument of national policy. But there were also demonstrations of comradeship and loyalty, of courage and of hope. All these positive attributes were present and were evidence that even in adversity the human spirit will triumph and that it does prevail.

PART ONE
THE EASTERN FRONT

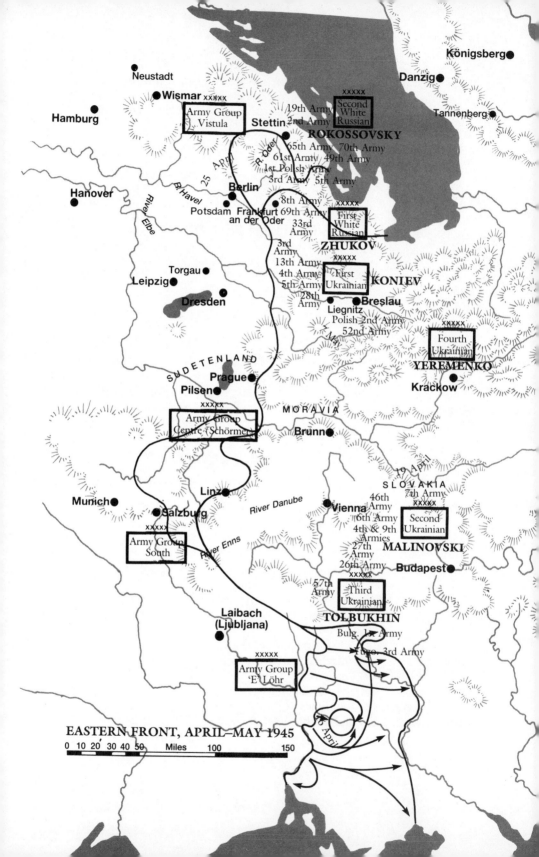

Neustadt

Königsberg

Danzig

Wismar ×××××

Hamburg

Tannenberg

Army Group
Vistula

19th Army
2nd Army

×××××
Second
White
Russian

ROKOSSOVSKY

Stettin

R. Oder

65th Army 70th Army
61st Army 49th Army
1st Polish Army
3rd Army 5th Army

Hanover

25 April

R. Havel

Berlin

8th Army
Potsdam Frankfurt 69th Army
an der Oder 33rd
Army

×××××
First
White
Russian

R. Oder

R. Elbe

ZHUKOV

3rd
Army

×××××
First
Ukrainian

KONIEV

Torgau

13th Army
4th Army
5th Army
28th
Army

Leipzig

Liegnitz

Breslau

Dresden

Polish 2nd Army
52nd Army

×××××
Fourth
Ukrainian

2 May

YEREMENKO

SUDETENLAND

Krackow

Prague

Pilsen

×××××
Army Group
Centre (Schörner)

MORAVIA

Brünn

19 April

Linz

SLOVAKIA

Munich

Salzburg

River Danube

Vienna

46th
Army
7th Army

×××××
Second
Ukrainian

×××××
Army Group
South

River Enns

6th Army
4th & 9th
Armies
27th
Army
26th Army

MALINOVSKI

Budapest

57th
Army

×××××
Third
Ukrainian

Laibach
(Ljubljana)

TOLBUKHIN

Bulg. 1st Army

×××××
Army Group
'E' Löhr

Yugo. 3rd Army

EASTERN FRONT, APRIL–MAY 1945

30 April

0 10 20 30 40 50   Miles   100   150

The Eastern Front was a cancer whose malignance weakened the German Army and ensured its eventual defeat. That bitter war fought between the Germans and the Russians made the Eastern Front the most important of the European theatres of operations. Not only did it have the longest battle line and the one on which the greatest numbers of men and machines were deployed, but it was also the Front on which two implacable enemies, ideologically and racially hostile, fought for the mastery of Europe.

The immensity of the task which the German Army had undertaken was soon apparent and this awareness crushed the spirit of the men who fought there. What caused the sickness of death in the German Army was the realization from the end of 1941 that Russia was a colossus that could not be toppled by military means, and certainly not by a country, like Germany, of limited means. The soldiers did their duty, but they realized the staggering losses which were being suffered, which could never be made good and they compared that knowledge with the realization that the Russians could recoup their own losses many times over.

To see them, the Ivans, rise up from the ground and just stand there, thousands of them, was really frightening. They would stand there, within range of our MGs, silent, withdrawn and not heeding those who fell around them. Then they would move off, the first three lines marching towards us. We soon learnt that behind the first wave there were others, waiting their turn to advance. When the Ivans charged, they would first halt, then close the gaps in their line and then, slowly, a sound would be produced, a long drawn out OOOOOORAH. The sound of that bellowing challenge was enough to freeze the blood. Just the sound alone terrified the new recruits – as it had once terrified us. It was not to be wondered at. There we were hundreds of miles from our homeland, isolated and facing an enemy who would show us no mercy.

And yet the war against Russia, Operation 'Barbarossa', had begun so well. Almost from the first day the pincers of fast-moving panzer groups had encircled whole Soviet armies, attacking and annihilating them. In the first months of 'Barbarossa' millions of Russian soldiers marched into German prisoner-of-war camps. Hundreds of thousands more lay dead on the steppes.

Contrasted against the flexible and dynamic control exercised by the German commanders, the handling of the Red Army by the Supreme Stavka*, seemed old-fashioned and incompetent. When they were faced with a crisis on the battlefield, Soviet commanders fell back upon the only tactic that had proved itself successful in the past. They mounted infantry attacks in which long lines of men marched, shoulder to shoulder, in successive waves. It is a remarkable fact that even in the last days of the war there were situations in which the tactic of the human wave was resorted to. The loss of life was prodigous. The long lines of men melted away in the fire of massed German machine-guns and if that attack failed another was immediately

---

*A Stavka was the command group of a major Red Army formation. Thus, at corps level there was a Stavka and one at every level up to the Supreme Stavka chaired by Stalin.

Above: in anticipation of the coming storm, but much too late, officials of the Nazi Party in East Prussia put the population to work on the construction of a Reichs Defence Line. **Below:** 'Ivan', the Red Army soldier – the man Goebbels's propaganda had made the German people fear. In this photograph, Red Army infantry are fighting their way towards Königsberg.

mounted. Any Russian soldier who turned back from the slaughter, or any units which refused to allow themselves to be butchered, faced the certainty of NKVD firing-squads.

The fighting bravery of the ordinary soldier, together with Russia's most reliable ally, a long and bitter winter, halted the German advance at the outskirts of Moscow, but with the return of campaigning weather in the late spring of 1942, Adolf Hitler ordered Army Group South to open a summer offensive. In that scorching summer of 1942, Germany was at the height of her powers. The whole of continental western Europe had been defeated by her armies or was allied to her through pacts and treaties. Those nations which were still neutral were nevertheless strongly influenced by the Reichs government. The West was safe. In the East the German Army had overrun the vast wheat producing areas of the Ukraine and the industrial complexes of the Don and the Donets. The 1942 summer offensive would gain much more for Germany. One arm of the assault would drive eastwards to the Volga while the other would advance southwards into the Caucasus. Then out of the high mountains, German Gebirgsjäger would descend upon the oil-producing centres around Baku. The success of such an advance would not merely obtain fuel for the German war machine, but would carry the war into a new continent, Asia, and threaten thereby the British military position in the Middle East. There is no doubt that victory was with the Germans during that high summer of 1942.

How cruelly deceptive are the prospects of military victory, how brief the triumph. Within months of the opening of the 1942 offensive, within months of battling towards the glittering prizes of victory, the German Army's reputation as master of the battlefield had been lost. By February 1943, Germany was mourning Sixth Army, which had been destroyed on the banks of the River Volga at Stalingrad. Later, rising above that defeat, a third summer offensive, aimed at smashing the Red Army salient around Kursk, opened on 5 July 1943. It died within days. Thereafter, except for tactical successes the Germans were forced to fight a defensive war by the wave of skilful new commanders who now led the revitalised Red Army.

The realization that they were losing the war, because no victory could ever be gained over the Soviet forces, was felt by the great mass of the German soldiers who saw with despair the growing power of the Red Army. Grenadiers lying in their trenches, subject to hours of bombardment by guns which never lacked for shells; panzer crews fighting in worn-out machines against armadas of Red Army tanks, all were aware of the terrible inferiority of their own army compared to that of their enemy. The strength and power of the German formations was gone and only the Führer could delude himself that those units whose positions he marked on the situation maps in the Berlin bunker were still at full strength. Everyone else knew that they were nothing but burnt-out remnants, undermanned and underarmed. Divisions were generally down to the strength of regiments and Sixth SS Panzer Army still held that title, commented its commander bitterly, because it still had six tanks left on establishment. The artillery formation of the

German Army were reduced to using oxen to tow guns, for there was no fuel for the prime movers. Ammunition was severely rationed, air cover for the ground troops non-existent. At the beginning of the war every Panzer Division had had so many vehicles that when they were tactically deployed each division had covered an area of twelve square miles. Now, the tanks were reduced to a handful of 'runners' and most of the remaining vehicles were drawn by cattle.

There were shortages of everything, but morale remained surprisingly high among the rank and file. The ordinary soldiers needed no propaganda to urge them on. They knew that they were fighting now to defend their own hearths and homes. All that was now left to the soldier was his skill in battle and his courage. Everything else, guns, planes, tanks, had been sacrificed to feed the cancer that was the Eastern Front.

The offensives that brought the Red Army final victory in Europe began during January 1945, when across the width of eastern Europe the might of the Slav empire concentrated on the last great push. By the end of March the Soviet Army was ready for the kill. A line of Russian fronts extending from Finland to Jugoslavia, went into the last battle. One month later, at the end of April, the disposition of these fronts showed that the war was indeed almost at an end. A few German 'fortress' cities were still holding out behind the Russian lines and there was also a strip of land to the west of Königsberg from which German civilians and soldiers were still being evacuated. In Berlin the Red Army was battling with the last few desperate pockets of resistance and within days the Red Flag was to fly over the Reichstag. Russian forces were preparing to thrust into the last, as yet uncaptured regions of Czechoslovakia and Austria, against the fierce, almost fanatical resistance of the German forces in those countries.

The armies of the Western and Eastern Allies met at Torgau on 25 April. Germany was split into a narrow, northern sector and a larger, southern pocket. Then followed even swifter advances and by the end of April the area of Europe that still remained in German hands was reduced to a few shrinking pockets of resistance and those towns which had not yet capitulated. The largest pocket was that on the Eastern Front, covering Bohemia and Moravia – the western regions of Czechoslovakia, and the capital city, Prague, as well as much of Austria, the Jugoslav province of Croatia and the northern regions of Italy. The pocket in the north of Germany extended as a narrow strip, from northern Holland and along the Baltic coast to Stettin. In the last days of the war the pocket on the Eastern Front was reduced to a north/south corridor extending from Bohemia to Marburg in Jugoslavia. The northern one was reduced to a few small pockets; one in northern Holland, one to the south of Denmark and a few others around towns still resisting capture. Eventually, the fighting stopped and at the end of those six years of blood-letting Europe lay prostrate. The single most important factor to emerge from the war was that the *de facto* frontier of the Soviet Union was no longer to the east of Brest Litovsk, but had moved westwards so that it was less than a day's drive from the Rhine.

Above: once the German Army had a great number of Panzer Divisions to combat their enemies; by the late winter of 1944/5, the anti-tank detachments were reduced to individual groups armed with Panzerfaust launchers. **Right:** Cossacks of a Soviet Guards cavalry regiment water their horses in the River Elbe, 26 April 1945.

This resumé of the war on the Eastern Front cannot conclude without reference to the bitterness of the fighting, unmatched by the battles fought in the West. In the first years of their overlordship the Germans had made strenuous efforts to win over to their beliefs the peoples of western Europe who shared the same culture as their conquerors. For the peoples in the East there was no consideration. The National Socialists saw the Slavs as sub-human, fit only for drudgery and exploitation. The war in the East was, therefore, not only a war of armies, but much more a racial conflict in which ruthlessness was a virtue and compassion evidence of weakness. When it is considered what suffering had been inflicted upon the Russian homeland, it is small wonder that when the Russians entered Germany they avenged themselves upon the people of that nation which had treated them so cruelly. Millions of German civilians and soldiers suffered and died because of the racial theories and evil practices of the men of the Third Reich. The deportation of the Volksdeutsche out of eastern Europe, the summary executions of Volkssturm men, the blindings, rapes and murders which were committed were a retribution, a revenge. So widespread and so frequent were the atrocities which the Red Army committed that many Germans believed the story which went round Europe. This was that before a Red Army unit stormed a German village or town, the men were read a hysterical exhortation by Ilya Ehrenburg on what the Germans had done in Russia which concluded with, not so much an incentive to rape and to pillage, as almost a direct and unequivocal order to do so. Such a command was superfluous.

That the men of the Red Army were not always under the firm control of their officers was soon evident and that the Soviet soldiers were capable of excesses soon became frightening common knowledge in the eastern parts of Europe. It was widely reported that women soldiers of the Red Army had, in effect, raped Hungarian men by ordering the Magyar males to have intercourse with them. The activities of Red Army units even in countries such as Poland and Czechoslovakia, which were allies of Russia, were notorious. Stalin in an acknowledgement of the atrocities committed by his soldiers asked Benes, the President of Czechoslovakia, to forgive them, by accepting the concept that soldiers are brutal and licentious creatures. The ageing President may have found it possible; the women, many of whom were pregnant and most of whom were diseased by their rapists, would have found it less easy to be so charitable.

This, then, is the story of the last days of the Second World War on the Eastern Front. It will range from the Baltic coast to Berlin, will describe the situation in Prague as that city waited for liberation and will conclude with an account of the fighting in Steiermark, the eastern province of Austria.

1
THE BALTIC SECTOR: KURLAND

The story of the Eastern Front begins along the Baltic where those few and understrength German corps and divisions that had once formed the mighty Army Group North stood, their backs to the sea, enclosed by the might of the Red Army. A succession of furious Russian assaults had reduced the formerly vast German-held territory and at the end of April that area was restricted to a few small pockets of land surrounding three ports: Libau in Kurland, Pillau in East Prussia and Danzig at the mouth of the Vistula.

They had been the principle objectives of the Red Army in its drive towards the Baltic, for into them came the weapons and men to sustain the German defence, and out from those ports sailed the ships carrying German civilian refugees fleeing the Red terror. The capture of those harbours would force the German military garrisons to surrender and would halt the evacuation of the civilians. The state of the refugees was pitiable for the only way of ensuring a place on the next ship was to queue; to stand, in the open, day and night until the next vessel tied up and embarkation could begin. Attempts to supervise an orderly evacuation through the distribution of embarkation cards collapsed quite early on when refugees rushed the ships in their desperation and scrambled aboard, defying the police to evict them.

The great masses of civilians gathered in each port waited in the cold and rain of early spring, enduring the bombardment of Russian guns, the bombing and machine-gunning by Red Air Force machines which now unchallenged, dominated the skies. Sudden rumours swept the crowds. One was of a very large convoy being assembled at Danzig. Thousands of those in Pillau responded to this rumour and marched at night across the narrow tongue of land between the East Prussian port and the city of Danzig. The sea was frozen along the east Baltic coast and for nearly half a mile from the shore line the ice was thick enough to bear the weight of human beings and their carts. The crowds at the back of the column, fearful because of the slow progress across the land, moved out onto the ice and marched in the dark over the frozen sea. At first light and throughout that day the Red Air Force swept over the long, long column. Bombs broke up the ice, plunging whole groups of refugees into the bitter waters. Those civilians on the ice forced themselves back onto the narrow causeway of land and the entire slow-moving mass waited, as dumb beasts wait in an abattoir, to be slaughtered.

There are no precise figures available. The estimated total of those in the German East who waited to be evacuated is more than seven million. The most determined efforts of the German Navy were not enough to carry off more than a third of that number for each ship lost on the evacuation run reduced the numbers of those who could be rescued – and there were many ships lost. To many came the bitter truth that they would not be evacuated and these moved inland into the towns and villages. There, amid a dread born of rumour, propaganda and, in a few cases, personal experience, they waited for the revenge of the Red Army to be loosed upon them.

———————

The huge, circular memorial at Tannenberg, erected to commemorate the defeat of the Russians during August 1914, stood silent and empty late in January 1945. The bronze coffin containing the remains of Field Marshal Paul von Hindenburg, the victor of the battle, together with the flags and trophies of his victory had already been taken away. The vast memorial stood empty and prepared for destruction. German Army engineers first demolished the towers encircling the central courtyard, then the walls were brought crashing down. This deliberate act had a significance greater than the mere destruction of a now vacant tomb. It was a recognition that Prussia, cradle of German militarism, was to pass under Russian overlordship. Of the destruction of the Tannenberg memorial the ordinary people of Prussia knew little and cared, perhaps, even less. Of more immediate and personal concern to them was that the Party bosses, the several Gauleiter of the Province, had betrayed them. It is, therefore, less the military operations in the northern flank of the Russian Front that hold our attention as the treachery of those leaders who should have, but did not, set an example to their people.

The Soviet winter offensive had begun on 12 January, against a weakening German front where ill-equipped divisions were ordered to hold to the bitter end territory of limited military importance and to counter-attack to recapture it when it was lost. This was a defence without reason and attacks without hope, but obedient to their orders the German divisions fought and bled.

When Fourth Army failed in its attempt to fight its way out of encirclement in East Prussia, Gauleiter Erich Koch* condemned it as a cowardly endeavour to flee into the Reich. Koch's telegram to Hitler, concluded with the heroic but untruthful boast, 'I am defending East Prussia with my Volkssturm.' That the Volkssturm was defending the Gau was certainly true. That Koch was with them was not. He paid lip-service to the belief in final victory, mouthing the slogans, and threatening with execution any whom he considered lacked faith. Secretly, he was preparing to abandon the people. He refused to organize the trek of the civilian population of East Prussia into Germany proper, condemning those who requested evacuation

———

*Erich Koch was Gauleiter of East Prussia and had been one of the chief administrators of the 'Eastern Territories'. In that capacity he was one of the worst murderers in the whole Nazi hierarchy. His political powers as Gauleiter were vast; and in the final stages of the war he became – as did all Gauleiter in threatened areas – a Reichs Defence Commissar with absolute power. Thus, he could overrule any military decision with which he disagreed and order military operations to be initiated. Even if these were lunatic, they had to be obeyed because in the role of Reichs Defence Commissar the Gauleiter spoke with the voice of Hitler.

as cowards and traitors. The civilians were ordered to stay in their towns and villages – and they obeyed orders. East Prussia would not fall, he assured them. It would remain German, he promised them. Hold firm, he demanded. What was needed were iron hearts, steel fists and firm resolve. Convinced by Koch and the Nazi propaganda machine the peasants stayed and suffered for their loyalty. The Red Army had been told that in East Prussia it would be entering the lair of the fascist beast and the Soviet soldiers behaved as though entering the den of a ferocious animal.

And Koch? What of Koch, the denouncer, the leader of the Volkssturm? As Reichs Defence Commissar he should have directed the defence of his Gau. He did not do so. Instead he supervised the loading of two railway wagons with personal possessions and sent them into the Reich. He then dispatched some very special personal property in an armoured truck before being flown to Libau where two icebreakers were waiting to carve a way through to safety for the Gauleiter and his staff.

In the Baltic port of Libau large numbers of civilians waited; people who had fled into East Prussia before the wrath of the Red Army and who, feeling themselves not bound by Koch's 'stand fast' orders, had trekked to the port hoping to be shipped to the west. In the bitter North German winter, with a cold so intense that the sea froze over large areas, the wretched refugees waited for a vessel. There was room in Koch's ship, but he would allow no refugees aboard. So far as he was concerned the Nazi political part of his life was over. Aboard ship he changed his brown Party uniform for Army field grey. The disguise of an officer and the forged papers he carried enabled him to escape arrest until 1949. The British, in whose zone he was caught, handed him over to the authorities in the East for Koch had been one of the most brutal of the German administrators in the Ukraine and in Poland. Surprisingly, he was not condemned to death, a sentence he certainly deserved, but was allowed to live in Communist East Germany. That the Soviets showed such leniency towards this major war criminal is not so remarkable. A large number of men, Müller of the Gestapo and Paulus of Sixth Army, to name just two, were given a plush living in East Germany because they could be of use to the Soviets. Koch was another such – it was the Russian belief that he knew the location of the Amber Room, a Russian art treasure which had disappeared when Koch left the palace in which the room had been fitted.*

Koch was not alone in his treachery. His Deputy Gauleiter had suggested that he might lead the civilian population of Königsberg to safety under the

*This was a room in the palace of Tsarskoe Selo, near Leningrad. The amber areas covered about 80 square metres and were interspersed with mirrors and candelabra. The Amber Room was dismantled on Koch's direct orders and was stored in a castle at Königsberg. It disappeared at the end of the war and has never been found, but it is believed that the crated-up room was on the ship *Wilhelm Gustloff*, which was torpedoed and sunk in the Baltic. Koch, despite being condemned to death for war crimes, was never executed, but is (or was until recently) still alive in East Germany. It is my own belief that the Reds did not execute him because they think he knows the location of the Amber Room and they are hoping to recover it.

cover of a military offensive. This man's own vehicles were ready and an escape route had been planned, but he was killed in the unsuccessful breakout attempt. Königsberg, the capital of East Prussia, finally fell during the second week of April. On that day and for two days after the capitulation the soldiers of the 3rd Belorussian Front released their frustrations and hate upon the Germans who fell into their hands.

'The life of a gunner in an Assault Gun detachment was hard; very hard and we were always in the thickest of the fighting. We were more effective than panzer and more manoeuvrable than conventional artillery. The infantry were always pleased to see us for where we were the enemy made no attack. Just a few SPs were enough to hold him in check. When Königsberg surrendered our CO told us we were not to destroy the guns or the vehicles. Everything had to be handed over to the Ivans in working order. The Reds promised us honourable treatment, food, protection – the usual things. I spent more than four years as a prisoner of the Ivans and was starved, beaten and humiliated. For years after my return I had nightmares about what I had seen in Königsberg. If I told you the half of it you would not believe me. The Ivans were out of the control of their officers and the things they did were ghastly – just blood-lust. But there was also brutality at Command level. I was told that most of the Königsberg Volkssturm men were shot by the Reds as partisans. In some cases tanks were deliberately run over wounded soldiers. The sickening thing

Right: Soviet armour rolling down towards the Frische Haff, east of Danzig, the embarkation zone for German civilians and soldiers being evacuated in the last weeks of the war.

was that the Reds had made our men lay the wounded on the roadway, very carefully lined up. Soldiers and civilians were tied together and set alight. There was nothing, no crime, no bestial act that they did not commit.'

While the last battles for the East Prussian capital were being fought, yet another National Socialist hero was deserting his post. Albert Forster, the braggart Gauleiter of Danzig, abandoned his fellow citizens in a luxury steam yacht. Except for his entourage the ship was empty. Thousands of refugees were in Danzig waiting patiently for ships to evacuate them. Among the vessels was an old ferry boat whose maximum speed was barely eight knots and then only in smooth water. The old ship, overloaded with people and sailing in the winter Baltic sea met difficulties. Heavy seas pounded her and threatened to swamp her. Forster's yacht sailed past the ferry loaded with its cargo of misery, ignoring the German Navy's signals to assist in the rescue. The Navy's patience snapped. One captain sailed his ship as close as he dared to the yacht and ordered her captain to turn about and tow the ferry. Forster appeared and began to browbeat the Naval Commander whose ship pulled away. Forster's glee at such an easy victory changed dramatically and suddenly when he saw the destroyer's guns trained on his ship. The ultimatum was clear. Either the yacht help the refugees or she would be sunk. The ferry was taken in tow until a safe harbour in the west was reached. The

destroyer then returned to the eastern Baltic where evacuation had become a rhythm; a race against time for the ships to be loaded, make the run to the ports of Schleswig-Holstein, disembark the passengers and return again to those freezing quaysides and open beaches where other frightened and huddled people waited and hoped.

Hitler had, of course, refused to permit the evacuation of the military forces from East Prussia, just as he condemned to death or to captivity the Army in Kurland. In one short and abrupt order, 'An evacuation of the troops in Kurland is out of the question', the Führer sealed the fate of the men and the divisions of that northern group. Those men had held their positions for months and by the first week of May had beaten back five Soviet offensives. The General Officer Commanding Army Group Kurland, Hilpert, surrendered his forces on 9 May, and forty-two Generals, more than eight thousand other officers and more than 181,000 rank and file of the Army Group, including the Luftwaffe's 1st Air Fleet, passed into a captivity from which their Commander and a great many of them did not return.

It may be asked what it was that these men of the Kurland army had defended so long and so tenaciously. The answer is that the port of Libau was vital for the supply of the German forces along the Baltic coast. This then begs the question; why were the forces in Kurland not evacuated and the answer is that given by Hitler – 'The evacuation of the Kurland Army is out of the question.' When the fifth Kurland battle ended in January 1945, a plan was produced and laid before Hitler who ordered that the Kurland army stand and fight. An attempt was made to change the Führer's mind by pointing out the burden that would be placed upon the Navy to supply the divisions and corps. The statistics demanded by Hitler showed that only twenty-eight ships were available to carry supplies. He brushed these figures aside and by a single sentence condemned the Kurland army to destruction.

A Strength Return produced at the end of the fifth Kurland battle assessed the Army Group's fighting capacity. This showed that the divisions were bleeding to death and that to produce men for the fighting line Luftwaffe and Navy unit had had to be converted to infantry battalions. Army Group prepared to meet a new Russian offensive. None came. The Red armies investing the Baltic were steadily reduced to bolster the assaults that were going in against Berlin and the other areas of the Eastern Front. The Soviet units surrounding the Kurland army were content to invest the Germans and to wait for the end of the War. There was military action, of course, but it was on a limited scale. The propaganda war increased and daily the little RATA planes flew over the German lines scattering leaflets which showed how deep the Allied armies had penetrated into Germany. All the phases of the battle for Berlin were shown on the Soviet propaganda leaflets and then, on 1 May, as a back-up to the paper war the Red Agitprop teams brought loudspeakers into the front line to announce that with Hitler dead the German soldiers could surrender with honour.

The Führer's death and the succession of Doenitz allowed the evacuation plan to be put into action. The thin trickle of men that had been returned by ship to Germany – the wounded and the specialist detachments – could now become a flood and the Navy would make every effort to lift off the civilians and soldiers from the ports and harbours of the eastern Baltic. But the moment had passed and a rescue operation that might have had a chance of success in late autumn had very little chance with fewer ships, fewer harbours from which to take off the waiting masses. Nevertheless, minesweepers, minelayers, torpedo-boats and trawlers ran a shuttle service to carry the evacuees from isolated Kurland harbours to other ports where they were transferred to larger vessels. But the end of the war was very near and with the capitulation of the Army Group all movement would have to cease. To beat that deadline German convoys assembled in Libau harbour. Every available ship in the eastern Baltic was to be loaded to capacity and would sail for Kiel, Eckenforde and Neustadt, risking the Soviet submarines rather than that the regiments and the civilians should endure captivity in Soviet concentration camps.

During the evening of 8 May several German motor torpedo-boats and five destroyers left the west for Hela to undertake the evacuation of the last patient civilians. With those aboard it was found that there was room for the military wounded. Then space was found for men of a few units. The whole area around Hela was a mass of flames and explosions as the rearguard destroyed what could be destroyed in those last few hours before the capitulation came into force. When there was nothing more that could be done the Colonel of one battalion of Engineers called his men together, thanked them for their loyalty and devotion to duty and then the unit waited in the cold, dark night for the Red Army to arrive.

The evacuation had brought more than two million people out of the eastern provinces of Germany and into the west. It was carried through despite the most appalling loss of life. Early on in the rescue operation one vessel, the *Wilhelm Gustloff*, was sunk by a Russian submarine with a loss of life that has been estimated at 8,000 people. That was the most dramatic disaster, but it will never be known how many other smaller ships and helpless civilians perished in the icy cold waters of the Baltic.

To the everlasting shame of the Swedish nation a large number of German soldiers who thought they had escaped the gulags and the concentration camps of the Soviet Union, were handed over to the Red Army. Many hundreds of thousands of the soldiers of the Eastern Front perished in battle or failed to return to the west, but in the gloom of those days there shone the bright beacon lighted by the German Navy which carried out what was, perhaps, the largest evacuation in history – an operation almost unknown to the peoples of the West.

The Kurland army and that in East Prussia; those forces that had in earlier days been known as Army Group North, achieved one last distinction; they were named in the last communiqué issued by the German High Command.*

*See page 245.

2
THE REICHS CAPITAL: BERLIN

At 05.00 hrs (Moscow time) on 16 April 1945, the guns of the Red armies positioned along the river Oder opened a barrage that was to roll, almost without cessation, until the fall of Berlin. Under cover of this, tanks and infantry poured across the Oder or broke out of bridgeheads already established on the western bank and moved into the attack. Operation 'Berlin' had begun.

Within days the front of Army Group Vistula, covering the German capital, had ruptured. The Ninth Army and the Fourth Panzer Army holding a salient to the west of Frankfurt an der Oder, were outflanked and Army Group Vistula was cut off from Schoerner's Army Group Centre which was holding Czechoslovakia. To the north of Berlin, Third Panzer Army had been driven back to a position north-west of the German capital. Only remnants of the armies that had held the line of the Oder still offered resistance to the advancing Soviet 1st Ukrainian and 1st Belorussian fronts which were racing each other to be first into Berlin.

Contrary to popular belief, the battle for Berlin was a short one, but around that battle has grown up a legend created by both the Germans and the Russians. It is a myth formed out of the unreliable material which was all that was available to historians in the immediate post-war years and projects a picture of an entire city defended street by street, almost house by house. It is a myth of a major metropolis ablaze from end to end; a modern capital in whose ruins the defenders fire Panzerfauste at giant Soviet tanks rumbling through the blackened rubble. Much of this picture is false. The truth is always less dramatic than the fiction.

The Red Army advanced from the Oder with great speed and struck Berlin from several directions. Spearheads drove through the outer suburbs towards the inner city so quickly that in many cases the German defenders were overrun before they could put up any resistance. There were a great many suburbs and districts of Berlin in which there was no fighting; merely an occupation, proclamations and the imposition of new mayors and civic dignitaries. German opposition to the Soviet advances did harden to the point of desperation as battle groups of the Red Army struck prepared and manned defences, and it is from that point onwards, that is to say from about 24/25 April, that the apocalyptic picture of the battle for Berlin becomes real. The inner defence zone in the heart of the city did have to be taken out almost house by house, often room by room, this new damage overlaying that which had been caused to the Government Ministry buildings by the heavy and repeated air raids of the Allied air forces.

The street fighting for the Reichs capital lasted no longer than nine days. On 20 April the first Russian artillery shells fell in the centre of the city. By the 25th assault groups had thrust through the outer suburbs and were striking towards the heart of Berlin. On 2 May, the city was surrendered. Other German cities had held out for weeks and in some cases even for months, yet Berlin fell after what was little more than token resistance. Soviet authors are determined to illustrate the bitterness of the battle and the severe losses which the Red Army suffered. West German writers, for their part, concentrate upon the overwhelming masses of men which the Red Army put into the battle and write, with great emotion, of Germans defending their city and their homes to the last round against an enemy pitiless in conquest. The truth of what actually happened in Berlin lies somewhere between the two extremes. That truth, however, will never be accepted because the myth is set so firmly in folk consciousness as to be ineradicable.

To the Red Army Berlin was the final objective; the true goal. With a strong reliance upon slogans the Soviet authorities described the German capital as 'the lair of the fascist beast' and all the energies of the Red Armed Forces were directed to the capture of that lair and to the destruction of the beast which lived there. It is a surprising fact that the Russians believed the powerhouse of Nazi evil was located in the Reichstag building close by the Brandenburg Gate. Red Army battle orders refer constantly to the importance of capturing that building; the Reichstag, which had no significance except as a reference point. The real 'lair of the Nazi beast' was in the Chancellery, between the Wilhelmstrasse and the Hermann Goering Strasse. Not that the Russians were absolutely certain that Hitler was in fact in Berlin. They assumed that he had left the city and gone southwards to Bavaria and the mountains. Not until quite late in the fighting were they aware of the prize which might be found in the German capital.

Because the fall of Berlin was equated with the destruction of the Nazi system and, therefore, with the end of the war, Russian soldiers felt they had to be first into Berlin, to demonstrate, as they saw it, the Red Army's achievement in single-handedly destroying the fascist hordes. This deep conviction was held by the rank and file, but at Supreme Stavka level there was a fear that Montgomery's army would strike quickly across the North German plain and seize the German capital before the Red Army could reach it. The political and military leaders of the Soviet Union were determined to prevent this because if the Allies took Berlin the implementing of the Russian plan for a Communist empire in Eastern Europe would be delayed and might, indeed, even be stopped. Stalin and his inner circle were determined to impose their will and decided to work at two levels. Militarily, they would force the pace of the Red Army's assault on the German capital with utter disregard for the losses which this would entail, and politically, they would apply pressure upon the Anglo-Americans so as to halt the thrust of the Allied armies towards the German capital.

On 1 April Supreme Stavka produced a timetable. It ordered that a blocking force be aligned along the Elbe river within a fortnight of the opening of the Red Army's Berlin operation. Thus, when the British and Americans reached the river they would find the Russians lining its banks and the Allies would have no justification for crossing the Elbe to continue their advance upon Berlin. The democracies would be forced to leave the capture of the city to the Russians who would, by that time, be deeply committed inside it. The most important factor, so far as Stavka was concerned, was to halt the eastward advance of the Western Powers.

Two Red Army Fronts would be directly involved in the battle for Berlin, with a third in a supporting role. Zhukov's 1st Belorussian and Koniev's 1st Ukrainian Fronts would make up the strike force, with Rokossovsky's 2nd Belorussian Front serving to guard Zhukov's northern flank and forming the right-hand claw of a great pincer movement. In the Stavka plan, the central mass of Koniev's Front was to pass to the south of Berlin and once it had passed the city the individual armies of this central Command were to strike north-westwards to the Elbe, thus forming the left-hand pincer. Only Koniev's right-flank army would collaborate in the capture of the city. Zhukov's battle plan was for three of his armies – 3rd Shock, 5th Shock and 8th Guards – to make the direct assault on the city and while his infantry force was driving into Berlin an armoured force made up of 1st and 2nd Guards Tank Armies would pass on each side of the city in an inner pincer movement.

The Stavka directive insisted that Koniev's main thrust be maintained westwards towards the Elbe and that any temptation to strike south was to be resisted. Berlin was the first priority; Prague would come later. For his part, Hitler had not assessed correctly the Soviet intention, for he had anticipated that the Stavka priority would be Prague–Berlin, and to block the Red Army's drive on the Czech capital he had moved down into the competence of Army Group Centre a great mass of the German Army's remaining armour. Thus when the Russian attack came in from the Oder to take Berlin it was made against a German Eastern Front whose forces were incorrectly deployed to meet it, with the armour in the hills of Bohemia and a mainly infantry force facing the Red Army's tank armadas, along the river.

When considering the problem of taking out Berlin, Stavka appreciated that so great an area; such a complexity of streets and buildings, of waterways and canals, could swallow up and dissipate the strength of an attacking army. The Russians had seen this happen to the German Sixth Army which they destroyed at Stalingrad, and Stavka had no intention of being drawn into a long, involved battle in a pit called Berlin. They decided that the city must be taken in a hard-hitting, uncompromising, all-out drive. To achieve this it was obvious that the great mass of men and material should not be employed in conventional assaults; too many units working within the restricted space would be dangerously unproductive. Instead, specially chosen assault groups drawn from veteran infantry units would be supported by armour and backed by massed artillery which would, quite literally, lay a red-hot path of destruction. Zhukov's artillery in the assault sectors had a density exceeding 450 guns per mile of front, and the most efficient and numerous artillery weapon in the arsenal of the Red Army was the Katyusha. This was a rocket launcher, a light and mobile recoilless projector, which did not need the elaborate, setting-up procedure of conventional field artillery, but which could be fired from almost any position. It was reported that during the fighting many were dismantled and carried into first-floor apartments to engage particularly difficult targets. Katyushas were the great feature of the battle for Berlin and the memory of the sound they made is an enduring one in the minds of our correspondents.

The news that the Red Army had burst out of the Oder river bridgeheads and that its divisions were driving onto the capital produced in Hitler the belief that he could destroy the Soviets at the gates of Berlin. In view of the actual military situation such a faith was pure fantasy. On the northern wing of the Eastern Front where once the powerful Army Group North had been located in the golden years of victory, there stood now, in the bitter days of defeat, a German force, Army Group Vistula, whose front had been torn apart by the Russian offensive. This Army Group had fragmented into disconnected groups: Third Panzer Army, Fourth Panzer Army and Ninth Army, understrength formations which were moved about at the orders of a Supreme Commander so out of touch with reality that he thought them to be at full strength and at the height of their powers.

The Red Army's swift drive into Berlin, together with other political factors, determined Hitler to remain in Berlin and fight. When the announcement came that Himmler had betrayed him by undertaking peace negotiations with the Swedish Count Bernadotte, Hitler decided to die in Berlin, by suicide. The senior military officers of OKW had already left the city and within the Führer bunker in the Reichschancellery building, Hitler considered the battle for his capital. Little did he realize that the city was indefensible. His troops were insufficient in numbers and matériel, and Berlin was a metropolis with a civil population of about four millions, for whose protection nothing had been prepared.

The organization of the defence of Berlin was an unbelievable mess. In the neuroses of the days following the unsuccessful assassination attempt nine months earlier, no one had dared to suggest to Hitler that the Russians might one day capture the city. Such a thought would have been taken to be a criticism of the Führer's conduct of the War; a defeatist thought, the utterance of which would be high treason. Lacking the courage to tell Hitler the truth; to make him understand the danger to Germany, his inner circle had fed him with lies and falsifications and in deluding him they deluded themselves. The scheme that was finally produced, planned for the city to be surrounded by a series of defensive rings, the one farthest removed from the capital merging with the defences of the River Oder. Closer to the city there was to be a first defence zone which corresponded to Berlin's territorial limits. Behind this was a second which included a 20-mile stretch of the elevated railway; a natural defensive position. This second zone was divided into battle sectors each of which was given an identifying letter. The letter 'Z' (*Zitadelle*) was given to the innermost defence or Citadel zone, within which were the principal government ministries, the Reichstag building and the Chancellery.

The military command structure of the defence was in just as chaotic a condition. There had been a succession of battle commanders, but the man who finally surrendered the city is the officer who will figure in our story; Artillery General Weidling, commanding 56th Panzer Corps. He, together with what remained of his Corps, had been pulled back into the city on Hitler's express orders to run the defence. Weidling had assumed, quite naturally, that as Battle Commandant of Berlin he was in command. He was mistaken. Hitler had given authority to fight a total war to his political officers. The Gauleiter (District Governors) were given the title of Defence Commissar and as such had unlimited authority, even over the local military commanders. The Gauleiter of Berlin was Josef Goebbels who had never been a soldier; his club foot had excused him from military service, but now, in April 1945, at Hitler's decree, he was the supreme civil and military authority in a city of four million people.

Goebbels had shown a naivety when considering the city of which he was Gauleiter, a naivety which was out of keeping with his acknowledged flair and brilliance. He refused to allow the evacuation of women and children – some had left because of the Allied air raids, but the majority had stayed behind and to their numbers were added the thousands who had fled into the city from Germany's eastern provinces. The city was swollen with people for whose feeding no proper plans had been prepared and for whom no shelters except the Flak towers existed. These were huge, concrete structures, really fortresses in miniature, each with its own electricity and water supply, and fitted with anti-aircraft guns which were used in an anti-tank role during the battle. As a result the towers were under frequent and heavy attack from Russian artillery and the Red Air Force, and it was as well that the walls were thick for within them sheltered a great number of bombed-out and homeless people. During the fighting the towers were also used as hospitals – perhaps because they had both power and water and were bomb-proof.

Berlin was unprepared probably because Goebbels intended to carry out his dire threat that if the Nazis went down they would drag with them the rest of the world in flames. It may be that he intended that the civilians of Berlin should suffer and perish in a *Götterdämmerung*, for such an end was very much in his nihilist nature. But even had he wanted to defend Berlin there was little he could have done without the help and co-operation of Gauleiter Stürtz, regional governor of Brandenburg, and Goebbels and Stürtz were bitter enemies. Any request from Goebbels for labour to help build the city defences or to dig anti-tank ditches was ignored. A direct order from the Berlin Gauleiter was met with bureaucratic pedantry. And these were the men charged with conducting an all-out war against a well-armed, ruthless enemy, superior in numbers and weapons. Then, interfering in this confusion came Hitler, the self-styled 'greatest military genius that the world has ever known'. And he issued military orders, too. To those who could understand what was happening the prospect of three commanders issuing conflicting orders for military actions in an indefensible city that had too few troops, guns or matériel, must have been horrifying. To many it must have seemed that there was a death wish on the part of those in charge of the destiny of Germany.

It is not possible to determine with complete accuracy how strong were the German units on the Eastern Front between Stettin and the Czech frontier; that is the force which made up Army Group Vistula. Not one of the units was at full strength nor had any of the component armies any reserves worth mentioning. Against a Russian Force numbering perhaps three million, the German Army Group could put up perhaps 320,000. In numbers of tanks and aircraft the imbalance was even more marked and was about 20 to 1. According to Schultz-Naumann, in his book *Die Letzten Dreissig Tage*, the military forces defending the capital were few. He lists them as being a mixture of fixed artillery and Flak, of 'alarm' units, reinforcement detachments, army schools, factory guards, local militia, the postal defence units, locally raised anti-tank groups, Waffen SS and Allgemeine SS formations, the Volkssturm and the Hitler Youth.

There was no large infantry force within the city except the Berlin Wach Regiment, which was part of the Grossdeutschland Panzer Korps, and Mohnke's Battle Group, of about one thousand SS men, whose task it was to defend the Chancellery. The remainder of the infantry forces, and I refer here only to active units, was made up of pupils from military schools, regimental depot staffs, convalescent soldiers and men on leave. Groups of these were formed into so-called 'Alarm Units' that had no experience of fighting together and were therefore, of doubtful military value. Then there were the units of General Weidling's 56th Panzer Corps which had been taken onto the garrison strength on the Führer's orders. Of the units of that Corps, only the understrength SS Division 'Nordland' and the equally weak 18th Panzer Division can be described as being operational. Neither the 20th Panzer Grenadier Division nor Mommert's 'Munchberg' Division, both on the Panzer Corps establishment, was capable of holding the Line, and 9th Fallschirmjäger Division, another component of the corps, had suffered heavily in the fighting along the River Oder. Thrown into battle before it had been completely raised, it had been smashed and now its remnants were in Berlin.

The other groups in Schultz-Naumann's catalogue of units in Berlin were more or less useless in the military sense. Of the least value were those units known as 'Landesschützen' made up of old men long past military age who could not be used on active service, but who were put to guarding depots and bridges. The Landesschützen were armed with obsolete foreign rifles for which no ammunition was available. Of only slightly more use were the replacement and reinforcement groups, while the postal defence units and the police detachments were quite good although poorly armed. Of the two principal non-regular military formations, the Volkssturm was a force whose

Above: the dream of a warrior's life – young men of the Hitler Youth, accompanied by their instructor, a highly decorated NCO, take part in a parade before being committed to battle. **Below:** what the warrior in the German Army really looked like – men of an assault group formed in the last days of the war.

value it is difficult to assess. Some Volkssturm battalions gave up after only minimal opposition while others fought with heroism as great as that of the Hitler Youth. The HJ as it was known was made up of children up to about 16 years of age. Few of them could remember a time before Hitler and it was to the Führer that they had sworn allegiance – to the death. For most of them if was exactly that. Armed chiefly with the single-shot Panzerfaust rocket launchers, these children waited until the Russian tanks were almost upon them before firing their projectiles. One of the more accurate elements of the story of the battle for Berlin is the role of the young boys of the HJ in the defence of their city. It was a crime that children should have had to be used – abused is perhaps the better word – in such a way, and the crime must be laid at the door of Hitler and his associates.

In artillery the defence was forced to rely on a gallimaufrey of guns of which the great majority were of foreign make and for which there were usually fewer than 30 rounds per barrel. In addition this artillery force was totally immobile. There was no fuel for prime movers to tow the guns nor were any horses available. The backbone of the artillery defence was 1st Flak Division whose four regiments had defended the city against allied air attacks, but who proved equally adept in fighting the Soviet armour in a ground role. It should also be added that the three principal ammunition depots from which the Berlin artillery was supplied fell quickly into the hands of the enemy. Appeals from Weidling for ammunition to be air-dropped resulted in a few missions being flown by the Luftwaffe and the total amount brought in amounted to about eight hundred rounds per barrel.

Subsequent examination of the Red Army's Berlin Operation shows it to have been less swift and decisive, given the imbalance of forces, than a first glance might indicate. The Red Army used their most experienced troops and rotated them quickly. Units would capture their objective and then hand over to a fresh group with a new target to achieve. There was, thus, a constant renewal of front-line units on the Russian side. For the German soldiers it was a matter of carrying on hour after hour, day after day, without relief, because there were no other troops to replace them.

The speed and efficiency of the Red Army in constructing battle groups by now equalled that of the German Army, and for the direct assault on Berlin their combat detachments were made up of skilled veterans. The following report by an Engineer officer was written upon his return to the German lines after a short period of captivity. He was taken prisoner along the Oder.

'The composition of a Red Army assault detachment is made up of soldiers who are disciplined and totally under the control of the regimental officers. I experienced no brutality from them although they did carry out the usual taking of personal possessions. The morale of those soldiers, many of them of non-European races, is excellent and their tactical skill of a very high order. We prisoners were given food and drink upon request. There seemed to be almost a daily norm for fighting. The 'day shift' would leave at about 7 in the morning and would return at about 6 in

the evening. The second shift which had arrived in the camp about 9 in the morning and whose members slept all day, would then leave. It was a two-shift system and it seemed to be effective.

During our second day support waves of infantry came through the positions in which we were being held. The soldiers of this wave can only be described as an armed and dangerous rabble. When they saw that we were prisoners they tried to rob us. Only the prompt intervention of our guards prevented this. The support troops burned houses and destroyed furniture merely, or so it seemed, out of viciousness. We all heard women screaming and volleys of shots being fired from close at hand, and could imagine what was occurring, but were, of course, powerless to intervene . . . The second wave travelled in a mass of Panjewagen (a peasant cart drawn by one horse) crammed full with booty including livestock. Other cattle and sheep accompanied the march of the second wave. It was almost like a scene from the Middle Ages – a migration, no less . . . In the morning of the fifth day of our captivity a panzer unit broke out of the woods . . . and released us.'

Waves of fresh Russian tanks crunched through the Berlin rubble, flaming, bombarding and machine-gunning the defenders, crushing them into the rubble. Where resistance was particularly determined the whole area was saturated with Katyusha rocket fire if necessary for hour after hour and then the tanks would go in to take out the first dazed survivors with fire and high explosive. Over Berlin the RAF and the USAAF no longer flew. The sky was now filled with Russian aircraft bombing and strafing in close-support operations. The defenders of Berlin and the civilians suffered bombardment from the ground and from the air. Stavka knew the strength of its own forces and could assess with a high degree of accuracy that of the Berlin defenders. It had not been expected that the advance would be so slow, and nagging by senior commanders at the tardy progress of their forces produced an interesting insight into that factor which bedevils those who write official histories – morale.

For the Red Army Berlin meant the end of the War. With the Reichstag captured it would be all over and Ivan could go home with the fascist loot he had accumulated. Contemporary accounts report the keenness of the young Communist soldiers to plant the Red Flag over buildings in Berlin and many of them may have been that keen, but it is more likely that there existed in the Red Army the same 'why me?' syndrome as existed in the Allied armies. There is a law of diminishing returns in front-line units. Those which are the most efficient are selected time and again to carry out dangerous tasks. Eventually they resent the reputation which they have gained; it brings with it only death and hard fighting. A cartoon by the military artist Bill Maudlin expressed this feeling. The picture shows two tired US infantrymen looking at a small Italian town. The caption reads 'This will be one helluva place to take, Willy. The CO says that our Company has the honour of liberating it.'

In Normandy, it was learned with some shock, that veteran British Divisions which had fought in the desert, in Sicily and in Italy had lost the aggressive edge which had been theirs in earlier campaigns. The rationale of the men was a simple one 'We've done our bit. Let some other buggers do theirs.' For a great many years it was supposed that the peculiar and sinister system of informers within the ranks of the Red Army as well as the brutal discipline under which its soldiers suffered, might have repressed the feelings of 'why me?'. It now seems that the same attitude of mind affected Ivan just as much as it did the Tommy or the GI Joe. Even the Soviet battle commanders at intermediate Command level appreciated that the men were fighting without their customary élan and were courageous enough to defend this caution in the face of condemnation by superior officers.

On the German side, one did not have to be a military genius to know that Germany was losing the war. Now in April 1945 the end was very near. The hopes buoyed up by stories of wonder weapons must have been cast down when these failed to appear, so in place of the V weapons there was now a new rumour of a miracle; one which was believed in from the Führer bunker to the front-line slit trenches.

This was the belief that the capitalistic Western Allies must inevitably clash with communist Russia and that this clash would occur in Germany when both armies met. This account of the Eastern Front will go on to show that even very senior officers believed this. Some even accepted that an alliance between the Anglo-Americans and the Germans against the Russians had been accomplished and that very soon the Western Allies and Germany would march together against the Soviet Union. This delusion was widespread nationally, and the German people pinned their hopes and offered their lives believing this alliance to be imminent.

Until the Tommies and the Amis came into the line it was simply a matter of holding out, killing the enemy and seeking to avoid being killed. Of course, the Allies would have to hurry – supplies of even the most basic military equipment were running low. There were too few panzer, too few aircraft, not enough petrol to fuel them, and the guns of the artillery were falling silent for lack of ammunition. Dependent upon miracles, the Germans lost the battle for Berlin even before the first shells from Zhukov's guns had fallen in the city. Dreams, hopes and beliefs do not of themselves stop tanks, deflect bullets or extinguish flame-throwers. The Germans gambled on a miracle. The Russians relied upon the Red Army.

In Berlin morale, already poor, must have diminished as day by day fresh waves of Soviet armour and new Red Army assault squads pushed forward covered by the screaming Katyusha shells and the shattering detonations of their explosions. Within the Führer bunker there was reliance upon another miracle; that the German armies fighting outside Berlin could combine, as the Führer had commanded and would smash the ring which the Red Army was throwing around Berlin. In the north a hastily cobbled collection of troops, called Army Group Steiner, had been ordered to strike southwards and cut off the armoured spearheads of Rokossovsky's and Zhukov's forces. To the south-west, Wenck's Twelfth Army, which had been fighting against the Americans, was to reverse its front and to engage Koniev's troops. To aid Wenck's drive, Busse's Ninth Army was to move from its positions to the

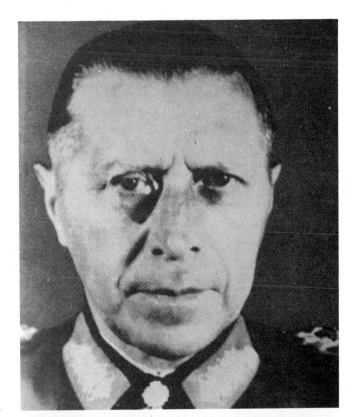

Right: General Weidling, Battle Commandant of the Berlin area, whose orders were frequently countermanded by Hitler or by Goebbels, the Gauleiter of Berlin.

Right: General Wenck, whose Twelfth Army was ordered to cooperate in the drive to smash the Red Army around Berlin.

south-east of Berlin, and join Wenck. The union of these two armies would provide enough strength to raise the siege.

Had those armies been fresh, at full strength and had air cover, they might well have carried out the task. As it was, they were overtired and understrength and, therefore, powerless to help their Führer. The armies of Wenck and Busse did not link up and their individual northward thrusts lacked the power even to hold their gained positions. Hitler had thought himself to be commanding armies of the strength of 1941. It was a delusion. This is not to say that on the German side there were no successes scored, no victories gained. An Army fighting for and on its homeland, and equipped with combat skills gained during four years of fighting has abilities which produce victories. And there were some achieved which, although only tactical, nevertheless had the power to cause panic among local Soviet commanders and a certain consternation at military levels up to Corps Commander.

The story of the day to day fighting for Berlin lies outside the scope of this book, but the foregoing pages will have set the scene for the final act. Before we go on to that ending let us see again the images that are associated with the term, battle for Berlin. These are, on the German side, a young boy in a dusty Hitler Youth uniform firing his Panzerfaust from behind a pile of rubble. On the Russian side it is a small group of Red Army infantry struggling to raise the Red Flag over a Nazi stronghold.

We are not dealing with the day to day battle, but since we must select some point in time at which to begin the narrative proper, let us select 29 April. The mental images which represent the phrase, battle for Berlin, had by that day become vividly true. The Red Army noose is drawn tight around the inner defence zone 'Zitadelle' – and Soviet infantrymen are less than five hundred yards from their final objective, the Reichstag building and the Chancellery.

The city's streets are rubble-filled ruins, yet from behind shattered walls and from ruined cellars the defenders, crowded together now because of the smallness of the area they are holding, are fighting the last battle. The entire area is covered with smoke. It is a gloriously sunny day, but the tired, red-eyed defenders and the confident, thrusting attackers see nothing of sunlight. Theirs is an opaque world of choking sulphur-coloured murk through which targets are only dimly seen. The attackers cannot see the defenders until a rocket's fiery tail betrays the position from which the Panzerfaust has been fired. Then a hurricane of fire pours onto the hiding-place. The red-and-yellow plumes of fire projected from flame-throwing tanks saturate the area. Showers of grenades explode and slowly an armoured fighting vehicle noses its way forward. In a shattered window a figure stands up, aims and fires. The Russian tank begins to burn, but the man silhouetted in the shattered window does not see his victory. He is already dead; blown apart by the shell fired by a follow-up tank. The dead man and the crew of the tank will be mere statistics, in the story of the battle for Berlin.

There was an almost surrealistic quality to life in the last days of the fighting of this communal nightmare shared by hundreds of thousands of soldiers and civilians, Germans and foreigners alike. In some streets soldiers fought bitterly alongside lines of women queuing patiently in front of food shops for something to take home and cook. There were other queues at stand pipes waiting to fill any sort of container with water, for the rumour was that the mains had been damaged in the fighting and would soon run dry. Those areas of Berlin in which the fighting was concentrated were overhung with dense clouds of smoke as houses blazed, out of control.

Dimly through the murk the queuing women might see a tank loom up, pass and then disappear into the smother, its great gun firing at some target shrouded in the fog. At times the screaming noise of Katyusha rockets, blocked out all other sound, but the women only pressed closer to the house walls and waited. A position in the queue was too important to be lost by seeking cover from high explosives. If this sang froid seems improbable, it must be remembered that Berlin had been the target for the British and American Air Forces' massive and destructive bombing campaign. Fire and sudden death had become the standard feature for the Berliners whose reflexes were so sharp that they could determine from which direction shells and bombs were coming, where these would fall and at what distance. Only when machine-gun fire swept above their heads did the queuers move away and then only into nearby doorways or cellars where each waited with eyes fixed on the doorway of the shop ready to rush forward when it opened.

Right: a picture that summarizes the Battle for Berlin – a teenage boy and a pensioner, with a single-shot Panzerfaust rocket launcher, ready to combat the tank armadas of the Red Army.

Above: a street scene in Berlin after the fighting for one of the bridges across the Spree. **Left:** Berlin women in the streets of the city watch in despair as tanks of the Red Army move towards the city centre.

Consider this horrifying picture. Clouds of dense smoke rising from one side of a street of damaged houses where stands a line of elderly women, dressed soberly and wearing hats, and all with their shopping bags, ignoring the noise and the danger. Along the street roar armoured fighting vehicles advancing to give battle. Soldiers are moving warily, dodging from doorway to doorway, flinging grenades into windows. Some are using Panzerfaust against enemy armour. Others are setting up an anti-tank gun on the cobbles and will fire off a round or two before limbering up and pulling out again. Neither of the groups we are observing seems to be aware of the other; each inhabits a different world. Each group has its own priorities. That for the women is to obtain food so that life may go on. The priority for the soldiers is to destroy the enemy. This is one part of the surrealistic picture which is Berlin in May 1945. There is another; below street level in the Führer bunker of the Chancellery. While in the streets of the upper world the noise and sights of battle are both plain and visible, down in the Führer bunker there is little to indicate the fury that is raging overhead. The chief sound in the bunker comes from the generators which supply lighting and run the air extractors. Shells exploding in the upper world are heard in that nether world as just dull thuds. For those in the bunker there is no realization of time. The hands of a watch may indicate that the hour is 2, but whether 2 in the morning or in the afternoon is of little significance. Life goes on with afternoon tea being served during what passes for afternoon. The atmosphere surrounding those trapped in the Chancellery bunker is, of course, tense but this tension is not that of the streetworld; fear of sudden death or mutilation. It is rather more the frustrated fury of commanders who feel that their troops are failing them. The German armies which Hitler has ordered to attack and smash the Russian ring around the city are held miles from their objectives and are fighting for their own existence. So far as their commanders – Wenck, Busse and Steiner – are concerned, their armies can not relieve Berlin for they have neither men, armour or aircraft in sufficient numbers to blast a route into the capital. The city is doomed and will fall. There is a simple solution. The Führer must revoke his declared intent of fighting for Berlin and break out, leaving behind a rearguard which will surrender and save the city from total destruction.

In the bunkerworld there was no idea that the fighting was now only half a mile away, nor were the people of that world aware that the rescuing armies had been halted. Out of touch with reality, they waited for the relieving forces to arrive. Instead, there came instead like blows upon a coffin the announcements of one disaster after another. Mussolini had been murdered and his butchered body, together with those of his companions, had been grotesquely hanged as a spectacle for the mob. Then came the news that the German armies in Italy had capitulated and this was followed by the radio announcement that Heinrich Himmler, acting through an intermediary, Count Bernadotte, had asked the Western Powers for peace. It may be that this treachery of the SS, of 'der treue Heinrich', (the faithful Henry) was the final blow to Hitler's hopes. Certainly from that time on the Führer determined on his suicide and agonized on to whom he should pass the succession. It could not be Goering, for he had proved himself a traitor. Nor could it be Himmler for the same reason. There remained in favour only those around him and those prominent Service chiefs who had not been tarnished by complicity in the bomb plot of July 1944. From those few men the choice would have to be made. It was a remarkable self-deception on the part of Hitler and his subordinates to think that those who would inherit the Nazi offices could ever be accepted as a legitimate German government by the victorious Allies. Hitler spent much of his last day on earth considering to whom the senior posts in the next government should be offered.

Admiral Doenitz in Flensburg was to be the new Head of State. Josef Goebbels, erstwhile Minister for Propaganda, to be Chancellor; Dr Seyss-Inquart was to become Minister for Internal Affairs and Martin Bormann was named as Foreign Minister. Were the situation in Germany not so tragic this Cabinet shuffling would have been farcical. A State with only days to live had nominated one man as Minister for Internal Affairs and another to be Foreign Secretary. What part of Germany would Seyss-Inquart control? What foreign policy could Martin Bormann initiate in a Germany cut off from the outside world? It was madness.

While in the claustrophobic atmosphere of the bunkerworld the entrapped leaders of the National Socialist system sat devising schemes and operations which could have no outcome and, while in the areas around the heart of the city there was bitter fighting, in other parts of the city for some civilians the war was over.

'We sheltered in the air raid cellar of our house when the fighting came very close. It would, I suppose, have been on 2 May, when we heard a series of thundering crashes which came nearer and nearer. One young boy in our cellar was brave enough to look out. He told us that two Russian tanks and a lot of soldiers on foot were coming and that the tanks were firing into the houses as they moved up the street. One tank was firing at the houses on the left. The boy suddenly jumped down from the slit through which he had been looking and almost immediately our house was struck by a shell. In North Berlin, where my mother lived, the Russian tanks fired shot after shot into the lower stories of her block of flats until the whole building came crashing down.

The noise moved past us. The sound of the firing grew less and less loud. We all sat quite still. Hunched up for lack of space and with only a flickering Hindenburg lamp to lighten the darkness. Each of us had our own thoughts. Mine were of my husband who was a sailor somewhere near Schleswig-Holstein. At least he would be safe now that the war was over. He was in the West and his job was with Signals so he would not be in the front line.

We all sat silent waiting, wondering and fearful. Very soon the Red Army would be here. Suddenly the door was pushed open and in the doorway was the silhouette of a man. Then another and another. Two pocket torches were switched

Left: a Russian heavy mortar team in action in a shop in the Alexander Platz, Berlin.

on and their beam passed from one face to another in the cellar. "Alles Kaput", shouted one of the silhouettes, "Komm", and we made our painful way up the shelter stairs and into daylight. There they stood, the soldiers who had come into our cellar, laughing and shouting. "Alles Kaput". They looked about sixteen years old. The Ivans had arrived.'

On 29 April it became clear to Hitler that the end was very close. Late in the evening General Weidling reported that the supply of ammunition and rations had failed. The air drops had produced only six tons of supplies including just 20 Panzerfauste. The General declared the situation to be a hopeless one which led to the inescapable conclusion that the city would fall to the Russians on the next day. This sombre assessment spoke the truth and Hitler must have realized it for he rejected Weidling's suggestion to break out in some of the few remaining armoured fighting vehicles. Then came the news, relayed through a third source for efficient communications had long since ceased, that the armies seeking to raise the siege could not achieve this.

The Führer's mind turned towards his own end. Little remained to be done. He had married Eva Braun and had dictated his last Will and Testament, copies of which were to be taken out of Berlin by reliable messengers. Orders were given for the following day, but no mention was made of any plan for a mass breakout from the city. Everyone had to remain at his post until the last bullet or shell had been fired.

Only hundreds of yards away from the bunker, Red Army infantry from two Divisions, 150th and 171st, prepared to make the final assault upon the Reichstag building. Into the most forward positions were brought special red flags to be hoisted over the last objectives so as to signal final victory. The idea of planting flags was not merely a good psychological move. It had a more practical purpose for where those recognizable flags stood marked the front line, the farthest point which the Red Army had reached. It was not peculiar to the Russians; the Germans had done the same during their successful advances.

But in Berlin the presentation of special banners had a strong political overtone. The Red Banners of Victory were handed to selected regiments who then presented them to the picked battalions whose honour it would be to plant them over the 'lair of the Fascist beast'. The unit to which was handed Banner of Victory No. 5, was the 1st Battalion of 756th Regiment, and shortly after noon on 30 April, its men flung themselves across the open space of the Königsplatz and into the battered Reichstag building. The German garrison counter-attacked, but the men of 1st Battalion forced their way up to the second floor and unfurled their banner from a window. More and more Red Army infantry were drawn into the fighting to subdue the SS defenders who included Frenchmen of the Charlemagne Legion. These men were battling with the terrible knowledge that this struggle could only end in their destruction. Late in the evening of 30 April, the Red Flag waved over the shattered dome of the Reichstag building, lit by the raging fires and by the shell flashes of the artillery which now concentrated upon the very last objective – the Führer bunker.

During 30 April, the fighting around the Reichstag building eased and the main efforts of the Red Army were then concentrated upon pushing the final few hundred yards against an opposition that had now become fanatical in its intensity as it neared the Reichs Chancellery and the Führer bunker. Within that underground complex there was feverish preparation and then three officer couriers were sent out, each carrying a copy of Hitler's last Will and political testament. Mohnke, the Commandant of the Zitadelle zone, reported that Soviet assault troops were now quite close and that their attack to take out the bunker might come at any time. The men of his SS group as well as the remnants of 56th Panzer Corps were fighting hard, but there was little time left.

Shortly after the officer couriers had left the bunker Kempka, in charge of the Chancellery's vehicle park, was ordered to choose two motor-cyclists for a special mission to carry a dispatch through the Soviet lines to Wenck's headquarters at Ferch near Potsdam. The text of this dispatch, signed by both

Martin Bormann and General Burgdorf was, 'Wenck, it is about time'. That these two officers were willing to sacrifice subordinates to carry out such a ridiculous gesture is a terrible condemnation of how out of touch they were. The dispatch-riders did not question the orders, but rode out; first because they had been specially selected, but also because they were soldiers under orders. One of them vanished completely and has never been traced. The other, apprehended by a vigilant German patrol in the Grunewald, and being dressed in mufti, was accused of desertion. The luckless cyclist was passed from one command post to another. None of the officers who interrogated him believed his story or was prepared to accept the signatures of Bormann and Burgdorf as genuine. Not until the following day was his release effected and he returned to the Führer bunker.

On the same day, after having several times taken leave of the personal staff and of those officers who had stayed loyal, Hitler and Eva Braun committed suicide. In discussions about his self-destruction the Führer had demanded the complete cremation of both bodies. This could only be achieved quickly by a petrol fire, and he thought that by using 200 litres there would be no remains which could be identified as his. In the early afternoon of the 30th Kempka suddenly received an urgent call from Günsche, Hitler's SS Adjutant, for that amount of fuel. There were supplies of petrol buried in the Tiergarten and these would have to be dug up and brought to the Chancellery. Kempka asked for time until the Russian shelling of the area had subsided for this had reached a new intensity and Kempka knew that to send men out to risk their lives would be unforgiveable unless there were a valid

Above: the entrance to the Führerbunker in the Reichs Chancellery. It was through this doorway that the bodies of Adolf Hitler and Eva Braun were brought.

and compelling reason. He had not yet been told that Hitler was dead and that the petrol was needed for the funeral pyre. Günsche did not tell him and refused to give reasons for the urgency over the telephone. If Kempka would not send his men into the Tiergarten to dig up the petrol he should set them to work siphoning the fuel from the tanks of the vehicles standing in the Chancellery car park. What was obtained might be sufficient for the task in hand. The fuel was to be brought without delay to the garden exit of the Führer bunker.

Kempka, worried by the unusual demand and by the hectoring tone of his SS comrade, set some of his men to work and himself hurried from the car park to talk to the Sturmbannführer. He was soon made aware of how urgently the petrol was needed and then it was reported that between 160 and 180 litres had been obtained from the vehicle tanks. The canisters were outside the garden exit. All was now ready. The small group of mourners burdened with the corpses climbed the twenty stairs from the living quarters of the bunker to the garden door. As the door opened they could see fountains of earth rising as artillery shells exploded in a continuous and shattering bombardment. They could see nothing but those fountains; could hear nothing but the thundering detonations and could smell nothing but the stink of explosives and the smoke of burning fires. To go out into the garden while this bombardment continued was suicide and yet it was their duty to do so; to carry out their dead leader's last orders. The mourners took a deep breath and charged into the bursting shells.

To the right of the door was a concrete mixer which had been brought in before the siege began. It had been intended to put down another layer of concrete so as to thicken the roof. Now it stood in the garden and just in front of it was a small hollow which had been caused as the mixer was dragged across the grass. Hitler's body, wrapped in a grey blanket, was laid in that slight hollow. One trouser leg was rucked slightly showing a dark sock. The black-shod feet were pointed at the bunker door. Eva Braun was placed, not quite alongside the Führer but at a slight angle. The shelling which had diminished somewhat in intensity as the bodies were laid on the grass broke out again with renewed fury. The mourners rushed back to the safety of the doorway, fearful that behind that frightening bombardment might come wave after wave of Russian infantrymen pouring into the Chancellery garden in the last charge. The Führer's body must be burned, but for anyone to go out again into the garden was to risk being blown apart by the heavy shells detonating all round. Linge, Kempka and Günsche each seized a canister of petrol, ran to the bodies, opened the caps and with shaking hands poured out the fuel. Eva's thin, black dress which had been blowing about in the wind fell still and unmoving onto her body as the petrol soaked into it. Once again the barrage reached an intensity but the men did not stop. Death had no fears for them now. They had a task to complete, a duty to fulfill. Three jerricans of petrol were poured before they were forced back into the shelter of the doorway. The petrol had been poured. Now it had to be lighted. The idea of using a hand-grenade was rejected. Nor could one of them go out and light the bodies for the grass all round them was saturated. Kempka seized a rag from the grass, tore it into strips and dipped it into a petrol tin. Goebbels produced a match. The wind created by shell blasts blew out the flame. Another match was struck. It went out. Kempka held out the petrol-soaked rag. Another match was struck and the flames ran quickly up the cloth. Kempka threw it through the air and it fell on the bodies. There was a sudden burst of flame. The cremation had begun.

Goebbels, Martin Bormann and Dr Stumpfegger stood in the doorway watching the flames above which a cloud of black smoke mushroomed. Caught by the drama of the scene and held by their emotions, the watchers came to attention and saluted their Führer for the last time. They turned to go; there was no point in staying and they left Kempka, Günsche and Linge to their grim task. Those three watched the bodies contort as the flames consumed them. The bodies were charred but not destroyed. They fetched six more jerricans of petrol and poured it over the blackened corpses. Another piece of rag, another match and then the flames rose again around the dead couple. The three men waited until the fire was completely out and then the bodies were again soaked in petrol and set alight. Then again and again. From the afternoon until 19.30 hrs the cremation lasted until the fuel had all been used and the three men were satisfied. The remains were unidentifiable. In the bunker the Führer conference called by the new Reichs Chancellor, Josef Goebbels, discussed the points that were to be made to Zhukov when General Krebs went over to discuss terms with the Russian commander. Towards midnight on 30 April, a German officer approached the Soviet lines and had soon made arrangements for Krebs to come into the Soviet headquarters.

At midnight it was the first day of May 1945; May Day. In Berlin the Führer was dead. In a shallow trench in the small garden of the Reichs Chancellery the corpses of Adolf Hitler and his wife lay burned but not totally incinerated. The flames of the pyre had died away several hours earlier and now, crouched in the exit doorway of the bunker, a group of policemen headed by Linge, the Führer's valet, was waiting for a pause in the furious Russian shelling. At last it came and in that brief interval the group rushed to where the charred remains lay and scattered the ashes. Then taking up those parts of the cadavers not totally consumed by fire they interred them in a shell hole near the wall of the house in which lived Kempka, the Führer's chauffeur.

The Reich that was to have lasted a millenium was in the last days of its life after only twelve years of power. All that now remained of the once vast territory of the Reich were small islands of land. One of these was a narrow strip of central Germany. There was another small strip in northern Holland and Germany, and the largest of all, a pocket extending over most of western Bohemia and much of Austria. Then there were a few 'fortress' cities which still held out although behind the Allied fronts. The Reich was all but dead and it was clear that within days those little islands of territory which were still under its control would be overrun by the Allies. The Reich had little territory and less influence. Its Navy had no role other than that of ferrying civilians from ports in the eastern Baltic to others in northern Germany and Denmark. The Luftwaffe was impotent and the Army all but defeated in the field.

At 03.50 hrs on 1 May, the German delegation, headed by Krebs, arrived at the battle headquarters of General Chuikov. Without preliminary discussion Krebs announced the death of Hitler and asked for an armistice. Did he speak for Berlin or for the whole of Germany, he was asked? The German plenipotentiary did not answer directly but prevaricated and after Chuikov had discussed the point with Zhukov, who then talked to Stalin, Krebs was told that only unconditional surrender to all the Allies was acceptable. Again Krebs demurred. He was empowered only to talk and not to act. There was a German government headed by Goebbels which would make the decision, but if Germany surrendered unconditionally there would be no German government to discuss terms. Then, too, there was the danger of other German governments being formed in southern Germany or by Himmler. What he, Krebs repeated, was seeking on behalf of the Goebbels government was a truce; he could not decide about surrender. What the government in Berlin was seeking was peace with the Soviet Union. Once again the point was put to him that only a total surrender to all the Allies was acceptable. Who would speak for the Berlin government? Krebs considered this and named Goebbels and Bormann. Would the German Armed Forces obey an

Above: General Krebs, here seen outside General Chuikov's headquarters in Berlin, where he had gone to arrange the surrender of the city.

order from Goebbels? Krebs thought they would. What about unconditional surrender first and then talks – and so the argument went round and round in circles.

Meanwhile some of Krebs's delegation had been returned to the German lines where one of them was captured and arrested by an SS outpost which would not release him until a direct order came from Bormann. When the captured officer, von Dufving, reported to Goebbels that unconditional surrender was being asked for, Goebbels refused this and demanded the return of General Krebs. With this accomplished the truce was at an end and at 18.30 on 1 May, a shattering bombardment opened up again, all of it directed against the Chancellery. Throughout the rest of that day there were local surrenders by the survivors of German units which had been overrun by the Red Army, and in the Führer bunker the final decision was made that the breakout, which Hitler had forbidden, would take place at 21.30 hrs that night. Whether the defence could hold until that time was uncertain as the enemy was drawing ever closer.

The atmosphere in the bunker was unreal. Marriages were arranged and entered into. There were farewell celebrations and there were suicides, one of whose was that of General Krebs. There were also mercy murders. Goebbels and his wife had brought their six children into the bunker and as both parents were determined to die by suicide, they decided to kill their children rather than let them fall into Russian hands. Whether the children were killed by injection as they slept in a drug-induced sleep cannot be known. So many of the events of those last hours in the bunker cannot now be determined with accuracy.

Late in the evening, Magda Goebbels, shocked by the death of her children and with the thoughts of her own imminent suicide, went up the stairs from the bunker's living quarters to the garden, leaning heavily on her husband's arm for support. He, sardonic to the end, joked that by committing suicide in the garden he and his wife had spared their comrades the necessity of carrying their dead bodies up the stairs. In the garden there was a shot and then another one or two – the evidence is unclear. Goebbels is believed to have shot himself and Magda took poison. An SS soldier carried out the *coup de grâce* as he had been ordered. The bodies were burned but not so thoroughly as those of Hitler and Eva Braun. For one thing there was insufficient petrol and two, the survivors were now more concerned with the breakout attempt. Groups were formed and left.

The group with Kempka worked its way through the tunnels of the underground railway moving northwards from the Chancellery to come out at the Friedrichsstrasse station. Not far away was the Weidendamm bridge which was still in German hands. Just south of the bridge, stood the ruined Admiral's Palace which Kempka named as the rendezvous for the group should they be separated by the shell fire. At the northern end of the bridge was a road-block held by exhausted German soldiers surrounded by their dead and dying comrades. The evidence of a bitter battle was everywhere to be seen. From houses on the corner of the Ziegelstrasse and Karlsstrasse

Russian snipers, machine-gunners and mortar men were directing a furious attack on the road-block. A few men might be able to filter through the Russian lines, was the advice which Kempka received, but most breakout attempts, he was warned, had been flung back with heavy loss before they had gone far.

At about 02.00 hrs on the morning of 2 May, Bormann's group arrived and joined Kempka. It was agreed that any breakout attempt could only succeed if it were made with panzer support. Bormann's luck held. In dying Berlin a squadron of three Panzer IVs and three armoured cars approached the road-block. The task of this small group from SS Division 'Nord' was to fight its way northwards out of the city. Quickly Kempka explained what his groups intended to do and under the protection of the first panzer the break-out attempt was undertaken with the vehicle moving slowly up the Friedrichsstrasse towards the Ziegelsstrasse. There was a crashing detonation. A Russian shell had struck and destroyed the tank. Naumann, aide-de-camp to Goebbels as well as Martin Bormann, who were the first and second in the short line of people, were both killed instantly.

With the Führer dead, burned and buried; with his successor, Goebbels, Gauleiter of Berlin and Reichs Defence Commissar, dead and burning, and with the political leaders of the Reich seeking to escape, the way was clear for General Weidling to offer the surrender of the city. No one could gainsay him now. All those who might have interfered were dead or had flown.

Even while Kempka and Bormann were preparing to undertake their escape attempt under cover of the last panzers, Weidling had sent radio messages to the Russians offering to send emissaries under a white flag. At 06.00 hrs he surrendered the city to the Red Army and was brought before Chuikov. Weidling did not know that his was only one of several approaches that had been made that day. These several proposals, in all of which Chuikov was involved, produced at last a document penned by Weidling and ordering that those who were still fighting in Berlin should lay down their arms.

It began to rain early on that morning of 2 May as the German troops came out to the general surrender. To emphasize to the determined defenders of the Reichstag building that it was pointless to resist, the Red Army mounted one last attack and shortly thereafter, a trickle of men and then more and more came out of the building, formed up into columns and were marched away.

Yet there were still some who would not surrender. Sometime late in the evening of 1 May, a rumour had spread among the fighting troops and some of the civilian population that Hitler was dead. That he had fallen in a hand-to-hand battle near the Chancellery. There were even those who claimed to have seen the Führer firing a Panzerfaust at the enemy. To a great many of those who heard that their Leader was dead the news had little impact. There were more important priorities, such as surviving. To many it was the end of the world they knew and of a government in whose triumphs they had participated. To a very great number, however, the Führer's death gave only the opportunity to escape from Berlin.

Above: fragments of the German Army are rounded up by the Soviets in the area south of the Spreewald.
Below: even while the fighting for the city continues, the people of Berlin come out of hiding to cut up the carcass of a horse that has been killed in the street. A Red Army soldier passes the spot, wheeling a bicycle.

Those who wanted to leave the city were of two contrasting types. First, there were those, and they were not all of them civilians, who had no wish to be in the capital when the Red Army began to celebrate the victory it had won. All Germany knew what had happened when Königsberg finally fell. The story was that the Red Army, in an act of vindictiveness, had paraded the prisoners and had selected one man of each rank who was then shot by firing-squad in the presence of his comrades. To compound this crime the Soviets had then shot all the Königsberg Volkssturm as partisans. Whether the stories were true or false is irrelevant. They were believed to be true and the wish to escape a possible summary execution put many on the road westwards out of Berlin.

There was a second group: those who would not give in because Berlin had given in, but who were determined to escape from the city and join a group which still maintained the struggle. And how would these two types of people escape from Berlin? Although in the heart of the city the Soviet regiments were closing in on the Reichschancellery there was still a narrow strip of territory as yet untaken by the Soviets. This salient ran westwards from the Chancellery to the bridges which crossed the Havel at Spandau. It was towards these bridges that those seeking to leave the capital were drawn. It was a sort of lemming madness, of course. To what were they heading? On the distant Elbe the Western Allies and the Red Army had met and were celebrating that link-up. All the territory west of Berlin and up to the Elbe was already part of the Soviet empire even though their occupying troops were few in number. To what, then, were the Berlin escapers fleeing? Encircled by the Red Army, their area of freedom was as closely circumscribed as that of a rat in a cage.

Either not caring, or perhaps not knowing that there was no real escape, vehicles raced out of the centre of Berlin. The lorries and cars swerved through bomb bursts, bumped in and out of shell craters, raced past the ruined Kaiser Wilhelm Commemorative Church and down the Kurfursten-damm in the centre of which was the dug-in turret of a Tiger tank firing down the length of that once elegant boulevard. Along the Heer Strasse, driving farther and farther westward under fire the whole time from the Red Army whose units formed a gauntlet along whose punishing length each escaping vehicle had to run. A long way away from Spandau the traffic jam began, a great mass of motor vehicles, horse-drawn carts and people on foot, all pressing towards the three bridges which had once spanned the Havel. One had been destroyed, and of the two remaining, one was in Red Army hands. Towards the German-held bridge the slow-moving traffic tried to force its way. The air was filled with Russian aircraft diving and climbing; strafing and bombing, while Red Army artillery bombarded the last remaining link with the west. Lorries, cars, tanks and carts crawled forward over the bodies of the dead and of the dying whose screams formed a counter-point to the firing of a handful of panzer and one or two German guns which were making a brief and ineffectual reply to the crushing Russian bombardment.

Above: a Berlin street scene after fighting has stopped. **Left:** a 'work commando' in Berlin's Frankfurter Allee fill in the shell and bomb craters with rubble, after the cessation of fighting.

*'To the east hidden under clouds of smoke that rose black and yellow into the sky is
Berlin. Underfoot are the bodies of those who had not made it as far as the bridge.
Sod their luck; let's hope ours is better for in a minute or two it will be our turn to
race across. Every man on our lorry is firing his weapon; machine-gun, machine
pistol or rifle. We roll onto the bridge roadway. The lorry picks up speed and races
across the open space. It is not a straight drive but a sort of obstacle race, swerving to
avoid the trucks, tanks and cars which are lying wrecked and burning on the bridge
roadway. There is a sickening feeling as we bump over bodies lying stretched out,
hundreds of them all along the length. At a collecting point SS Military Police
armed with machine pistols halt us. "Arm of Service?", they ask. "Grenadier".
"Over there; join that group, collect ammunition." A battle group is being formed,
an "alarm" unit was its proper name. The struggle for Berlin may have ended for
some, but the war continues for the rest of us.'*

During the middle of the afternoon of 2 May, the Russian guns stopped
firing. The battle for Berlin was over. A war that had begun when Operation
'Barbarossa' had opened on 22 June 1941, and during which the Red Army
had suffered terrible losses, was nearly over. The old Bolshevik ideas of
warfare, tied to Marxist/Leninist dogmas had been false. New ideas brought
in by fresh men, using modern battle techniques, had produced victory. The
misery, the heartbreak, the destruction and the horror that had once been
unleashed on the Russian people, had been requited. As the Red Army men
looked around at the ruins in which they had fought, the burning destruction
of Germany's capital city, they must have felt that the victory though worth
it, had been bought for a terribly high price. They did not know – at least
most of them did not – that the world was about to change because the
balance of power in Europe had altered.

For those Germans who were prisoners of war much of the future was
uncertain but one thing was clear. There would be a very long period of
imprisonment for each of them and for the really unfortunate ones their
indeterminate sentence would be hard labour in one of the lead- or
coal-mines of the Soviet Union, where there was little food and no safety
regulations. Those who did not wear the German eagle on the right breast as
the Army did, but wore it instead on the left sleeve, were known to the Red
Army as 'arm eagles'; SS men and therefore, candidates for special treatment;
imprisonment of so rigorous a nature that few would ever get home to
Germany again. That prospect was in the future. In the grey Berlin drizzle of
the present, jubilant Red Army men strolled, enjoying the luxury of being
able to move upright and without fear of being killed. Soviet soldiers
marshalled the tired, hungry and lousy German prisoners into open spaces
and told them to wait.

*'We prisoners, waiting as soldiers always have to wait, sat in the exhausted daze
that the end of a battle brings. There was such a depression that we hardly talked,
but dozed off into light sleep or smoked, waiting to know what was our fate.
Suddenly the guards began to run away. Surely the fighting was not about to begin
again? No, it was not. A Russian soldier had found a wine shop. These had all been*

shut since the battle opened and this one had most of its stock intact. The guards just abandoned us. Well, there was no place to which we could escape, so they knew it was safe to leave us while they got their share of the booty. It was soon clear that Ivan had no head for strong drink. They began firing in the air and as darkness fell the soldiers, now very drunk indeed, fired off Very lights and tracer into the dark. We were marched away southwards and onto the airfield at Tempelhof which seemed to be the collecting point for prisoners of war.'

For civilians, too, it was all over. The immediate danger of being killed had passed. Now the concern was to survive the first excesses that Nazi propaganda had foretold: rape, murder, pillage, hunger. Once all that had passed, and it might take months, would come the time of Occupation; the imposition of Slav rule upon the Teuton peoples and God alone knew how long that sentence of living death would last. The past had been a horror, the future would be frightful. Today was not much, but at least one was alive. That was a bonus.

Above: when the fighting died in Berlin, both sides were totally exhausted. Here Red Army men sleep in the street by the side of a dead German.

'We were living in one of the huge Flak towers that had been put up during the war for anti-aircraft defence. It was being used by a great number of people who, like us, had been bombed out and to begin with it was quite comfy and very safe. There was light, warmth, efficient ventilation and a communal kitchen which issued stew and bread for which we have to give up only half coupons. Once the fighting began seriously none of us wanted to go outside and do our shopping. Of the actual fighting I saw nothing but we all heard a lot because the walls were not so thick that they kept out the sounds of shells and bombs bursting against the Flak tower walls. The tower soon became an emergency hospital and we were all expected to help. Not in the medical sense but by carrying out domestic duties, carrying the wounded, feeding them and cleaning up the mess. That sort of thing. Thank God, we had light all throughout that difficult time. It would have been frightful without it. More and more wounded were brought in and a lot died. Burial parties took the bodies outside and because there were not enough men to dig proper graves the bodies were just put into shell holes and covered with a sprinkling of earth. We had a military chaplain with us in the tower who was worried because he could not report the details of the fallen. If he could not record these correctly and report them to the proper authority the dead would merely be listed as missing. There were suicides in the tower, as well. It was a ghastly time and when the shelling began to come really close it was clear that the Russians would soon be at the doors. We all knew what that meant and some of the girls decided not to wait until the Ivans came but to end their lives there and then.

One afternoon there was no noise of shelling. In the huge tower we all stood and listened. Someone opened the heavy steel door and reported that there was no shell fire, no aeroplanes dropping bombs, but that there was some machine-gun fire a long way off. Slowly people went out into the fresh air although many were fearful that this ending of the barrage could be some sort of Russian trick. We could see the devastation. It was shocking; unbelievable. Lots of fires and dead bodies all round, although a lot of these must have been those taken out of the Flak tower.

Some German soldiers came up and told us that Berlin had been surrendered to the Russians. Hitler was dead and Admiral Doenitz had taken over. It started to rain. The strongest memory of that day is seeing my city alight, smelling the smoke of the fires in the air and feeling the rain drizzling down.'

3

THE BELEAGUERED FORTRESS: BRESLAU

By 2 May, Berlin was just a city in the Soviet zone of occupation. The principal one to be sure, but it now formed no part of Soviet military strategy, but rather was an important political pawn. Even before General Weidling had ordered its surrender green posters had been pasted up announcing that the supreme authority in Berlin now resided in the Red Army. Some boroughs in the city had had mayors and city councils imposed upon them by the Russian authorities as early as 25 April. Now, on 2 May, Berlin was completely under Soviet occupation and yet miles away to the east Breslau still fought on despite an encirclement which had begun shortly after the opening of a Soviet offensive, on 12 January.

Hitler had appreciated the importance of Breslau as a centre of communications and ordered that the city be held to the last. As early as September 1944, the city had been declared a fortress, but no well-armed and trained troops had been placed at the disposal of the battle commandant, General Krause. He was expected to defend Breslau with infantry formations consisting of old men and young boys. Among these military bodies of doubtful value was a battalion made up of local volunteers and another of Landesschützen, old men well above military age. These poorly equipped and almost untrained ancients were backed by six batteries of Fortress artillery, a Company of Engineers and another of Signals. It had been the German High Command's intention to have at least three conventional divisions in position around each of Germany's 'fortress' cities, but the deteriorating military situation forbade this and Breslau was virtually without adequate defence. As early as September, aware of how weak were his forces and being unwilling to risk the life of women and children on a modern, urban battlefield, General Krause proposed that two hundred thousand civilians be evacuated from the city. Gauleiter Hanke turned down this and other proposals to spare the non-combatants until, at last, on 19 January, he finally gave his consent and sent out treks of evacuees in the depth of winter and in the middle of a major Soviet offensive.

Determined to raise new military formations Hanke ordered the most ruthless and total conscription of manpower. This comb-out produced four regiments. A fifth was raised as a result of an even more thorough weeding-out and during February 1945, the 269th Infantry Division, withdrawing in the face of the Russian advance, was ordered into the city where it then formed the principal defence force. Like their comrades in Berlin, the boys of the Breslau Hitler Youth were soon in action with Panzerfaust and during one three-day period destroyed seventy-six Russian armoured fighting vehicles. Deliveries of gun barrels from a local factory increased the garrison's artillery strength and then to support the struggle

Above: Gauleiter Hanke addressing men of the Volkssturm in Breslau. **Below:** men of the Breslau garrison at a street barricade.

two whole train loads of radio-controlled, explosive tanks, the Goliaths, were brought into the city.

It must not be thought that the defence of Breslau was a passive one. The SS Fortress Battalion 'Besselein' went quickly and aggressively into action and wiped out a Red Army bridgehead on the Oder during 8 February. To counterbalance this success, an attempt by German forces thrusting from Liegnitz, failed to break the Russian ring. By St. Valentine's Day the city was completely cut off and isolated, miles behind the Soviet front. The Red Army then launched attacks to probe the defences and to test the morale of the defenders. Four Soviet divisions carried out one head-on assault which penetrated the city's outer defences. On its own sector Besselein's SS battalion was soon engaged in bitter house-to-house battles. The Red units were driven out of the suburbs by a staunch defence backed by the No. 311 Assault Gun Brigade, working with the SS battalion. Life as a civilian under fire was heroic to begin with, but soon lost its glamour and became in the final days an agony of unimaginable suffering, as the following report shows.

I should think that there were still more than half the civilian population in the city when Breslau was finally cut off. We heard nothing official about the treks that had gone out on 19 January, but unofficially – I worked as a civil servant and the news spread quickly among us – the treks suffered horribly. Many were overrun and cut to pieces by the Red Army panzers. Hanke, our Gauleiter, ordered as a propaganda slogan "Every house a fortress", and I must say that as a 20-year-old girl the idea of being a German hedgehog working against the Russians and delaying their advance, was initially exciting. It became less so as the truth slowly dawned that Germany had lost the war and that Breslau would not be, as we had been told, a springboard for a victorious advance, but that it might very well be razed to the ground and we Breslauers destroyed along with it.

There were many acts of bravado at that time. I was told that the men of an SS battalion put up a huge sign facing the Russians. "Besselein's battalion is defending this sector". It seemed to work. The SS battalion was not attacked by infantry as often as the units on other sectors, but the SS did have to endure really long artillery bombardments.'

During the battles, which endured until May, there were other acts that may have been courageous, but made no sense from a military view-point. Late in the afternoon of 20 February, Captain Seiffert's 55th Volkssturm battalion carried out a frontal attack against the Red Army's positions in the city's southern park. The old men and young lads of Seiffert's battalion advanced bravely enough across the open lawns into heavy machine-gun and mortar fire, but were soon driven back in a short but bloody battle which left more than a hundred of the Hitler Youth dead on the battlefield.

Gauleiter Hanke, now Reichs Defence Commissar, was the supreme authority in the encircled city. At last even he became aware of the dangers which the citizens faced and of which he had been repeatedly warned by the military. His plans for Breslau were either to fly-in trained paratroops so as to produce a 'Cassino on the Oder', or alternatively, to organize a mass breakout

Above: a Red Army anti-tank rifle in action during the house-to-house battles that took place during the siege of Breslau.

westwards. Two battalions of specialist soldiers were indeed flown into Breslau. The Russian reaction to this move was to intensify efforts to capture the city's airport. This they finally achieved, so with landing facilities denied them the garrison turned the Kaiserstrasse, one of the city's longest and widest thoroughfares, into a runway for aircraft. Planes landed under fire, discharged their loads, took on wounded and took off again. In one of the machines which risked the landing was General Niehoff, who had been flown in to take over from General Krause as battle commandant of Breslau.

By the first week of March, Russian infantry had driven back the defence in a great number of places and street fighting was approaching the inner city. Supplies were running low and improvised explosives were produced from oxygen and acetelyne bottles which replaced conventional materials. The town was dying. There was a shell shortage so that the German guns could not respond to the Russian bombardments. Lacking men to relieve the units in the front line, short of food and of ammunition, the exhausted defenders battled on. The numbers of wounded increased alarmingly and doctors worked 18 hours a day to help those who could benefit from their surgery. Special Red Cross flights of German transports took out six thousand of the more badly wounded, but there were many, many more for whom there was no place in an aircraft.

Late in March, Stavka became impatient. Breslau had to be cleared away so as to release troops for the Berlin operation. This resulted in an increase in the weight and number of attacks. Soon the defenders were fighting in the sewers beneath the city and the German defence perimeter at street level shrank with each new Russian assault. On the day that Berlin surrendered, Breslau's battle commandant advised Schoerner, commanding Army Group Centre, that he too must soon surrender the city. It could not hold out much longer. The troops were too few, the number of suicides was alarming, there was civil unrest, near revolt, and rations were at starvation level. Schoerner refused to allow the surrender. Two days later, on 4 May, a delegation of churchmen begged the Commandant to give in. Gauleiter Hanke was spared the embarrassment of meeting delegations or the need to make so painful a choice as the General was being called upon to do. Hanke flew out of the city in a Fieseler Storch, abandoning to their fate those whom he had exhorted to hold out until final victory. His reason for leaving was that Hitler had named him to be the new Chief of German Police and also Reichsführer SS in place of Himmler. To take up these pointless tasks, he fled the city and vanished completely. He has never been found. Niehoff would hold out no longer. On 5 May his officers were briefed on the situation and on the following day, at 14.00 hrs, the city surrendered to the commander of 6th Red Army. It was all over. Berlin had held out for nine days; Breslau had resisted for more than seventy. On 7 May, the day on which the act of unconditional surrender was signed at Reims, the Red Army marched in.

'Rape began almost immediately and there was a viciousness in the acts as if we women were being punished for Breslau having resisted for so long. There is no point in recalling those acts. Let me say that I was young, pretty, plump and fairly inexperienced. A succession of Ivans gave me over the next week or two a lifetime of experience. Luckily very few of their rapes lasted more than a minute. With many it was just a matter of seconds before they collapsed gasping. What kept me sane was that almost from the very first one I felt only a contempt for these bullying and smelly peasants who could not act gently towards a woman, and who had about as much sexual technique as a rabbit.

We women were put on rubble clearing gangs. Unless we worked we were not fed. There was no distribution of rations against coupons. Instead there were soup kitchens. We would be marched at midday to the kitchen to receive our portion of soup and bread. One day something strange happened. There were Red Army troops of whom the ordinary European Russian was terribly afraid. We were working as usual, then we noticed that the guards were very jumpy. We heard singing, loud, strong, masculine voices singing Red Army marching songs. But yet there was something not quite right; the rhythm was wrong. In the first years of the war I had studied music and the cadence of western military marches was, of course, familiar to me. The voices singing those Russian songs were not singing them in a western rhythm. The Red Army men who were guarding us told us in bad German to run away and hide. The Mongols are coming, they told us. Very bad men. You go quick. Go quick.

This really was a case of a pot calling the kettle black. These were the same men who had come into our town about 10 days before and had carried out practices and orgies of unbelievable savageness. Yet they were telling us that this new group of approaching Soviet soldiers were bad. They were terrified that the Mongols would come near the street which we were clearing. They were really afraid. It is strange how the mind works. I seldom recall the days when I was young. Yet when I hear a military choir singing then all those days come back. All the senseless destruction that the Ivans carried out. The burning of two of our most beautiful churches, St Barbara's and the Mary Magdalene. Of course, now, our Breslau is Wrocław, a Polish city.'

Breslau had held out to the end and at a cost of 29,000 military and civilian casualties. The Red Army suffered 60,000 dead and wounded. General Niehoff, the battle commandant, received no treatment becoming to an officer and a gentleman, nor the treatment that is usually given to an honourable opponent. Instead he spent ten years in solitary confinement in a Soviet concentration camp. Another of the Breslau Generals, Ruff, was hanged for alleged war crimes, and the German rank and file were treated to specially harsh conditions. Perhaps the men of 6th Red Army resented the fact that a German garrison of 40,000 men, many of them grandfathers and others mere schoolchildren, should have resisted for so long the vigorous and sustained attacks of 150,000 well-armed Soviet troops. The men and women of Breslau paid dearly for their staunch defence of 'Cassino on the Oder'.

4

THE CENTRAL SECTOR: PRAGUE

During 1 May, on the northern sector of the Eastern Front, the Red Army was completing the capture of Berlin, was overrunning the north German coastal areas and was compressing those few remaining pockets of Germans who were still resisting along the Baltic. On the southern sector of the Eastern Front, as we shall presently see, some units of the Red Army had captured Vienna and were pushing towards the River Enns while others were fighting hard in the mountainous province of Steiermark.

This section of the book deals with the central sector of the Eastern Front, Czechoslovakia, where the westward drive of the Soviet forces had been less spectacular than on the northern and southern wings. The reasons for the slow advance were several. There had been movements of men and matériel away from the central sector to strengthen the Red Fronts on each wing. Then, too, the terrain difficulties had not allowed either 4th Ukrainian nor 2nd Ukrainian Fronts to move as swiftly as their commanders had hoped. Finally, the German Army Group Centre had been handled so vigorously by its commander, Field Marshal Schoerner, and had fought so well that the pace of the Russian advance had been slowed dramatically.

Thus, on that first day in May, there was a large German-held salient, separating the Red Army Fronts in Germany from those in Austria, and that salient formed one of the last pockets or islands in central Europe which were still in German territory. While to the north and south the German capitals of Vienna and Berlin were already under Soviet control, the Slav land of Czechoslovakia was still held, and firmly held, by Schoerner's Army Group Centre.

Into this military situation there then intruded an important political consideration. At least to the Europeans it was important; to the Americans it was an irrelevance. It was, quite simply, which of the two Allied forces, the Red Army or the American Army would capture Prague. In the last days of April US armoured spearheads had driven into the western regions of Czechoslovakia and the US 2nd Infantry Division was about to capture Pilsen. The distance from Pilsen to Prague was not great, and to the leaders of the Soviet Union the prospect of a Western salient was frightening. The fact that they held the capitals of all the lands in the eastern half of Europe and that the frontiers of Russia had advanced from Poland to central Germany, was less important than the presence of a Western-style democracy breaking the solidity of the western wall of the Soviet bloc. As Stalin saw it, it was imperative that the Red Army seize Prague before the Americans did. Had he but known it, the US had no intention of capturing the city and using it as a political counter. To them the destruction of the armies of the Third Reich was the prime, indeed the only, consideration.

As he considered the disposition of the Soviet forces, Generalissimo Stalin could appreciate that neither of the two Fronts in Czechoslovakia would be able to reach Prague before the Americans. However, if he were to turn the 1st Ukrainian Front in a ninety degree wheel from its battle area to the west of Dresden, this would change the line of its advance and the objective, Prague, might be gained more quickly. The danger of such an operation was that Schoerner, feeling himself to be outflanked, might withdraw and concentrate around the capital city. The attention of the German Field Marshal had to be held, therefore, and his Army Group caught and destroyed in a pincer operation to the east of Prague. While the 1st Ukrainian Front was using its main force to drive from Dresden through the mountains of northern Bohemia and then down to Prague, a secondary thrust would strike behind Schoerner's forces with the aim of meeting the pincers of 2nd Ukrainian Front. That Force would be advancing to capture the line of the River Moldau and the capital city no later than 12/14 May. It was accepted that 1st Ukrainian Front might have already seized Prague before the 12th, but if it had not done so the 2nd Ukrainian would. Either way, the capital city of Czechoslovakia would be part of the Soviet empire by 14 May. To ensure this the Americans must be subjected to political pressure to halt their movement into the Czech republic.

The martyrdom of Czechoslovakia, the first, non-German victim of Nazi aggression, had begun in 1938. In the autumn of that year the republic had been forced to hand over to Germany her western province of Sudetenland. It was, perhaps, possible to accept Hitler's statement that he had demanded the Sudetenland because historically it was German and its population was overwhelmingly Teuton, but there was not the same justification for the aggression which led to the occupation of the purely Czech provinces in the March of 1939. This demonstration proved to the leaders of the Western democracies that the promises of the German Führer were not to be trusted; that Hitler was determined to use aggression as a State policy. The Czech republic died and the country became a Protectorate of Nazi Germany. Its Protector in 1943 was the SS General Heydrich, following whose assassination, the title and power passed to the General of the SS, Karl Hermann Frank.

In the last months of the Second World War, the western regions of the Protectorate were among those few parts of the Third Reich which had not been overrun by the Allies, but the fall of the Bohemian 'island' and those other, as yet uncaptured, areas of Greater Germany was only a matter of time. In those 'islands' the provincial governments of the Reich continued to run a scheduled air service to link the remaining cities still in German hands, which produced the bizarre situation that officials isolated in one Nazi 'island' were able to move to some other 'island' by simply flying over those regions of their Fatherland which had by that time passed under Allied control.

As if to commemorate the six years which Czechoslovakia had endured as a vassal of the Reich, a Red Army offensive opened during March 1945, raising Czech hopes of an early liberation. Great masses of Soviet corps and armies struck towards Berlin and Vienna. But the thrusting arms of these great offensives swept past Czechoslovakia both in the north and south. It is likely that the Soviet Supreme Command, was determined to capture the two German capitals before the Western Allies, in order to complete a chain of outposts in eastern Europe, which the Russians saw as essential to protect the territory of the Soviet Union against any future aggression on the part of a Western Power.

While to the north and south of Czechoslovakia German cities were falling to the Soviet forces, and the armies of the Western Allies were occupying the provinces and states of north and central Germany, Prague, in the heartland of Europe, exhibited an air of calm, order and normality. The location of the city so deep inside Europe had protected it against the massive air assaults which had destroyed the cities of the Reich, and although air raids had damaged parts of Pilsen, the rest of the country was so untouched by the effects of war that the Protectorate was the area into which schoolchildren and bombed-out families from the Reich had been evacuated.

During the last months of the war, Soviet spearheads seemed to be concerned with gaining ground in the west. It was certain that Czechoslovakia would become a vassal of the Soviet Empire. Moves had been made, both in England and in Russia, for the eventual assumption of power within the Republic. Nationalist groups of partisans had been formed and committees of action set up. With that astounding naivety that European Socialists always show, Benes, the Czech leader, flew from London to Moscow convinced that he would be allowed to set up a national body to rule the country on the lines of the pre-1939 government. Stalin had other ideas. During the years of occupation Communist cadres had infiltrated and gradually assumed control of the partisan organization. There was no doubt that once the Germans had been driven out there would certainly be a Czech government, but it would not be that of Benes and his Social Democrats, but one set up by the Communists, whose will would prevail because they had the guns and the organization and the Red Army to back them.

But in the last weeks of the war, German military power in the Protectorate was sufficiently strong to be a deterrent against any open revolt either in the country or within the capital city and it remained so until almost the end. It is true, however, that there had been isolated incidents in the capital as a result of which individual German soldiers had had their firearms taken from them. There had also been small acts of sabotage both in the cities and in the rural areas, but there had been nothing that would provoke a harsh response from the German occupying forces, for the Czechs knew only too well how swift and ruthless was the retaliation to any serious act of provocation. Word was passed to the civil population, particularly in Prague; keep calm, keep quiet, do nothing provocative. At the right time there will be a signal for a national uprising which will sweep the Germans out of the land.

The Czech people obeyed these instructions and remained calm. Let us imagine ourselves in Prague on that first day of May 1945. As we stand on Kinsky Hill and look down upon the golden city we might well be deceived into thinking that life is normal in the capital. From our forested elevation we can see a city over whose buildings the swastika still flies, buildings that are undamaged, public transport that runs punctually and elegant streets and squares filled with well-dressed men and women strolling in the warm sunshine of this May Day. One would think this to be a city at peace. There is no sound of gunfire and only occasionally does a single Russian plane fly low over the city, heralding the slow approach of the Red Army. Otherwise all is normal and Germans who have lived in Prague during these days state, almost without exception, that life is being lived at almost a pre-war level. The severe rationing laws applicable throughout Germany proper are not enforced so strictly in the Protectorate. There is rationing, certainly, but the ration cards are always honoured and in full measure; which is not always the case in German cities following a heavy air raid. There are goods to buy in the shops of Prague and the Reichs Government pays good wages to those who work in the Skoda heavy engineering work at Pilsen or in the smaller factories which produce optical equipment and small arms for the German military machine.

Many Germans whom I interviewed about life in the Protectorate insist that the Czechs were given preferential treatment by the Germans and that Heydrich was so popular with the Czechs because of his liberal rule as Protector of Bohemia, that he could drive through the streets of the capital without an armed escort. Despite his assassination and other attempts to foment unrest among the native population, the German occupation of Czechoslovakia lacked the severity which characterized its rule in other occupied lands. No: according to many Germans, life in the Protectorate had been lived at an almost peace-time pace. Thus, even on the first day of May 1945, the city of Prague was quiet and peaceful. Order reigned and the commands issued from the government palace, the Hradschin, were obeyed promptly and to the letter by Czech as well as by German officials. May Day was gloriously spring-like, with a cloudless blue sky and a warmth almost of summer. It was a holiday. May Day, the workers' festival, a national holiday to be enjoyed by all.

The glorious weather, like the calm itself was a delusion. The cold of late April came back and together with the return of chill and snow showers came the news that Hitler was dead; news which sharpened the realization of the Czechs that the end of the war and, with it, the liberation of their Homeland was at hand. That the war was coming to an end had long been obvious to the Germans as well as to the Czechs. Only SS General Frank had refused to accept the obvious, but the military disasters of the recent weeks had convinced, finally, even him. The defeat of the Reich was inevitable and now he would have to act on his own initiative independently of Berlin, to make preparations to meet the oncoming catastrophe. In common with most of those in the senior echelons of the Nazi Party, SS General Frank was politically naive and was convinced that when the meeting of the military forces of the capitalist Western Allies and of the Communist East occurred there would be clashes which would lead to a new war between the victorious nations. The Minister for Propaganda, Josef Goebbels, had often proclaimed the historical inevitability of such a clash and his words had found in Frank ears that were prepared to hear.

Frank was a senior SS officer, notorious for the atrocities which he had committed. He knew the Soviets would give him short shrift. But he convinced himself that if he could hand over to the Anglo-Americans the entire Protectorate of Bohemia as a bulwark against the East, Churchill and the brand-new US President, Truman, might well be prepared to be lenient and to forgive him the crimes of which he was guilty. It was a naive hope, but Frank believed it and sent emissaries by JU 52, to a military headquarters near Munich from where the members of the Mission set out to contact the local US military commander. That American officer refused to even meet Frank's men. The attempt to offer Czechoslovakia as a counter in the barter for leniency had proved abortive. In view of the deteriorating situation it was time – and now even Frank accepted it – for the Germans to leave the city of Prague.

For centuries German-speaking people had been living in Prague or in the Czech lands, for the former Kingdom of Bohemia had once formed part of the Crown lands of the Habsburg Empire of Austria-Hungary. The greatest number of these Austrian/Germans lived in Sudetenland, the westernmost province of Czechoslovakia, and in such numbers that they formed there the principal racial component of the population. Even in Prague there was a large German-speaking element among the city's population, relics of the old Empire, who were concentrated in certain districts of the city. These were, in effect, German ghettos in Slav cities, whose people had lived among the Czech peoples for generations and considered themselves as citizens, with all the rights of citizenship. With the imminent destruction of Germany none could say what would be the fate of the German ethnic minorities. There would certainly be unpleasant times ahead and plans were made for those who wished to join the official evacuation from the city which was to be organized by Frank and the officers of the German administration. Most of the Prague Germans elected to stay. They had lived in the city and in the land for so long that they were as much rooted to the country as were the Czechs themselves.

In those days the frontier between Czechoslovakia and Germany was a two-day trek for the marching column which Frank had planned. The main body would have to go on foot for there was not enough petrol for the great mass of vehicles which would be required to carry all the people, the files and the essential equipment which the SS General and his subordinates intended to take with them. Frank and his staff should have made their preparations months or even weeks earlier for the feeding and accommodation of the evacuees; but they had not. Everything was ad hoc, improvised, cobbled together. What Frank's mass of government officials, policemen, soldiers, SS men and refugees would do once they had reached Germany had not been considered. There seems to have been no policy other than the attitude of Mr Micawber; they would wait for something to turn up.

Banner headlines on the German-language newspapers of 2 May, proclaimed within a thick, black border the message, 'Our Führer, Adolf Hitler, has fallen in the battle for Berlin'. Reports spoke of a Hitler fighting Bolshevism to the last gasp and falling – implied but not stated – in battle.

Counsel from the underground national government to the Czech population was, for the moment, to remain passive, but there were small things that could be done to unsettle the occupying forces. One such was the rumour that spread through the city – German currency was no longer legal tender and only the Czech crown had value. Loudspeakers were sent out by the German authorities to assure the population that the Mark was still official currency, but Czech shopkeepers generally refused to exchange their goods for a money whose worth they knew had a limited life span.

In certain streets during the evening of 2 May, German-language signs were removed leaving in position only those in Czech. German advertisements, the proclamations of the Reich and its notices were torn down. Where this could not be done, paint or whitewash covered the words written in the hated language of the occupying Power. Everything in German was removed and yet the German war flag still flew on government offices. The streets were still filled with German soldiers and SS men. A Cossack Division that had been raised to fight for the Führer was rumoured to be en route to Prague. The White Cossacks, like the SS, could be expected to repress with brutal ferocity any Czech insurrection, for the men of the renegade division, like the SS, had nothing to lose by being brutal; they would be shown no mercy when the time for revenge came.

Out in the country during that night, on the roads which lead westwards towards the Bohemian forest and the German frontier, there is considerable movement. Behind the groups of German guns, tanks and infantry trudge the long, straggling columns of refugees. The columns are constantly enlarged as from every side-road small groups of carts join the trek. These new-comers are local peasants; Sudeten Germans, women and children for the greater part, who have been sent away to safety in Germany before Nemesis in the shape of the Red Army or the Czech partisans overtakes them. Rumour flies faster than the speed of the Russian tanks and rumour says that the Soviets show no mercy.

The horses pulling the new-comers' carts are fresh and clean, in contrast to the weary nags which are struggling with the wagons of the main column, for these have come from eastern Slovakia, from Hungary and even from Roumania. The people of the main column who are now the old hands on the trek, are verminous and are suffering from dysentery. There has been little chance to keep clean. Polluted water, bad food and privation has brought on the flux.

So that the tired horses can still pull the wagons the old hands have lightened the loads and have flung out articles they once thought indispensible. The roads are littered with stoves, clothes and even furniture; memories of happier times. In the wagons there are now only those too young or too old to walk and those whom dysentery has prostrated. Cooking utensils and the bare essentials of food are kept, together with a minimum of bedding. This is less an evacuation than a flight. All the westward-leading roads in the Protectorate – the roads which lead towards Germany – are filled with bewildered civilians, hungry, tired, cold and fearful. And to what future are they heading; what is now left of the Fatherland that they are hoping to reach?

'Our family had farmed land near Saaz since the sixteenth century. In April the men began to discuss what we should do when the Russians came. At about the middle of April the Kreisleiter called us all together and said we should wait until the very last minute before sending the women away into Germany. Some men, he told us, would have to stay in the village to guard the farms and the cattle against partisan attack. Others would go with the women to act as escorts in case of attack by Czech bandits. We were all to be armed and we were to wear our Volkssturm brassards to show that we were members of a properly established military group.

Our family farm was only about ten miles from the frontier, but we were not allowed to march independently into Germany. We had to join an official trek as the columns were called. This did lengthen the journey but it did provide security. Also it meant that our army would not have every road choked with refugees when it had to go into action in a counter-attack. Another thing that stopped us moving independently was the fact that there were not only minefields laid out in the Bohemian forest, but also defensive positions had been set up. Anyone blundering about could come to a lot of harm.

By the end of April we were all very worried. We could pick up nothing on the wireless from the stations on the Deutschlandsender net. We could still get Prague station but it was very indistinct. Then we read that Hitler was dead. It was time to leave. Those of us who left on the night of 2 May, expected that we should be away for a month or two, well, until the fighting had stopped and things had settled down. We did not expect that we should never see our homeland again. We thought a month or two of exile and we would all be back farming again.

As had been planned, all our livestock was collected and handed over to those who were staying behind to guard the beasts. They would be fed and milked at least, but there was little we could do about the growing crops. We left our village at eight in the evening and by four in the morning had reached the western highway. It was crammed, filled, overfilled, with every sort of cart and vehicle that you can imagine. There was no moon and it was not quite daylight. It was a grey, cold dawn. The weather was icy cold and there were light snow showers. In that cold grey dawn I thought I was looking into the jaws of Hell. In several army trucks there were wounded soldiers, just piled one on the other. People told me the government in Prague had given orders that one of the military hospitals had to evacuate all its patients. So the wounded were ordered to march without food, proper clothing or arms, on foot to the German frontier. The hospital was to be used as an overnight stopping-place for SS General Frank and his staff when they had to leave Prague.

The memory of what I saw in those trucks upsets me even now and my anger rises at the callous indifference of Frank and his lot to the suffering they inflicted upon front-line soldiers. A small column of carts heading for the main highway had passed through the village in which the hospital was set up. A mile or two down the road from the hospital the people in the carts saw the first of the wounded. This was a group made up of men with leg wounds, in plaster casts and with open wounds. The soldiers were hobbling along on sticks and crutches. Farther along the road there were some blind soldiers and others less seriously wounded. These were carrying stretchers on which the really badly wounded lay. At the front of this procession of misery there were those who were wounded but who were fit in the legs. A small group of them was striding out for the main road where they intended to halt the trek and to bring some carts for their comrades.

That main road was miles away. Many of the soldiers were weak from wounds. There were probably about two or three hundred of them, all told. Some were just sitting by the roadside crying because they could not force their bodies forward. They cried because just ahead of them lay the hills that marked the border and they were afraid of being caught when the war ended, in the Protectorate where they would be at the mercy of the Red Army. In those early days we had not learned that the Czech partisans were a worse enemy than even the worst of the Ivans. That lesson in frightfulness was still to come.

One of the villagers unhitched a horse and galloped away to tell the main trek that the wounded needed help. Eventually, a group of empty wagons came up but by that time many of the wounded were already on our carts. When these reached the main column the wounded were put into lorries which already held many other wounded. The stink was sickening. There were medical officers and nurses who did wonders, but so many people died on the trek; soldiers as well as civilians. The trek was so slow-moving that it was possible to dig a shallow grave, to give the corpse a proper service and then to return to the column to find that it had moved forward only a few hundred yards.

On 3 May, the Russians made their first air attack with stubby, little fighters which roared over the column and machine-gunned us. At about midday bombers came and attacked the army trucks which were at the head of the column. The soldiers put up a hail of fire, chiefly from machine-guns, but bombs hit some trucks and blocked the road. While the army was pushing the burning vehicles into the fields the fighters came back and machine-gunned us again. I call it murder. Those Russian pilots were so low they must have seen that there were only civilians, mostly women and children, between the army at the head of the column and the army rearguard. They must have seen that for they flew so low and must have seen the people running into the fields to avoid the bullets.

Our small section of the trek buried over 80 dead that day, all of them victims of the air raids. How many the army lost or how many other parts of the column lost I cannot say. In our area we did not dig individual graves. There was just one big hole into which all the dead were put and a cross above them on which was written that in the grave there were the victims of Russian air raids.

I remember 3 May well for that air raid and for the fact that the weather turned cold and that snow fell. It was a miserable time and we had only just joined the trek. There were some people who had been on the move, on and off, since the previous autumn.'

Despite the refusal of the American military commander in Munich to treat with Frank's emissaries, the SS General sent out other groups, one of whom was fired at by US tanks as the staff cars roared up the road to Klettau. Strong American armoured groups were now well inside Czech territory, moving eastwards through the dark, vast and silent Bohemian Forest. The US troops moved cautiously for the forest undergrowth could conceal Wehrwolf men with anti-tank rockets and nobody wanted to have the dubious honour of being among the last to be killed, particularly at the hands of some grubby little Kraut hardly old enough to be in long trousers.

Once out of the confining and claustrophobic woods, the American armour drove along empty roads towards Pilsen and other cities in western Czechoslovakia. The tanks passed through villages and small towns from whose houses, often from every window of every house, protruded poles on which white flags of surrender were flown, for this was the German-speaking area of the Czech lands and its inhabitants were the enemy. The white pillowcases, tablecloths or sheets might indicate the surrender of the civil population, but there might still be pockets of determined soldiers to be overcome. So, God help any village if a shot was fired at the US troops, or if a rocket flare disclosed a Panzerfaust team was in action. In such cases the American commander on the ground called down an airstrike and anything that survived the fury of the aircraft was smashed in the systematic and prolonged bombardment of tank guns. It was a prodigal use of ammunition, but it did save lives and served to reinforce the point that instant and frightful retribution followed any hostile act against the tank men of Patton's Third Army.

Meanwhile the situation in Prague had become tense, and there were clashes in Wenceslas Square, the focal point of demonstrations and rallies, between German soldiers and mobs of Czech youths. Under orders not to be provocative, the servicemen did not react to the insults, the threats and the intimidation with their accustomed swiftness and ruthlessness. Sensing this hesitation the mob grew more daring. German power began to slip away. In the afternoon the defacing and removal of German signs had spread to the main streets and squares of the old city. German shop windows were shattered by stones and all over the city enamelled shields bearing German place names crashed to the ground to the applause and laughter of the crowds. The mobs grew in number as workers left factories, offices and shops.

Militant Czech officials of some government departments in the Hradschin Palace went so far as to demand that their German colleagues and in some cases, their superiors, leave their offices and turn over to the insurgents the task of ruling the emerging nation. The decay of German rule was not confined to just the capital, for reports received by the Secretary to the Protector detailed spreading anti-German feeling and demonstrations in a great number of towns. There were still some German officers who were determined to maintain control and sent out army and SS patrols. Wherever the well-armed and disciplined battalions appeared the shouting, the window smashing and the casting down of German signs suddenly halted and the mob melted away into side-streets and alleys. But the situation had deteriorated to such an extent that German soldiers no longer walked alone or even in pairs, but only in groups strong enough to resist the partisans.

Throughout the final hours of 3 May, throughout that night and the following day, pressure within the city built up to a danger point where one incident could cause a blood-bath. The Czech knew that the situation which the Germans faced was a hopeless one. Hitler was dead and the government of Admiral Doenitz had neither the authority nor the influence to control events. The Third Reich existed in only a few shrinking pockets of territory in southern Germany, on the Baltic or in Czechoslovakia. The Czechs felt that there was no purpose in the Germans holding on in the Protectorate. They should hand over political power and go back to Germany – all of them. Not the Nazis alone, but also those relics of Habsburg rule and especially those who had arrived in the country during the seventeenth century and had dispossessed Slav farmers in the Sudetenland. All the hated Teutons should be encouraged to go. As the hours passed the mood of the civil population hardened to cold hatred. Those hours of transformation changed the mood of the Czechs from desiring the departure of the Germans to a desire to destroy anything and everything German; to nothing less than complete expulsion of the German population; forcibly if needs be.

The German authorities in the Protectorate were still unaware of the depth of that hatred or to what degree they had lost control of the situation. They were still undecided as to what should be their course of action. Berlin was no longer the seat of Reichs authority and no orders had come from Doenitz to Frank. In the absence of orders from his superior, Frank stayed in Prague and issued no orders to his subordinates. Doenitz *had* issued a proclamation in which there had been a vague demand for the need to hold the Eastern Front intact – and Prague was in the East, but there had been no further directives. Frank decided to continue as if nothing had happened while all around him the pretence of authority crumbled. The loss of power had so manifested itself that some Czech officials had demanded that power be transferred immediately to them so as to prevent a general uprising on the part of the Czech population and its concomitant of war in the streets.

There were now very few German Army units still in Prague. Warned by the radio that American troops were inside the Protectorate and that Russian armies were sweeping down from Brunn, the German commanders swung their units south-west to avoid capture. The western regions of the Protectorate still had a certain number of military formations but the only troops which remained in the Czech capital were SS detachments, those in hospital and certain rear echelon army troops. Then the news spread that the German Army Group in Italy had surrendered to General Alexander and this was followed by the rumour that an armistice would be signed within a week. Czech officials who pointed out these facts to their German colleagues asked them directly; what are you waiting for? Leave now before it is too late.

Prague slept that night of 5/6 May, in a fever of excitement. Eager hands pushed flags into maps to show how close the Allied armies were to the city. Like an inexorable tide the Red Army was sweeping down from the north while the Americans were driving in from the west. A spectator on the Kinsky Hill on the cold, starry night of 5/6 May, would have seen to the north and to the north-west the lightning flashes of gunfire which proclaimed a battle in progress. Tomorrow, or at the latest in two days, the soldiers of the Red Army must arrive in the capital.

There were other natives of Czechoslovakia to whom those days were not exciting but terrifying. I am referring, specifically, to the Volksdeutsche who had farmed the Sudetenland for generations. Their pride of race had once been an advantage. Suddenly being German had become a liability – more than a liability, it had become a sentence of death. What the Sudeten Germans underwent was not unique to them. It was a horror repeated at a great many places on the Eastern and South-Eastern Fronts and the martyrdom of the Sudeten Germans detailed in the following pages represents the suffering that was general.

'The robbings and the beatings began at dawn on the 9th. The Czechs, punctilious as always to the letter of the law, did not attack us during the night of the 8th/9th even though the war had ended and we were their captives.

The trek had been halted at a crossroads high in the hills. The war ended at midnight and the trek was ordered to halt at that time. We were not allowed to go any further until it had been decided what the victors would do with us. We were at this crossroads. The middle of vast forests often contain very big patches of ground on which no trees grow and where even the grass is sparse, for the soil is thin. The whole of our trek was stuck at that crossroads in that empty, flat plain. Each road leading towards the crossroads was a mass of wagons and carts packed with refugees. At some time during the night some of the refugees lit the first campfires. The war was over. There was no need now for black-out precautions.

I was woken about four in the morning. It was my turn to stand guard and I saw many fires along our column as well as on the other roads. All the fires formed, so I thought, the shape of a Cross, the fiery symbol of the Passion that we were to suffer. As soon as it was light enough we could see whole areas filled with masses of partisans, many with red flags and all armed to the teeth. There were lots of trucks and lorries; vehicles that had once belonged to the German Army. Groups of partisans started to shepherd our people towards the crossroads and eventually we were all gathered there in a jostling mass. We had to leave our carts and these stood empty. Everybody had to go to the crossroads, even the children and the sick. Loudspeaker vans ordered us to hand over all weapons, even pocket-knives. The German soldiers were marched away – eastwards, towards the Soviet Union and Siberia and that left only us civilians, defenceless and frightened.

A loudspeaker van ordered all Sudeten Germans to assemble at one certain point, Reichsdeutsche at another place and other Volksdeutsche – that is those from

Hungary and from Roumania, in a third place. From somewhere close at hand there was a burst of firing and this seemed to be the signal for the Czechs to plunder our unguarded carts. Some of our men started to run towards the carts intending to stop the looting, but the partisans shot them down as they ran. This caused our women to scream and to cry. And that caused one particular partisan, a bald man of about forty years of age, to lose control. He had a dog lead in his hand and he rushed into the screaming women lashing at them and flogging them with the steel end of the lead. His action started the real terror as other partisans followed his example.

What happened then is so terrible that I do not even like to think about it. Men who tried to protect their womenfolk were shot as they knelt or crouched over the bodies of the women. Then came the robbing of the women. Those with gold chains around their necks had them stolen. Wedding rings were taken. In fact, anything of value was torn off. Although I cannot remember seeing any of the partisans drinking a great many of them were very drunk and this made them even more violent.

The Reichsdeutsche and the Volksdeutsche were marched away and we Sudeten Germans, about five hundred in number, were soon alone. The men were separated from the women and children. We all had to stand in ranks and we had been standing there for some time when groups of partisans walked through our ranks and selected men at random and led them away behind some carts. There were shots heard and the Czechs came back and laughed at our fear. Then they picked out fresh victims. There were about twenty in number. This group was ordered to kneel down in front of the rest of us – about 50 yards in front of us. There was a clicking of bolts then one of the partisans swung the barrel of his rifle along the line of kneeling men. He fired. One of the men fell forward. Another partisan stepped up and traversed his rifle along the line of men now shaking with fear. There was another shot but this time nobody fell. The partisan had deliberately aimed wide of his target. A third Czech pointed his rifle and pulled the trigger. There was no explosion. He roared with laughter. He had not loaded the gun. It was a huge joke. Then a fourth partisan fired and killed a man from my own village. So it went on. How long we stood there while they slowly selected their victims in that line and tormented them before murdering them, I do not know. Eventually, all the twenty or so were dead.

If we moved while standing in line we were beaten with sticks or gun butts. Sometimes we were beaten for no reason at all. It was well past midday when a group of partisans rushed into the crowd of women and there was a lot of screaming. We could guess what was happening. The Czechs were dragging out the young women to rape them. The older ones tried to form a circle so as to protect the girls, but against an enemy who is willing to kill you all the passive resistance in the world is no use. The girls were taken out and then stripped. Then the rapes began. Not just by one man of one girl but the multiple rape of one girl by a whole group of men. There were also some of the rapists who had abnormal desires. When the attacks began we rushed forward to show the partisans that we were determined to protect our women. Bursts of machine-gun fire over our heads caused only a slight hesitation and as we ran on the Czechs opened fire with machine pistols and killed *or wounded about forty of our group. We were flogged back with whips and clubs and some of the wounded were bayoneted. It was a humiliating experience to be so helpless and to be able to do nothing to help the poor girls. I will not dwell on what happened. It was humiliation that even now makes me burn with a sense of outrage and shame.'*

The two groups of Sudeten Germans, men and the women, were kept standing in that area all day. It was particularly hard on those unfortunates who had dysentery, for they were not allowed to break ranks. Some groups of men were led away; it was thought that they would be shot but they had been selected to bury the dead, to carry away loot for the new masters or to perform some other task for the Czech overlords. The arrival of some Czech army officers stopped the rapes, and they were able to organize food for the two groups, although this was not distributed until the following day. During that day the partisans drove away with the carts and soon the only sign that there had been a trek was the broken furniture, torn clothing scattered by the side of the road and the fresh graves. Czech Army doctors also came up and tended to the wounded.

'Late in the afternoon of that second day we were told by loudspeaker that as German swine we were not wanted in Czechoslovakia and that we were to leave the Republic within twenty-four hours. We were allowed to take nothing with us except what clothes we stood up in. Those of our people who were too weak would have to be carried as would those too old or too ill to march. There would be no transport for German swine. Anybody who was left behind by the side of the road would be shot. Anyone found on Czech soil after the twenty-four hours had elapsed would be shot.

We marched! No we didn't! We shuffled along the roads carrying on our shoulders the weak and the sick. The women carried the girls who had been raped. They wouldn't let the men go near them. It seemed to be such a long way to the border. The last mile or two was uphill. How many died on that trek I don't know, because I do not know how many began it or how many finished it. What happened to the groups of Reichs and Volksdeutsche, I do not know. I never saw them after we were separated into national groups.

It goes without saying that we were beaten constantly during the trek to the frontier. When we reached the frontier there was a whole mass of Czechs waiting. They fell on us like locusts, stealing whatever was left. Lots of them subjected our women to what they termed 'body searches', to see if they had any jewels concealed – you can guess the nature of those searches. The men were not allowed to cross over until about forty-five minutes before the twenty-four hours expired. The partisans delayed our departure as long as they could, but when they finally let us go they forced us to run the gauntlet. Blows came from every direction. What the Czechs wanted to do was to knock us insensible so that we would still be on Czech soil when the time expired. They would then be justified in shooting us. We left behind there only three people and they had died under the blows of that gauntlet. The corpses were dragged away by the partisans.

We had hoped to be in safety once we had passed into the Reich, but the guards on the German side wore the Red Star, too, and began to attack the women. We had passed out of the hands of the Czech partisans into the hands of the Red Army. Eventually, we did pass into a Displaced Persons camp and I escaped from there, together with my family, during the Hungarian rising of 1956. I had spent eleven years of my life behind barbed wire.

In those years as a DP I was allowed back only once to Czechoslovakia. I had to sign some papers passing ownership of our family farm over to the Czechs. I passed close to the village in which our farm had once stood. The whole area was a wilderness of concrete anti-tank defences and anti-tank minefields. There was nothing growing at all. Three centuries of good husbandry had gone forever.'

There were still some major formations in the slowly disintegrating German Army that had the power and the morale to take the offensive. One which was still capable and aggressive was the 2nd SS Panzer Division 'Das Reich' and one of the regiments of that formation carried out its last military operation in Prague; an unusual and interesting mission.

In the last week of April 'Das Reich' Division had been given a series of conflicting orders, evidence of the confused political leadership within the German government. Attempts to obey these contradictory orders had resulted in the component regiments of the Division being widely dispersed. SS Panzer Grenadier Regiment No. 4 'Der Führer' had concentrated in the Budweis region and was under orders to go into action in the area of Brunn. SS Panzer Grenadier Regiment No. 3 'Deutschland' was in Linz area, while divisional headquarters, together with the Panzer Regiment, the artillery, the anti-aircraft regiments, the Engineer battalion and the Signals battalion were en route to the area of Dresden. It had been proposed to use 'Das Reich' in the offensive to relieve Berlin, but there had been no time for the division to deploy before the Red Army's advance caught it with the Grenadier regiments detached from the main body. Each element of the SS Panzer Division battled where it stood and was destroyed, piecemeal. Although the actions of each of those units is interesting the following account of the fighting in Czechoslovakia recounts, principally, the operation in which 'Der Führer' regiment was involved.

On 30 April, the Regimental Commander, Obersturmbannführer Weidinger, was ordered to report to the SS Commandant of Prague. During the morning of 1 May, the commander and his escort set out and reached the Czech capital without incident. The SS Commandant of Prague, Obergruppenführer Puckler, explained to Weidinger the principal difficulty which faced him. He might have to evacuate all those civilians who wished to return to Germany. How many might wish to avail themselves of this opportunity he did now know, but he did know that there was no motor transport to convey them, nor was it possible for them to be evacuated by train. The Protector, Karl Hermann Frank, had proposed that any evacuation be made on foot or by horse-drawn cart. A strong and reliable military unit would have to protect the columns of civilians.

In response to Weidinger's question as to why nothing had been prepared earlier to meet such a possibility, Puckler offered the excuse that a premature evacuation might well have encouraged the Czechs to rise in revolt. Weidinger was assured that Prague was quiet and was likely to remain so. The regimental commander, naturally, accepted these assurances by the SS Commandant, for Puckler was the man on the spot and should know the true situation. How was Weidinger to know that his superior and, indeed, the whole German political apparatus in Czechoslovakia, was out of touch with the true situation in the Protectorate? Before Weidinger returned to his regiment, he did discuss with Princess Stephanie zu Schaumburg-Lippe* the plans which she had begun to make for the evacuation of those German civilians who wished to leave Prague.

The battlefield conference of 'Der Führer' regiment during the evening of 1 May, was overshadowed by the news that Hitler had fallen during the battle for Berlin. Weidinger stressed in his briefing that although the regiment had carried the Führer title as a regimental distinction, the chief loyalty had been and was still pledged to Germany. The Führer's death had not released the SS men from their oath; rather did the name on their cuff band demand of them a firmer discipline and a stronger need for courage and for loyalty. Almost as an afterthought Weidinger mentioned that in view of the changed political situation it was unlikely that the offensive by Wenck's Army to relieve Berlin would now take place. He touched upon the probability of providing an escort for the German civilians in Prague and ordered that the regiment move closer to the Czech capital.

During that move, on 5 May, the Grenadier battalions of 'Der Führer' regiment saw strong evidence of the dissolution of order and discipline within the army. For mile after mile, as the Regiment's vehicle columns made their way forward, the SS men could see abandoned arms and equipment; trucks, half-tracks and even tanks in working order, scattered and abandoned by the sides of the roads. This evidence of the collapse of good order and discipline within the German Army was paralleled by evidence of the growth of partisan activity by the civilian population. Even in rural areas road signs had been defaced, Czech flags were flying and the occasional barricade was met although few of these were manned by armed insurgents.

In the regimental concentration area on the night of 5 May, two orders came for Weidinger. The first told him that the deteriorating military situation made it no longer possible for the Regiment to link up with the remainder of Das Reich Division. With immediate effect 'Der Führer' was therefore placed under the direct command of the Army Group Commander, Field Marshal Schoerner. The second message was an order from Schoerner that the Regiment was to open and to hold open the road to Prague; that it was to put down the insurrection within the city, to link up with General Toussaint, the Army Commandant of Prague, and to carry out such orders as

---

*As a German aristocrat, and as a person with extensive contacts among the Czech leaders, she was the obvious choice of the German authorities to organize the evacuation of their people from Prague.

he might issue. Schoerner's message urged the necessity to complete the mission with the utmost possible speed. Weidinger could well feel disconcerted by the change in political events. Only seventy-two hours earlier the SS Commandant of Prague had assured him that the city was quiet. Schoerner's insistent order made it very clear that this was not the case and that in fact there was rioting of such proportion that the city garrison and the government of the Protectorate were isolated and virtual prisoners.

The flexibility of the German army was ably demonstrated in the construction of battle groups – Kampfgruppen or KG. Units would be selected to form a battle group which would be given a certain specific task upon the completion of which the KG would be broken up and its component parts returned to their parent units. In Weidinger's opinion speed

Right: with the cities of the Reich threatened by the advance of the Allied armies, it fell to the citizens to erect anti-tank barricades. Many of these were so flimsy that they were completely useless; but the one being constructed here would have been sufficiently deep and firm to hold back an enemy advance.

was more important than heavy armour and he built Kampfgruppe 'Der Führer' on that premise. To the three Grenadier battalions of the Regiment he added one armoured reconnaissance Company of the divisional reconnaissance battalion, a second similar Company, taken from an Army Division, plus the 2nd Battalion of the Das Reich divisional artillery together with two of the Division's medical Companies. In view of the Army Group Commander's call for speed Weidinger ordered that the Kampfgruppe should be ready to march out at 05.00 hrs.

While the SS Regiment was preparing itself for the undertaking, the situation inside Prague had deteriorated alarmingly, owing to rumours concerning the entry of the American Army into Prague and the intervention of German Army Cossack units on the side of Czech insurgents.

Punctually to the second, the first vehicles of KG 'Der Führer' swung out of the area in which regimental headquarters had spent the night and drove in bright sunshine towards Leitmeritz. The vehicles had all been properly serviced, fuel tanks had been filled, the road was smooth and the convoy made good speed for the first miles. The signs of German collapse became more frequent as groups of soldiers were encountered, usually without weapons – which they explained had been taken from them by partisans. Road-blocks became more frequent, but most were of such flimsy construction that they could be smashed aside by the armoured reconnaissance vehicles.

Then, as the column approached the suburbs of Prague, it came to a road-block which resisted every effort to push it over. This barrier was not the usual rural one of a couple of farm carts or tree trunks laid across the road, but was of stone. In those days, the suburban streets of Prague were surfaced with small square cobbles. For hundreds of yards these had been torn up and used to build a barrier nearly six feet high and nearly as thick, placed at a point in the road where the column could not bypass it. To turn back to Leitmeritz was unthinkable and the SS Grenadiers were put to work to dismantle the barricade. A patrol returned quickly, having found no civilians who could be made to help the SS men. Leaving only sentries on duty in a few vehicles to guard against surprise attack, Weidinger set the remainder of his men the task of removing the thousands of stones.

Schoerner, to whom Weidinger had reported responded with the sort of message which Generals usually send hard-pressed commanders in such situations. 'The honour and the reputation of Der Führer Regiment depends upon it reaching the inner city of Prague by 7 May.' There were other messages coming over the air, for reception was, and remained, perfect throughout the operation. From these it was clear that Prague radio station had been captured by the rebels. Inflammatory announcements urging the Czech people to rise in revolt were interspersed with appeals to the Allies to hurry to prevent the city becoming a battlefield and with other statements that the Americans had reached the city and that the war was at an end. The radio station was set upon a hill on the left of Weidinger's line of march and the SS commander decided that he could spare the Army Recce Company to recapture it from the rebels in a short, swift assault.

The afternoon wore on and then the evening, and the SS were still busy tearing down the wall. To ensure that his men remained at work, Weidinger drove a line of trucks forward, removed the hoods from their headlamps and switched on the lights. In this blaze the SS soldiers presented fine, distinct targets to partisan riflemen lying concealed in the dark. Fire was answered with fire and machine-gunners in the recce cars sprayed bullets at any muzzle flash. Late in the evening of the 6th a gap had been made wide enough to allow the vehicles to pass through and soon the column was moving fast to make good the time that had been lost. The great mass of vehicles roared through the night with blazing headlamps ignoring the occasional sniper fire and machine-gun aimed at the column.

At the Troya bridge in Prague there was more determined resistance and as the first vehicles crossed they were met with a hurricane of fire which forced them to withdraw. Weidinger was now faced with a choice. Either he accepted the Field Marshal's challenge and pushed on or he halted the advance and waited until daylight. To such an experienced soldier as the SS commander it was obvious that any attempt to force a crossing of the bridge would embroil his battle group in costly house-to-house fighting. Schoerner's demand for speed and action would have to go unmet, but preparations could be made for an attack to go in at first light.

Shortly after dawn on 7 May, the SS artillery opened fire and, supported by machine-gun and cannons, the SS Grenadiers thrust across the bridge and into the attack. Fire from houses commanding the exits from the bridge was heavy, sustained and accurate. Casualties mounted and soon twenty-five SS were dead and three times that number seriously wounded. During the battle a Czech officer arrived at Weidinger's battle headquarters and offered to act as an intermediary between the battle group and the partisans, first demanding that the KG cease fire and that Weidinger and his men return to Leitmeritz. Weidinger rejected the second proposal out of hand and agreed to the first only if the Czechs first ceased their fire. The battle group had been halted at the approaches to the Troya bridge for the greater part of that day. Darkness brought all firing to an end. It also brought an end to Weidinger's patience. He was furious that the partisans should obstruct the movement of his SS battle group and very early next morning he flung his force across the bridge and established a small perimeter.

Over Prague radio, now once again in the hands of the Czechs, came the announcement that the war in Europe would end at midnight that night. Whether or not the Czech announcer was speaking the truth was not important to those of the battle group who heard him. What was important was that 'Der Führer' had been given a task to complete and it was already behind time. Now they had to break out of the perimeter. Shortly before the KG formed up ready to drive into Prague a second Czech officer appeared who offered to liaise with the partisan forces and with General Toussaint, the German Army's Commandant in Prague. Weidinger put his viewpoint succinctly but firmly. His orders he explained were to drive to a square in the old town and to liaise with Toussaint, and he intended to do just that. If the drive could be accomplished without incident that would help, but alternatively, the SS were willing and able to fight their way through to the rendezvous. An officer of the German Army accompanying the KG offered to go with the Czech as his bona fides. Before the two officers left Weidinger issued a warning. If the German had not returned by 15.00 hrs the SS would consider the truce to be broken and the guns would open up again. At the appointed time there was still no sign of either officers and when by 16.00 hrs neither had reported in, Weidinger gave the order to open fire. Suddenly there was a commotion; the two officers had returned bringing with them news that an armistice had been agreed between the partisan forces and the German commanders in the Hradschin Palace. The barrage was halted.

Meanwhile SS patrols had swept the streets and squares in the immediate area and had found military ration stores, ammunition depots and fuel dumps. Lorries, motor-cycles and cars which had been abandoned by German soldiers were collected, fuelled, fitted with extra petrol cans, and ammunition was distributed. It was a paradox that within hours of the end of the war, the regiment was at full war establishment in every respect. Even the three Grenadier battalions had been brought up to full strength as convalescents and volunteers came in to join the strong and resolute group. The regiment had accepted the armistice between the Army Commandant and the insurgents, but were determined to resist with force any hostile action made against them. And they had the strength to carry out that threat.

The last conference before the KG moved out on the final stage of its mission planned what was to be done. The German civilians waiting for the arrival of 'Der Führer' would be loaded on the vehicles. If necessary the trucks would be overloaded, but nobody would be left behind. The column would make for Pilsen and if the Czechs kept their side of the bargain all road-blocks would have been removed and signs would have been erected to guide the convoy through the night. Weidinger laid great stress on correct behaviour. There was to be no alcohol consumed. When the regiment drove into captivity it would do so in correct military fashion with each man clean and sober. Because of the armistice there would be no firing, but weapons would be loaded and manned, ready for action.

Before the battle group set out to link up with the Army Commandant, the SS Commander sent out the two final messages: one to the headquarters of Das Reich Division and the other to Schoerner. Both signals announced that when the mission had been completed the regiment would surrender to the Americans and each signal ended with a patriotic slogan.

Sharp at 19.00 hrs the Kampfgruppe drove off to the rendezvous point with a Czech officer standing on the running-board of the lead vehicle to guide the way. Czech sentries at each dismantled road-block saluted as the SS swept through. The slow drive took just under an hour and as the vehicles drove up and parked in formation it was clear that a certain confusion reigned. Czech officials were trying to forcibly eject German civil servants while Frank was firm in his conviction that the armistice had still a day to run. Weidinger informed him quite bluntly that German power in the city was now numbered in minutes and that the convoy must soon be loaded up and on its way. To add to the confusion General Toussaint proposed that the Kampfgruppe try to reach Austria, having forgotten perhaps that Vienna and the eastern provinces of Austria had been occupied by the Russians for more than a week. The SS officer insisted that the orders which he had issued be adhered to. He could not change them now. All his people knew that Pilsen was the objective; the destination and the route could not be changed.

Fresh complications arose. There were several ambulance trains filled with German wounded. The trains could not be moved. The Czech railway staff had abandoned them. The wounded would have to be brought from the trains and loaded onto the battle group vehicles. Then in came a group of female SS signallers and places had to be found for them. Finally all were aboard. The civilians, the wounded, the women soldiers, the administrators and the men of 'Der Führer' regiment. The column was made up of nearly one thousand vehicles.

At 21.00 hrs on 8 May, the convoy, few of the vehicles recognizable as military and all of them overloaded, moved away from the rendezvous area and headed towards Pilsen. The journey was completed with only one interruption which came on the morning of 9 May, when a German General and a Czech Colonel halted the column and demanded that all arms be handed over. Weidinger's response was to order all firearms to be rendered useless before they were thrown away. During this enforced halt the Commander took the opportunity to hold the last pay-parade. The regimental cash-box was opened and the contents distributed among the men.

Just before nine on the morning of 9 May, the objective was reached and the civilians and the wounded were unloaded. The SS women elected to stay with the regiment. An hour later and the lead vehicles of 'Der Führer' Regiment, carrying Weidinger and his headquarters staff, made contact with troops of US 2nd Infantry Division at Rokiczany. Without ceremony the American soldiers ordered the SS officers out of the vehicles in which they were travelling and directed them to a field where their camp would be set up. Contemptuous of the dusty, unmilitary GIs of 2nd Division, the SS commander brought his headquarters group to attention and marched them as an organized and military body, into captivity. On their tunics were the awards and decorations honouring six years of war. At their waists the pistols they had been allowed to retain; on their cuffs the title band of their allegiance and on their collars the insignia of their rank.

The small group of SS officers marching in step across the grass had not gone far when they were surrounded by American soldiers each of them keen on obtaining some souvenir from the SS. The marching group was halted and pulled apart and in vain Weidinger demanded to see an officer of the US forces. There seemed to be none on hand. Within minutes the German group had been stripped of everything that could be classified as a memento and the same undignified fate awaited the men of the battle group as, throughout the day, they came in to surrender.

It was a tragedy for the Germans. They had intended to overawe the Americans with their martial bearing and with soldierly qualities maintained even in defeat. The US troops saw the marching SS groups as a sort of mobile shop counter where good souvenirs could be had for the taking and were so little influenced by the awesome Prussian discipline that the history of the 2nd Division does not even mention 'Der Führer' by name. It was lumped among the miscellaneous detachments which came in as a result of the surrender. Not to be recognized for what one is – or what one thinks one is – is the final humiliation.

Of all the tragedies that occurred during the Prague crises in the first week of May, none was sadder than the intervention of the anti-Communist Cossack cavalry units of General Vlassov's army.

The invasion of the Soviet Union by Germany in June 1941, had produced in the areas overrun by the Wehrmacht national liberation movements which were violently anti-Communist and anti-Russian. Out of a burning desire to fight against Soviet tyranny military units had been formed in the Ukraine, the Cossack lands and the Caucasus, which had placed themselves at the disposal of the German Army. Hitler opposed the formation of such an anti-Communist Army until very late in the war, by which time it was too late to produce the result which might have been obtained in 1943 or 1944. Nevertheless, without the Führer's consent or knowledge, native formations had been raised and these were commanded by men of influence and great ability. Among the most successful of these leaders was General Vlassov, a former Red Army General and dedicated communist who had been captured by the Germans and who had subsequently volunteered to lead a crusade against Bolshevism. When in the last months of the war permission was given reluctantly by Hitler for an anti-Communist military Force to be raised, Vlassov's zeal and efficiency soon had two Cossack Divisions under arms. It is with Bunyachenko's 1st Cossack Cavalry Division that we are concerned.

The 1st was the only one of Vlassov's two divisions that had actually fought alongside its German comrades in arms, and in a bitter battle it had been badly mauled and suffered severe losses. Bunyachenko had withdrawn his depleted sabre regiments from the line and rejecting the demand of Field Marshal Schoerner for them to be used in penny packets without reference to Cossack needs, had marched his regiments through Czechoslovakia to Beraun, south-west of Prague. It was to this encampment that the Czech underground leaders came to discuss with the Cossack commanders a joint action against the Germans. The Czechs were well aware that Schoerner had threatened to have Bunyachenko shot for refusing to obey orders and that the Cossacks were depressed from the battle in which they had suffered such heavy losses. It proved no difficult task to convince the General and his men to support the projected rising and within hours patrols of Cossacks were cutting down with sabres or shooting the German troops they encountered. The next thing was for Bunyachenko to move his Division into the city. He sent out strong patrols, which entered Prague on 2 May, and had soon made common cause with the partisans. The Cossacks were the heroes of the hour. They were the men who would help to free Prague when the call came. They were the first liberators, and pictures of Vlassov and other leaders were soon displayed in shop windows.

At that time, there was no German military unit in Prague strong enough to oppose the Cossack advance. The combat formations of Army Group Centre were well to the east of the capital. The government was not a military body nor did it have a unit under its command strong enough to take on Bunyachenko and his Division. There was one single chance. The 2nd Training and Replacement Battalion of the SS was indeed made up of recruits but it might have the power to challenge the Cossacks. Orders went out to Sturmbannführer Oettinger, the Battalion Commander, that he and his unit were to prevent the main body of 1st Cossack Division from entering the city. How he was expected to accomplish this was not made clear since among his orders was one that forbade the SS to make use of firearms. In the event the problem did not arise; the Division was already in the city and its 1st Regiment had soon surrounded the Prague-Rusin aerodrome on which the SS battalion and Luftwaffe personnel had prepared defensive positions. Fighting broke out between the two sides.

By late in the afternoon of 7 May, the Cossack banner and the Czech flag were flying side by side as patrols from both forces moved through the streets. Outside the city heavy fighting was continuing at Rusin where the Cossacks had lost three hundred men killed in frontal assaults against machine-gun positions. An ultimatum to the SS and the Luftwaffe troops to surrender or be hanged when taken prisoner was rejected and fighting continued throughout the night.

The morning of 8 May saw Prague covered in a sea of red flags and to the Cossacks it was horribly significant that the pictures of Vlassov had been removed from shop windows and replaced by those of Stalin. During that last day of the war a provisional government was formed in Prague, most of the members of which were Communist. The anti-Communist Bunyachenko and his men were, in the eyes of that local government committee, double-dyed traitors with whom they would have no dealings. The only advice that the committee gave to the Cossack General was that his Division should surrender to the Red Army, whose arrival was expected hourly.

With no qualms of conscience Bunyachenko returned to the Rusin airfield, called off the attacks by 1st Regiment and made his peace with the German garrison. He was an ally again. During the night the 1st Cossack Division and the SS garrison moved together out of Rusin and marched south-westwards to Beraun. There were incidents. During one, Czech partisans opened fire and overran the column's rearguard detachments. Nothing has ever been learned of the fate of the men of that rearguard group.

In the afternoon of 9 May, the Cossacks reached their former camping ground at Beraun and halted there while the SS went on to surrender to the US forces in Pilsen. In the late evening Bunyachenko and his officers were to dine with Czech liaison officers who would negotiate with the American Army the surrender of this special formation. The location of the dinner party was well away from the Cossack encampment and the meal was a pleasant one, enlivened with toasts to all and sundry. The armistice commission arrived, but its members were not American officers but men of the Soviet secret police, the NKVD. Those among the Cossacks who were fortunate were those who died quickly. Most perished miserably; beaten to death, blinded, tortured and pushed into vats of acid. With their officers dead, the men of the Cossack Division could not organize resistance so that when the killer squads of the NKVD arrived in the encampment, it was no difficult task to destroy the Cossack dream.

Self-deception is the cruellest of all self-inflicted wounds and nowhere is it more cruel than when it is grounded in racial or national hopes. The Cossacks knew who they were and assumed that the rest of the world would know that they represented a demand for liberation. It was a delusion for Vlassov and his men to believe that their actions would be seen as anything but base treachery. They chose the wrong road and paid the penalty of treason. Whether these many thousands of men were traitors or not is a moral judgement that I shall not make. I state it only as a fact that the Cossacks were not the only ones guilty of treachery in Prague during the last days of the war in Europe.

Above: the people of Prague greet the Red Army as liberators, 9 May 1945.

5
THE SOUTHERN SECTOR: AUSTRIA

Vienna had fallen in the middle week of April, a defeat that provoked from Hitler the cry that 'Berlin would remain German and that Vienna would become German again.' As a propaganda slogan it had brevity, clarity and punch. As a statement of military ability it was without hope of realization.

The geographical shape of Austria makes it confusing to deal with as a single battle front and it will be handled here as part of three separate fronts. The fighting in the province of the Steiermark (Styria) will form part of the story of the Eastern Front. Kärnten (Carinthia) will be included in that section of the book which details the war's end in Jugoslavia and Italy; that was the Southern Front. The battles fought in Tyrol and Salzburg will form part of the narrative of the Western Front.

During that period of the war with which this book is concerned, the French, the Americans and the Russians were all fighting on Austrian territory. The 1st French Corps had captured Vorarlberg and parts of the Tirol. US armies were driving down through the provinces of Upper Austria and Salzburg, while in the east, Tolbukhin's 3rd Ukrainian Front had taken Burgenland and its armies had fought their way past Vienna and into Lower Austria. To the south of the capital Russian forces had effected a penetration of the heavily forested province of the Steiermark, had been held there and, in some places, flung back in disarray. This chapter of the book will concentrate on the fighting in the Steiermark, but we cannot deny the capital, Vienna, a place even though it was, by the time of this story, no longer a battlefield but a zone of occupation.

Although Prague had suffered little and the 'golden city' had lost nothing of its gilded splendour, Vienna, the former Imperial city, had been fought over and showed it. The great Gothic cathedral of St Stephen was a burned-out, roofless ruin, as was the Opera House. The bridges across the Danube and the Danube canal had either been destroyed completely or were so badly damaged as to be unuseable, while in the Prater, that great pleasure park of Vienna, the bodies of fallen soldiers were still lying putrefying in the warmth of the early spring days.

Although, as a result of the fury of war, some of Vienna's architectural glories had been lost, there was compensation in something that had been restored to Austria. For the first time since March 1938, there was an Austrian government led by the veteran Socialist, Karl Renner. Established by the Russians, it was strongly left-biased, but it did embrace all the traditional parties and it was a new beginning, a rediscovery of democratic ways. In May 1945, the tasks which faced Renner's government were daunting. It had legal authority, but only in Vienna, and it had no power. With the war not yet ended, the Red Army could spare very little to aid the process of reconstruction, although Red Army engineers had built emergency bridges across the waterways and had also organized civilian work gangs to clear the streets choked with the rubble of destroyed buildings.

The Red Army divisions which had battled their way through Vienna had, by the end of April, moved north-westwards into Lower Austria, leaving behind them a city dazed and damaged, but now out of the war. In that interim situation the people of Vienna knew now the answer to the question that each had silently asked. What would it be like in the final days and hours? Now they knew and they had survived the horrors. They had come alive through the ordeal and surely nothing could be as terrible as the passion through which they had passed. During the war they had been subjected to massive air bombardments; to cascades of napalm and thundering explosions. The Viennese had survived them. The thundering barrages of artillery fired by the Germans and the Russians and the terror of the street fighting. These, too, they had escaped. Then had come the Red Army and the rapings and the senseless destruction of property by drunken soldiers. Few had been spared the indignity of theft, not even Chancellor Renner. When the Soviet authorities were told of the whereabouts of this famous Socialist politician they sent a Red Army Major to the modest house where the old man lived. The Russian officer greeted him with the words, 'You Renner. You Socialist. Good. Come with me,' and held out his hand. As Renner extended his own the Red Army officer in a single, fluid movement removed the Austrian Chancellor's gold watch.

Among the problems with which Renner's provisional government had to struggle was the complete breakdown of law and order. The prisons had been emptied during the fighting and the released criminals had erupted onto the streets of a Vienna devoid of policemen, for these had been put into battle as soldiers and the survivors were in prisoner-of-war camps. The city was flooded with thousands of assorted foreigners, soldiers and civilians, who had moved out of their own countries ahead of the Red Army. In eastern Austria and the capital there were more than one hundred thousand Hungarians. Adolf Schaerf in his book, *April 1945 in Wien*, wrote of seldom hearing German spoken in the streets of Vienna in those early days.

The population of a large city that has come through the horrors of modern war and the passage of an avenging, enemy army requires food, peace and news above everything else. Such a population is docile, easily cowed and helpless when confronted by organized bands of professional criminals. The lawless elements of Vienna carried out the looting of the food stores while a great number of the ordinary Viennese and the Red Army were occupied in emptying the wine and spirit stores. When some people intervened to prevent the wholesale removal of foodstuffs they were shot at by the thieves who had armed themselves with the machine pistols which littered the streets. Electricity was not restored until the end of April and with it not only did the tramway system function again, but the radio now broadcast news which countered the wild rumours that had swept the city. There had been no way of establishing the true situation for lacking electrical power to turn the printing presses, no newspapers had been produced and the wildest stories of mass deportations and executions had been spread. It was a time of confusion and fear for a population whose fate was now in the hands of an alien, occupying Power.

'Bread came back into the shops about the same time as we heard that Hitler was dead. His death was not important and the impact it made was negligible. What was important was that food distribution had begun again. We used, if I remember correctly, exactly the same ration cards that we had had under the Nazis. The food was little enough, but at least we could buy something with money instead of having to barter with a soldier.'

Rape reached almost epidemic proportions in the numbers attacked, and many women tried to disguise themselves as boys or as old women in order to avoid becoming victims. One story which spread was that the Russians did not attack prostitutes for fear of contracting VD, but post-war medical reports were to show that syphilis and gonhorrea were very common in the Red Army and that the milder forms of venereal disease were endemic. Viennese women staying at home for fear of rape on the open streets, took to applying heavy cosmetic make-up and wearing provocative clothing if they heard the screams and firing that heralded the approach of licentious soldiery. Then, if the Soviets broke down the door in their search for women, the housewife would like on the bed and invite the Russians to take her. They seldom did – or at least so it was said. The prime targets for the Russian rapists were either very young girls in whom, so the soldiers believed, the disease had not developed, or else very old women who, by the simple logic of these unsophisticated men, could not be diseased, otherwise they would not have lived to such an age.

The attitude of the Red Army towards the Austrian civilian population varied between the very friendly and the shockingly brutal. A Viennese passing too close to a building that housed a Russian Kommandantura might be summarily arrested and would be lucky to escape with just a beating. If he were less lucky he might be herded with other civilians, arbitrarily kidnapped from the streets, to be sent eastwards in cattle-trucks as slave labourers in the mines of the Soviet Union. The Viennese kept wary watch and avoided groups of people being urged along under guard, en route to God knew what fate. It was soon learned that at intervals the Russian guards would stop the group and conduct a head count of the prisoners. If one or two had dodged the column, substitutes for the missing could be easily obtained by plucking from the pavement any civilian stupid enough to be in the vicinity. The male population of Vienna seemed suddenly all to have had their arms broken. A plaster cast was an effective aid to avoid conscription into a Russian-organized street clearing group. The removable casts and a supporting bandage were fitted before venturing into the streets where no young men were to be seen. The streets of the capital were crowded with foreign refugees or squads of Red Army men busily engaged in dismantling machinery. This was another problem with which Renner's government had to contend: the wholesale removal of machinery and factories to Soviet Russia. The Soviet leaders claimed that this was 'Fascist' equipment and, doubtless, much had been erected, installed or built during the lifetime of the Third Reich. But such equipment was, of course, vital for Austria's own recovery and its removal made the task of returning to a normal life that much more difficult. Perhaps the confiscations would have made sense if the Russian dismantlers had treated the machinery with care, but it was left on railway flat cars unprotected, so that when at last the trains did leave Vienna it was rusty and had been vandalized.

'In every street one could see the same picture. A broken-down civilian motor car or coach with a ring of Red Army men clustered around the bonnet and all offering advice. Hammers were used quite freely and it was also a normal picture to see horses harnessed to pull the motor cars. The civilian car was a prestige object for Russian officers – even if it had to be horse drawn. One amusing sight, I saw one afternoon, was some Red Army officers sitting, all carrying parasols, in an open car being pulled by horses.'

Totalitarian governments all follow predictable courses of action and they are great organizers of 'spontaneous' demonstrations and marches. A May Day demonstration in newly occupied Vienna, organized by the political officers of the Red Army, was the same type of 'spontaneous expression of the peoples' joy and thanks', as had taken place in the days of the Third Reich.

'The Nazis had had flags, red with a white circle and a black swastika. All that the Reds did was to take out the swastika and dye the central white section. Not only were they the same flags; the same people carried them. Those who had been the most ferocious Nazis were now the most dedicated Communists. The Ivans had organized a march for May Day and a great number of people went – because they were told that at the end of the march there would be a food distribution. Each marcher received half a loaf and a tin of some sort of meat and I am convinced that most marched for the food.'

Schaerf records in his book that there were political compromises made during the May Day marches organized in his district of Vienna. The Socialists outnumbered the Communists. If Schaerf and his comrades marched behind the Communist Party banners the impression would be given that the Red participation was predominant. So Schaerf and his colleagues wore the red carnation emblem of their Party to distinguish themselves. How quickly the horrors of the immediate past were forgotten in Party rivalry and while the parties of the Left conducted their political trading in Vienna and while in the capital city a peacetime life-style was evolving however slowly, in the province of the Steiermark the war went on. The General Officer Commanding of Sixth Army had used the time when the Russians had been fighting for Vienna to improve his Army's positions in the Steiermark. His battle line ran north to south from the high mountains of the Semmering to the low hills around Radkersburg where the River Mur formed the frontier with Jugoslavia.

The Freyung in Vienna after the rubble caused by bombing had been cleared by gangs of women and students.

Army Group South held the right wing of the German armies on the Eastern Front, but in the last week of April was faced with a new problem. The US forces thrusting through Austria were at its back. To Rendulic, the Army Group Commander, were sent orders to hold the east at all cost for, in the words of the OKW, 'It is decisive to the fate of the Reich'. The Americans whose attacks would soon overrun the Army Group's supplies and bases were to be met with such resistance as 'compatible with honour'.

Rendulic needed no advice on the importance of holding the Eastern Front intact. He knew, just as did all his subordinates, that were Tolbhukin's armies to sweep westwards through the Steiermark it would be a triple disaster. Not only would it fragment the Army Group, but it would also turn the southern flank of the whole eastern Front. Thirdly, it would cut off the German formations of Army Group 'E', which were withdrawing out of Jugoslavia. Of all Rendulic's armies, the Sixth was the most important for it held the crucial sector. It is upon just two units of that Army that the following account deals. Both were Gebirgsjäger (Mountain Rifles) formations and both held positions in the mountainous area of northern Steiermark. They were the 99th Regiment of 1st Gebirgs Division and 13th SS Gebirgsjäger Battalion which eventually, formed part of 9th Gebirgs Division.

The battles which will be described below lack the scale and movement of those offensives on other sectors in which millions of men were involved and in which there were swift advances over great distances. But these smaller operations in the mountains of the Steiermark had an unusual ferocity and intensity. They were among the few actions of the European war which can be truly described as having included hand-to-hand fighting.

It is with the SS Gebirgsjäger Ausrüstungs und Ersatz Batallion, No. 13 (The 13th Training and Replacement battalion of the SS Mountain Rifles), that we first deal for it fought in the most difficult terrain, on the Semmering Pass at the northern boundary of the Steiermark. As its title indicates the role of the battalion was not intended to be a combatant one. The greatest number of its soldiers were Volksdeutsche from Roumania or Jugoslavia who had had no pre-military training. The officers and senior NCOs of the battalion were Reichsdeutsche and were veteran soldiers who had been posted, chiefly from the 'Germanic' divisions of the SS. It was their task not merely to pass on their knowledge of front-line service, but also to instruct the Volksdeutsche in the more disciplined Reichsdeutsch attitudes and habits.

The crisis which occurred during the last week of March, when it was feared that the Red Army would drive into the Steiermark, produced an order from Gauleiter Ueberreither for the SS battalion, untrained though it was, to be put on an active service footing. The Gauleiter was the senior Nazi Party officer at provincial level and, in each Gau threatened by the Allied advance, had been given by Hitler the authority of a Defence Commisar. Thus he had powers which, in military matters, overrode those of the local Army commander. Ueberreither was resolved to hold the Steiermark for the Führer and to defend it to the last as Hitler had ordered. In his military capacity, animated by that spirit of do or die, he ordered those units as yet uncommitted to battle to be put into action. Among the formations which received the movement order was the 13th SS Training and Replacement battalion.

In those days the supply column of a Gebirgsjäger formation was a mule train. If the 13th was to move quickly upon the Gauleiter's order motor transport would be needed to increase the battalion's mobility. Hauptsturm- führer Grunwald, the CO of the 13th, gave orders that every unauthorized vehicle passing through the sector was to be confiscated and handed over to the battalion Transport Officer. A great many of the vehicles were seized from officers hoping to escape the Eastern Front and to reach the west. Any protests which the malingerers made to Grunwald were swiftly silenced. The threat of a drumhead court-martial stilled all protests. The SS Flying Courts-Martial were notorious and the military units in eastern Austria knew that they were merciless. In less hectic days than these, captured and convicted deserters were sent by the Army authorities to Graz, the provincial capital, and there formally executed by firing-squad. Such legalistic niceties were abandoned as the war reached its end. The SS officers who made up the tribunal were not only the accusers, but also the judges and the executioners. Sentence was swift and immediate. The condemned were hanged from the nearest tree or lamp-post.

'I had been walking for several hours and was on the road called the Ries that runs into Graz. We (my mother, aunt and I) had left the city. We had been evacuated to the eastern suburbs of Graz so as to avoid the heavy bombing. As I walked along the winding Ries road I saw on a tree growing along the road-side a man hanging. His face was sunk forward on his chest and he was just dangling there. Along the roads in some parts of our County there were in those days fruit trees growing and that man was hanging from one of them. He had a hand-written notice round his neck. It read "I was a coward". The sight of that terrible hanging thing frightened me and although I did not want to look at it, it kept drawing my gaze. It was a horrible sight. The man's face was blue-black in colour, although his hands were natural colour. I walked on quickly, trembling. Then I saw another body hanging, and then another. The rest of that frightening journey to Ragnitz was horrible. I had to pass so many of those dead men and I was alone on the road. Even in broad daylight and on a warm day I was shivering. Not all the dead men had placards around their necks. Those that did had some sort of message that they were cowards or traitors or had betrayed Hitler. Sometimes there were several bodies as if a group of men had been hanged together.

When I arrived home it took me a very long time to get the memory of those hanging men out of my mind and before I had really forgotten them we had to leave and go into the Weststeier because the Russians were moving towards Graz and were about to overrun the whole province.'

Under such threat, the threat of flying courts martial, therefore, it was not long before the battalion's transport column was a mechanized one, although the vehicles were of all types and ages. The only properly maintained and uniform group were those appliances of the Budapest fire brigade which had accompanied the Hungarian Prime Minister, Szalasi, when he fled into Austria.

When the order came for the battalion to march out and fight much of the essential equipment for its seven Companies could be taken forward by lorry or car, the remainder was carried by mule or by the troops themselves. The 13th were ordered to plug a gap in the battle line around the Semmering. There was no time for the battalion to call in its Companies which were scattered on training exercises. The advance to the battle area could not, therefore, be made as a cohesive formation, but was carried out by individual groups marching independently. The only constant thing in the whole battalion was the order which each contingent received. They were to march from Leoben, the battalion depot, northwards to the Semmering Pass and to maintain the advance until Russian resistance was too strong to be overcome. The exact location of the Red Army's units was uncertain. It was known that strong Soviet forces were driving south-westwards from Wiener Neustadt with the intention of seizing by *coup de main* the strategically important Semmering Pass through which their units would pour down into northern Steiermark. If the Russians gained the high ground they would have turned the left flank of 1st Gebirgs Division which was blocking the advance in the Oststeier. That Division would then have no choice but to withdraw. Such a course of action would allow the Red Army to flood into the Steiermark and then advance into Jugoslavia and Italy. To prevent that catastrophe the 1st Gebirgsjäger Division must hold the Soviets pressing from the East, but they could succeed in this only if a firm and reliable unit on the Semmering protected the Division's left flank. Although this account concentrates upon the 13th SS Battalion, it did not fight the battle alone and unaided. Ueberreither's 'alarm' call set a collection of military units marching to the summit of the Pass where a thin fighting line had been established. The German Army's skill in forming Kampfgruppen has already been mentioned and on this occasion that ability enabled a battle force to be welded out of the variety of units which arrived in the area.

The baptism of fire for the first Companies of the 13th that reached the Semmering was an easy victory. They wiped out a Red Army group led by one man playing a piano-accordion and a second carrying a Red flag, which was marching along a road to a Russian post established behind the German line. The SS men let them enter the killing-ground, then opened fire and within minutes the Red Army men had fallen. From the day they arrived in the combat zone until the last day of the war, the battle for the Semmering Pass continued almost without pause. On the rare days when the Red Army infantry made no attacks Russian artillery was still active and fired massive barrages of Katyusha rockets which crashed around the battalion positions. Austrians who lived in hamlets and in the scattered houses around the battle area speak of massive guns being towed by teams of men, up the steep slopes of the Semmering to firing positions high in the mountains. The teams manhandling the guns were not always Red Army men. Sometimes German prisoners of war and even local civilians were conscripted to the tow ropes. Nor was the task without danger. In addition to the risk of being caught by German shells or machine-gun fire, a broken rope, an uneven pull, a sudden strain could and sometimes did bring the heavy weapon rumbling downhill, crushing everything in its careering course.

For more than a month the SS Battalion held its allotted positions and all the time it was fighting a 'subaltern's war'. Any orders received from Corps headquarters were ignored. The tactical situation changed too rapidly and the fighting was of too confused a nature to admit of interference from a body higher than the battalion. In mountain warfare the personal example of junior officers or sergeants, their strength of personality, courage and ability were the factors that held the battle line. Orders from Corps were irrelevant to the situation on the ground. For example, an order was issued that all offensive action by German units was to be scaled down. No attacks were to be launched, nor counter-attacks made. No patrols were to be sent out. Men and ammunition were to be conserved for one massive counter-attack. Inevitably, as soon as the soldiers of the Red Army realized that the Germans would not fire at them they held parades in the open air in full view of the frustrated Jäger. Such a ludicrous situation could not long be tolerated and one morning the order was completely ignored. Fighting flared and the Red Army men dived into their foxholes again.

Slowly the battle line at this crucial point in the Semmering defences was strengthened by fresh units, brought in by the Gauleiter's conscription order, one of which was the permanent staff of the Army Artillery school at Dachstein. Thanks to the first-class abilities of these artillery specialists, the 13th Battalion was able to rely upon good support in its own attacks and, equally, a firm defence against the Russians. Less fortunate than the men of Oberst Raithel's artillery school were those officers and men of the Luftwaffe's 'Boelcke' Squadron. Because of the lack of aviation fuel the squadron was disbanded and a few of the best pilots were posted to other operational units of the Luftwaffe. The remaining personnel of the squadron were transferred to the infantry as replacements for the SS Battalion.

Casualties drained the strength of both armies. The ability of the Red Army soldier to dig an almost undetectable foxhole in a very short time meant that if the Russians gained any ground they constructed a battle line so quickly and so well laid out, tactically, that each foxhole had to be attacked and destroyed individually. These minor operations proved very costly to the German infantry. The scale, weight and punctuality of the Red Army's infantry attacks was horrifying to those who witnessed them, and the Jäger believed that the Russian soldiers were either drugged or drunk. No other explanation could account for such suicidal tactics. Attacks would come in at set intervals; across the same stretch of ground and at precisely timed intervals. Whole waves of brown-overcoated infantry would march forward, shoulder to shoulder, stamping their way uphill towards the German positions. In their advance they ignored the dead and wounded, marching across the bodies without wavering, into the hammering fire of massed machine-guns. As gaps were torn in their ranks the survivors closed them so that an unbroken front was always presented to the machine-gun fire. The first ranks melted away leaving those single soldiers who had not been killed to continue stolidly and unflinchingly marching until they were killed or absorbed into the second wave of the assault. At times the lines of tramping men swept up to the brink of the Jäger forward defence zone, and came so close that the steam of the Russians' breath could be seen as they panted their way uphill and their look of determination as they advanced into the fury of massed machine-gun fire.

The SS Jäger suffered from an inferiority in fire power. Nearly every Russian soldier, certainly every second one, was armed with a machine pistol, compared to the one in five which was the scale of issue of automatic weapons to the SS. The battalion commander learned that there was a weapons store only a few miles away and sent out a requisition party. In vain did the military storeman in the armoury demand written authority before he would release the MP44 assault rifles. The SS officers ignored his protests and broke into the store, taking enough weapons to supply each of their men with a first-class, fully automatic rifle. This increase in fire power came at a time when losses to the battalion had reached a critical level. A machine pistol for each man did produce a high volume of fire with fewer men, but the lack of numbers told when guard duties were shared, when patrols were sent out or when counter-attacks had to be launched. When May came in the battalion had been in the line for thirty days without relief or replacements. The tired Jäger maintained a high morale and on May Day they flew the challenge of the Reichs war flag from the highest point of the Semmering.

Fresh units, scraped together from the last manpower resources of the Reich were brought into the battle line and their arrival at last allowed the very long front held by 13th battalion to be reduced. Now it was possible to withdraw men from the forward combat zone and put them into reserve so that they could change their clothing which they had worn uninterruptedly for weeks, and could bathe and delouse themselves.

Together with the tactical changes there had been changes in organization. The battalion was now part of Oberst Raithel's newly formed 9th Gebirgs Division which he moulded into a fighting force. The artillerymen of his Dachstein school were complemented by the Admont Gebirgsjäger NCOs' training school. Together, these two experienced units formed the trained nucleus around which 9th Gebirgs Division was constructed. The remnants of the 13th SS Battalion and those of the 'Boelcke' Squadron formed the next most battle experienced group. From convalescents and unit depots other men were obtained, sufficient to form two more complete battalions. These, backed by local Volkssturm battalions, acted as supply details, portering supplies and ammunition to the battle line. Starting from nothing the 9th Gebirgs Division had been created and handled so firmly by its commander that it held a front extending across twenty-four miles of mountainous terrain, from the Schneeberg to Rettenegg. At that point the 9th's right wing touched the left wing of 1st Gebirgs Division.

Supply difficulties reduced the supply of artillery ammunition and the gunners were ordered to reserve their shells for emergency actions. It was no longer possible to give artillery support to infantry operations and the Red Guard Division, obviously aware of the German shell shortage, came in more strongly and more frequently. In attack and counter-attack, in blazing sunshine or in thick fog, by night and by day the unequal struggle went on. If a position was lost to the enemy it had to be retaken as quickly as possible for the Jäger had learned that if a place was left in the hands of a small number of Soviet soldiers it became overnight a jumping-off point for a fresh assault in battalion strength.

On the night of 7 May, Raithel called his senior officers together to pass on the orders he had received. In the house which was his headquarters only the faint flickering of trench lamps illuminated the faces of the men who heard their commander set out the immediate tasks. The Division's principal duty was to form the rearguard and to hold the line while the bulk of Sixth Army marched away westwards to the demarcation line of the River Enns. They held, and at last the time came when the mass of 9th Division itself could begin its westward move. No. 3 Company of the 13th Battalion was detailed to form the divisional rearguard and to man the trenches while behind the shield which they formed Raithel's Division moved down the mountain slopes and headed towards the Enns.

The Company held the line until 07.00 hrs on 8 May and then struck out with platoons leapfrogging by bounds as they withdrew westwards. At a given point the Company was dismissed and fragmented into small groups which continued independently. The distant River Enns was reached by forced marches through the mountains. The SS men, tired from weeks of combat, undernourished and battle exhausted, had nothing to sustain them in this last effort but the fear of falling into the hands of the Soviets. Some men of No. 3 Company and other groups from 13th Battalion crossed the Enns and went into American prison camps; other battalion groups suffered the fate of the men of 1st Gebirgs Division, most were overrun and passed into captivity in the Soviet Union.

The battle that 1st Gebirgs Division fought paralleled those of 13th Battalion, but there were certain unusual events. We join the 1st Gebirgs Division at the conclusion of a brilliant little encircling operation fought out in central Steiermark (die Obersteier). The counter-attack by Sixth Army, a feature of which was the encirclement battle, did not merely halt the Soviet attempt at a breakthrough south of the Semmering, but recaptured important tactical features in 99th Regiment's sector during which Balck, commanding Sixth Army, used both the terrain and the fighting ability of his mountain troops to gain victory. This frustration of Russian military plans brought about a short period of what was described as 'quiet' in the OKW communiqué. The War Diary of 99th Regiment reported the south-westerly movement of Russian vehicle columns heading towards other sectors of the front where they might achieve the breakthrough which the Gebirgsjäger had thwarted.

A situation described as 'quiet' in the front line is a relative term and the keeper of the War Diary is scathing of German communiqués that used it to describe the Southern Front. The diary reported heavy enemy counter-attacks against all the three battalions and recorded that along the front of one battalion four thousand shells had fallen during the course of a single day. The bitter little battles among the trees and mountain tops of the central Steiermark were dismissed laconically in subsequent communiqués as 'the Bolsheviks carried out only local thrusts'. Life in the front line is an amalgam of many, a great many, unpleasant factors in which boredom and fear predominate. In normal conditions relief from the forward zone gave the opportunity to move back into a village or even a town; to enjoy for however brief a period, some of the benefits of civilization. But warfare in the mountains was not normal and there were no towns to provide rest and recreation. The troops stayed isolated in the mountains, devoid of any comfort. There were few cigarettes, little alcohol, no women, the food was poor and spring in the high country is a time of unending rain and freezing fog. Only those born and bred to the harshness can truly master the misery, the deprivations, the despair of day after day and night after night of damp mist or drenching rain. Then, too, there were the bombardments whose detonations reverberated, echoed and re-echoed; the machine-gun fire and the sudden, spectral appearance through the mist of the enemy making one of his hopeless assaults. Hell is not necessarily a place where souls are roasted; it can be a bare mountain top in wartime.

The strain of battle fought without rest, with little food, without the opportunity to change soaking clothes, had its demoralising effect upon the soldiers of both sides. Parties of Red Army men came in to surrender, waving leaflets which they had kept hidden but available against such an eventuality, but the traffic was not one-way entirely and, during the early hours of Wednesday 2 May, most of No. 3 Company of 1st Battalion went over to the enemy.

'One thing that kept us going was our belief that the Americans were coming in from the west and that we and they would join forces in a new war against the Soviets. The Führer's death went generally unremarked. There were more important things, and in any case, we all knew what we had to do. We had to stand fast, to hold the eastern wall and to prevent the Ivans from advancing into the Steiermark until the Amis came.'

The Russians still tried by thrusts and patrols to find a weak spot in the Regiment's front which could be exploited and widened and their attacks continued throughout the 2/3 May, in fog and icy rain.

'These days when I think back to the fighting in the Styrian moutains, I wonder how it was possible for me to do such things. You cannot imagine the fear when the mist came down and visibility was measured in yards. Being on sentry duty was

really unnerving. Ivan's snipers were first-class, even in foggy conditions and, of course, in such weather one has to look out more frequently and for longer periods if one wants to be really vigilant. Fog distorts so that distances are over-estimated and figures are huge, ghostly and frightening. One moment there would be nothing. Seconds later there were these great shapes lumbering, inhuman, through the mist. And when I think back we were subjected to such experiences sometimes four or five times each day and for weeks on end.'

This 'local activity', to use the correct military description, meant that there was a steady drain in men killed, wounded or missing for whom no replacements came through from the regimental depot. Some reinforcements were received, but they were more a liability than an asset. One group of forty, officer-grade paymasters, arrived unannounced at Regimental Head-quarters, not one of whom had had any experience of combat. They were described in the War Diary of 99th Regiment as being 'unlikely to inspire confidence' and were promptly returned.

During the morning of 7 May several companies of the 99th mounted successful but unnecessary attacks and gained some yards of frozen mountain top. At Eisenhower's Headquarters in Reims, Jodl had already signed the document of surrender and the war in the west was at an end. But of that significant event the Gebirgsjäger on the foggy Obersteier hills, knew nothing. Their most important news was that the men of the regimental mule train had deserted *en masse* taking with them all the animals and vehicles. This blow meant that the only available food and ammunition was that still held in the regimental area. No fresh supplies could be expected. The realization that there would inevitably be a cut in rations was more important than anything else.

'Priorities in the Line were less what was happening at OKW level than whether there were any cigarettes, whether anybody had some schnapps and whether there was the chance of a hot drink.'

The ignorance of the ordinary soldier in the German Army of the events of the past days did not last. The sky to the east of Sixth Army burst into light at 04.00 hrs on 8 May, as Red Army gunners opened fired. When the shells exploded there was not the thundering crashing detonation to which the Germans had become accustomed, but a sharper, shorter, less intense cracking sound. The explosion was just sufficient to burst the shell casing and to release thousands of leaflets. Marshal of the Soviet Union Tolbhukin was advising the rank and file of his enemies that the war was over. There were sectors of the battle front where those leaflets rained down upon empty positions because the formations which had held them had already withdrawn. Some units, of which the 1st Gebirgsjäger was one, had held the line to cover the withdrawal of the rest. In order to understand the necessity for this sacrifice we must leave the combat zone and the ordinary soldier and concern ourselves with the situation as seen from the viewpoint of the senior officers and of the political authorities in the Steiermark.

Graz, capital of the province of Steiermark, is the second largest city in Austria and in the Nazi era it had been given the title, 'town of the popular uprising', in recognition of the part which its citizens had played in helping to bring about the Anschluss with Germany.

Siegfried Ueberreither, a dedicated National Socialist, was the Gauleiter of the Steiermark and was determined to hold the province to the last. Armed with Hitler's authority to act as a Defence Commisar, Ueberreither set about the task of organizing his people to fight a total war and thereby to defend the province and its capital against the Red Army. The Russian advance in the first weeks of April had seemed to be irresistible and Graz had become a front-line city. Emergency measures were employed to meet the situation; a stricter conscription of the remaining men was undertaken, the Volkssturm battalions were called out and women and children were evacuated; a move long overdue in view of the heavy raids by the Allied Air Forces.

Ueberreither's emergency measures also included the erection of barricades at road crossings and defences set up surrounding the Schlossberg, a small hill around which the city had grown and on which the Gauleiter had his office. Local defence Companies had been organized as well as an anti-tank detachment. Everything was made ready to turn the old university city into an Austrian Stalingrad. The battle would be violent and bloody and fought against an enemy superior both in numbers and in weapons. The slogans which were offered were the German-language equivalent of Churchill's 'Blood, sweat, toil and tears.' Every sacrifice must be made to bring forth a victory at any price. Meanwhile the Red Army was pushing forward into the eastern areas of the province, the Oststeier, capturing villages and small market towns.

'When the Russians first came into our village I found them very friendly and correct in their behaviour. Of course, anything portable, like watches and chickens went immediately, but there were none of the rapings and burnings that we had heard about and which we had been frightened of. Those first units moved on and then in came second and third echelon troops. These were bad, but the permanent occupation troops who followed them, were a shocking lot. However, one speaks as one finds. I found the first troops to be very good. We had some billeted with us for more than a week; an officer and twenty men. The front line was actually a couple of miles away towards Feldbach and the detachments in our village carried out reconnaissance patrols through the German lines.

The Russian troops were well fed. Their bread was the best I have ever eaten. They did not live off the land as another rumour had said, but they did take our chickens. They still smoked a tobacco called Mahorka which I remembered from the First War when I had served in Russia. The smell of Mahorka took me back twenty odd years to the early campaigns of the Kaiser's war.

In those days in our village we nearly all spoke or at least understood some Serbo-Croat. Very few of the people do today. Serbo-Croat is very much like Russian so we and the soldiers had a few pleasant evenings together; the Red Army men and we the elderly men of the village. One evening I asked why they had shot some local men who had been out hunting for fresh meat. In explanation the Russian officer took down my jacket off the peg behind the door and told me to look at it properly. He pointed out that it had shoulder straps, was field grey in colour. It had green facings, had a dark green collar and was buttoned. It looked like a German Army tunic. Wasn't it easy, the officer asked, for one of his men to make a mistake in identification? If he saw a group of men in what looked like German uniform, moving stealthily through the forest and carrying guns, might he not, at first glance mistake such a group for a German patrol? He was right, of course, mistakes like that did occur and it was from such mistakes that rumours of brutal and unprovoked murders spread.'

News that Hitler was dead did not weaken the Gauleiter's resolve, nor would he accept orders that were being issued by Doenitz's government in Flensburg, but deemed them to be statements issued by an enemy radio station. For Siegfried Ueberreither and the Gau officers the war continued. While he and his men were making feverish and amateur efforts to turn Graz into a fortress, other heads, wiser and more experienced, had met in the house of General Ringel in Graz, to determine the action that would have to be taken when the end came, as soon it must. Army Group 'C' in Italy, had already capitulated and Army Group 'E' in Jugoslavia was pulling out of that partisan-infested land, closely pursued by a force made up of the armies of Marshal Tito and his Russian and Bulgarian allies.

Kesselring, the Supreme Commander South East, who chaired the conference in Ringel's house, informed the assembled senior officers of the imminent capitulation and asked for suggestions on future action. He accepted the proposal that units of Sixth Army would have to form rearguards and hold until the men of Army Group South had passed into American captivity. Loehr, commanding Army Group 'E' was concerned that his forces would not be able to complete their withdrawal from the Balkans very quickly. He stressed that any premature surrender on the part of Army Group South would cause his own formations to fall into the hands of the Jugoslavs. General Ringel was ordered to drive to the River Enns and to offer the local American commander the chance of moving swiftly into eastern Austria.

It is truly surprising to read from contemporary correspondence and diaries, how naive were the most senior officers of the German forces. In addition to Ringel's offer, the Chief of Staff of Sixth Army, was sent to ask General Patton to supply US troops to bring forward medical supplies to German forces on the Eastern Front. This astounding request was followed by the suggestion that the US General should allow German units to pass, from west to east, through the lines of his Third Army so as to thicken the Eastern Front. It is incredible that such senior men really did believe that the Western Allies were willing to align themselves with the Doenitz government in a war against the Soviet Union. The attempts by Ringel and the Sixth Army's Chief of Staff, both failed as did a later attempt by Rendulic himself. Accepting that no alliance between the Western Allies and Germany would be made, he faced the true situation and issued orders. The first two laid down the schedule for capitulation. The ceasefire against the Americans, that is on the Western Front, would become effective at 08.00 hrs on 7 May. The other Order was directed at the Eastern Front. The Army Group Commander appreciated that any precisely timed ceasefire order might have disastrous results and his order laid down no exact time. The commanders of Rendulic's four armies were merely instructed that they were to disengage their formations from the Soviets after last light on the evening of 7 May. All units were to move westwards at such speed that the demaracation line – the River Enns – would have been crossed before 09.00 hrs on 9 May.* After that hour all military movement was to halt; troops would remain where they were until they were taken into captivity by the army against whom they had fought their last battle.

Some unit commanders in Army Group South acted within the terms of operational freedom that Kesselring had given them and did not wait until last light on the 7th, but began to thin out the rear areas as early as 6 May. The Second Panzer Army, holding the sector between Radkersburg and Bad Gleichenberg, put into action plans which had been prepared weeks earlier. Under cover of a final artillery barrage the great mass of the Panzer Army pulled out, unnoticed by the enemy for nearly a day. Balck, commanding Sixth Army, ordered the motorized formation, 4th SS Panzer Corps and 3rd Panzer Corps, to move off, shielded by 1st Gebirgs Division and 9th Gebirgs Division. The order that German troops were to surrender to the soldiers of that nation against whom they had last fought was interpreted by Balck in a certain way. His orders were that his men were to reach and *cross* the River Enns even if they had to fight against American attempts to halt them. The Americans would then be the last troops to be fought against.

The military operation designed to save men from Soviet prison camps was soon in full swing, and the few mountain roads on the east-west axis in Sixth Army sector were packed with traffic as the columns poured onto them. In the mind of every soldier was the intention to reach the demarcation line between the American and the Soviet forces. Behind those units escaping down the clogged roads were the Gebirgsjäger of the 1st and 9th Divisions still holding the Line; an order that was the equivalent of a death-sentence. On other sectors other units had also received and had obeyed the order to stand fast. Along the length of the battle front in eastern Austria, throughout 7 and 8 May, there were small groups of men, some who had volunteered, some who had been chosen by lot, some who were under orders, to form the rearguard. The soldiers did their duty while behind them most Party officials made good their own escape. The bravura plans of Gauleiter Ueberreither

---

*The River Enns was approved by the Western Allies and the Russians as the halt line for their armies. The Enns had always formed a natural dividing line; Upper Austria is so called because it is above the Enns, while Lower Austria is below that river. It was a natural, obvious and distinctive halt line. For the Germans fighting in Austria, to cross the Enns meant that they were escaping Russian imprisonment; hence their strenuous efforts to reach and to cross it.

Above: Lieutenant-General Walter H. Walker, commanding XX Corps of the US Third Army, greets Lieutenant-General Birukov, of the Russian Fourth Army, on the Enns bridge, Austria, 8 May 1945.

had had no hope of fulfilment without the support of the Army, and Balck of Sixth Army had soon made it clear that he had no intention of sacrificing his men in a senseless battle in a war whose end was so close. Balck, on a visit to Graz, found the Gauleiter contemplating suicide because his dreams of a Styrian Götterdämmerung could not be fulfilled. Balck dissuaded him; Ueberreither holstered his pistol, left his office in the Burg and vanished. It was not until many years after the war. that he was found living in the Argentine. Other Nazi Party members who had held office in the provincial government organized false papers for themselves and escaped to Alpine chalets or to discreet little villas where they lived until the furore of capitulation had subsided. Some stayed in order that provisional administration might continue to function and among these few were Kaspar, Mayor of Graz, and Professor Dadieu who, as Gauhauptmann, held the office of a political Lord-Lieutenant of the Province.

Representatives of political parties proscribed by the Third Reich in 1938 and headed by the last freely elected Deputy Lord-Lieutenant, the Socialist Reinhard Machold, met in the town hall of Graz. The transfer of power from Dadieu to Machold and his group was a simple one, after which the Nazi officials, having laid down their authority, left the meeting. A second conference created a provisional government, the greatest number of whose members were from the left wing parties. The whole thing went very smoothly and the Machold administration prepared to meet the Russian forces which were heading for Graz.

While on the Semmering and in the northern mountains, the rearguards still held fast, away to the south motorized units of the Red Army had driven across territory devoid of German troops and had reached the outskirts of the provincial capital. A deputation of Red Army officers entered the darkened city to arrange with the new Chief of Police, a Socialist, the routes along which the Russian troops would enter the city. On the morning of 9 May the population of Graz awoke to find the Red Army in occupation. The Styrian provisional government, which convened to greet the Soviet military commanders, was brusquely informed that it had no authority. Executive power lay with the Russian military government alone; a verbal declaration that was soon confirmed by posters proclaiming that fact.

The General Secretary of the Austrian Communist Party arrived in Graz, charged by the Soviet Government with the task of forming the new and official Styrian government. He, too, chose Machold to lead it. The Steiermark was now a Russian province. The war was over and life could return to normal. Although there had been promises made by senior officers of the Red Army that they would keep their troops in check, this proved not to be completely possible. The local Russian commandant declared that the Red Army was in the Steiermark as a conquering force and not as a liberating one, an interpretation with which the Russian rank and file agreed and acted.

As in Vienna, rape, robbery and casual killing were commonplace. For an Austrian civilian to ride a bicycle in the streets was an unbelievable act of folly. Its confiscation by the first Red Army man to be met was immediate. Inhabitants soon learned to greet a Russian request to be told the time with a polite smile. Inevitably there were stories of Red Army men firing machine pistols at clocks whose alarms had begun to ring; of Soviet soldiers with looted watches up and down the length of each arm. It was obvious that the ordinary soldier had no experience of flushing a lavatory, and basins filled to the rim were emptied by the simple expedient of kicking a hole in them. The search for liquor by some soldiers who were billeted in what had been the SS Medical Academy led them to drink the fluid in which specimens had been preserved. It was an intoxicating time for one and all and one fraught with incident.

'One evening just after the Ivans had taken Graz, I was sitting in my flat when there was a banging on the door. When I opened it there were three Russian officers standing on the stairs. They demanded schnapps and I told them that I had none.

They pushed past me into my flat and began to open cupboards and drawers. I speak a bit of Russian and asked them what they were looking for. Schnapps was what they wanted.

We got talking and they asked me where I had learned Russian. I had picked it up on the Eastern Front where I had spent two years. Arm of Service, they asked? Infantry. So were they and we got on well talking in broken German and Russian and lots of arm waving. How was it that I was at home and not a prisoner of war? I told them that I had been discharged as politically unreliable; that I was an anti-Nazi. They believed me. In truth our unit commander had discharged us all on 29 April, when it was clear that the war was ending and he saw no point in our getting killed for nothing.

The Russians again demanded schnapps, cigarettes and sugar. I had none and they left. About half an hour later they returned with four bottles of schnapps, ten packets of cigarettes and a bag of sugar. This they ate by the spoonful after every fifth or sixth glass of schnapps. They liked our cigarettes better than their own issue ones. The officers put the stuff they had collected on the table and we drank and smoked all night long. Then they left. Later during the day I met a neighbour who lived in the basement of our house and who acted as a caretaker. He told me how that previous evening three Russian officers had entered his flat and stolen all his schnapps, all his cigarettes and his sugar.

The Russians were like that. Very generous. They would give you anything even if they had to steal it to give it to you. In Russia there was such terrible poverty that the poor devils had little opportunity of being generous. In our country which must have seemed like an Aladdin's cave to them, they could give presents and be generous even if they had stolen the stuff in the first place.'

Some soldiers of the Red Army, seduced by the evidently higher standard of life in the West, deserted and went up into the mountains where they lived off the land, preying upon the frightened peasants. In those same hills were SS men who had determined not to surrender themselves and who also terrorized the peasants. Then, and for months to come, the sound of automatic pistol fire in the quiet hills, announced that two opposing groups had clashed. The war was over but the killing went on.

PART TWO
THE SOUTHERN FRONT

SOUTHERN FRONT, APRIL–MAY 1945

0 10 20 30 40 50 Miles 100 150

Coblenz

Frankfurt

Dresden

Prague

Nuremberg

Strasburg

BLACK FOREST

xxxxx
Army
Group G

Munich

River Danube

Lake
Constance

Salzburg

Berchtesgaden
Golling

Kufstein

Feldkirch

ALPS

Innsbruck

TYROL

Leoben

xxxxx
Army
Group C

Brenner Pass

Hinterbichl

St. Veit

River Mur

Lienz

Graz

Bolzano

Klagenfurt
Völkermarkt

Villach

Lugano

Lake
Como

xxxx
10th

Trento

River Drau

xxxx
14th

Laibach
(Ljubljana)

GRAZIANI

xxxx
Ligurarian

Como
Bergamo

7 May

Vicenza

Treviso

Milan

Brescia

Gradisca

Trieste
Kocevje

Turin
Pavia

Padua
Verona

Piacenza

Cremona

25 April

River Po

Venice

Fiume

Genoa

Mirandola

Poggio

xxx
IV
xxx
II
xxx
XII
xxx
V

River Reno

Pola

20 April

Modena

Lake Comanchio

La Spezia

Bologna

xxx
IV
xxx
II
xxx
XIII
xxx
V

TRUSCOTT
5th

xxx
X

8th McCREERY

Florence xxxxx

15

CLARK

APENNINE MOUNTAINS

There had been a time when the German southern theatre of operations had extended as far south as Rhodes, had threatened Turkey and had spread its influence across the whole of the Balkans. Even in November 1943, the South-Eastern Front had been strong enough to mount a successful combined operation against a British force on the islands of Kos and Leros, but under Allied pressure and during the following months the Corps of Loehr's Army Group 'E' was pushed back north. Greece was evacuated; the Front in Bulgaria pulled back and soon the south-eastern section of the Southern Front was concentrated along a line from Hungary to the Italian frontier at which point it joined the area held by the South-Western Front where Army Group 'C' was deployed.

Behind both these Army Groups of the Southern Front, work had begun on a fortified line extending from Switzerland to Hungary. It was incomplete and even in those sectors where there were any sort of defences these were usually positions which had been constructed during the First World War. This weak defensive chain would be manned by overstretched and under-strength formations who would be expected to hold their positions to the last.

And so, as the days lengthened and spring was already in the southern lands, both sides prepared for battle. The Allies were confident that one final effort would overthrow the German Army Groups confronting them. The German troops were not unaware that the war was going badly. Not only was Germany now bereft of allies but from east and from west great armies of Allied troops had invaded the Reich. Vienna had already fallen to the Red Army; Berlin was under threat. The end was very near, but for as long as they were able to Grenadiers of the German divisions would defend the Fatherland.

'I was with the Regiment down near Bosnia. I can remember what a beautiful day it was. There was a tree in blossom near the house where we had been billeted. It was a pleasant spot. A circle of mountains – peace and quiet. We call it in German – Bergfriede – the peace of the mountains.

I was standing at the front of the house working on greasing the wheel sockets of a panje cart and not really thinking about anything at all. There was a sudden, loud explosion and I looked up to see the blossom falling from the tree leaving the branches bare and empty. The Titoists had begun their grand attack and this was the start of their barrage. That attack did not stop until the surrender in May. Nearly thirty days we retreated and as we withdrew northwards it seemed that spring had preceded us. It was a really beautiful spring – or it would have been if we had not been at war.'

In the splendour of a Mediterranean spring the armies of both sides waited for the signal that would launch them into battle.

6
JUGOSLAVIA

The three most significant factors in the story of the events in Jugoslavia at the end of the Second World War are the defeat of the German Army Group 'E', the genocide practised against the ethnic minorities and, thirdly, the attempt by Jugoslavia forcibly to change the frontiers of Europe. This naked aggression was challenged by the Western Powers and the ensuing political crisis brought Europe to the brink of war only days after the Second World War had ended.

To comprehend Jugoslavia's racial problem we must recall that before the First World War a nation known as Jugoslavia did not exist. That present-day country was then made up of the independent kingdoms of Serbia and Montenegro together with other, largely German-speaking, territories. These latter were part of the Austrian Empire. Out of its ruins and around Serbia and Montenegro the new Kingdom of Jugoslavia was built. Not all the former Austrian territories went to Jugoslavia. Istria and the coastal towns were passed to Italy, to the chagrin of the Jugoslavians who felt that they had a legitimate claim to that territory, much of which was Slav-speaking. In short, at the end of the First World War, Jugoslavia was a predominantly Slav nation, but containing minorities who were determined to regain for themselves some degree of autonomy from the central government through very active political campaigns. Racial hostility was thus a feature of Jugoslav political life during the inter-war years.

In 1941 Germany invaded Jugoslavia and had soon defeated King Peter's royalist forces. A number of army men, known as Chetniks and led by Draza Mihailovitch, undertook to liberate Jugoslavia and to restore the King. This they planned to do through guerrilla warfare. Not until Germany's attack upon the Soviet Union were there any Communist Party partisan detachments. British and later, Allied, support was first given to the Royalist cause, but then Balkan politics and racial hostility bedevilled the situation. The harsh but efficient Communist Party welded the partisan bands of the left wing into a single strong and powerful Force. The Red partisans obtained their weapons by attacks upon the Chetniks, and were known to betray Mihailovitch's men to the Germans in order to divert the enemy occupation troops from their own areas of operation. In an attempt to fight back, the Chetniks sought to establish a *modus vivendi* with the Germans with whose help the common enemy would be destroyed. Once aware of this situation, Allied aid was diverted to Tito's forces which had now grown large enough to become the Jugoslav Army of National Liberation (JANL).

The growth of partisan power from isolated weak bands to a strong national army was a phenomenon and by the end of 1944, having defeated numerous German major offensives, the JANL had reconquered a great deal of national territory, including the capital, Belgrade. Reacting to this partisan pressure, Field Marshal Loehr's Army Group began its fighting retreat out of Jugoslavia towards the Austrian province of Carinthia (Kärnten). Thus, in the final weeks of the war Army Group 'E' was spread across north Jugoslavia and was pulling slowly back towards Austria. The Group was predominantly German, but included units racially or politically hostile to the Slav-dominated, Communist-controlled partisans. There were serving with Army Group 'E' Croats who had formed a separate State, independent of Jugoslavia; also Slovenes who on 3 May, declared their own independence. There were royalist Chetniks, Montenigrians, White Russians (former deserters from the Red Army whom the Germans had formed into rifle regiments), Bosnians and other disaffected groups. This great mass of people, civilian and military, hoped to escape partisan revenge by crossing the Austrian frontier. What they did not know was that Tito had laid plans to annex those same southern provinces of Austria towards which the migration was headed. For Tito had looked beyond the battlefields on which the war's last battles were being fought, towards the peace negotiations which would follow.

To avoid the territorial disappointments of 1919, the Jugoslav government did not intend to wait to have territory doled out to it by the major Allies, but decided instead to present those Allies with a *fait accompli*. To bring this about the western wing of the JANL, the 4th Army, would seize the Istrian peninsula together with the cities of Fiume, Trieste and Pola, while from the south-east other armies would invade Carinthia. In all these seized territories rigged elections would be held and the results would be seen as clear proof of the desire of the native peoples to unite with the republic of Jugoslavia.

Personally and militarily, Tito felt secure. He was a Moscow Communist who had always followed without question the Party's line, and his partisans had become a strong, well-equipped army. The Jugoslav leader felt sufficiently confident to challenge Great Britain. Churchill was aware that if this Jugoslav aggression succeeded there existed the danger that Soviet influence would extend across South-Eastern Europe and might roll westwards to influence Italy and thereby bring her within the Communist camp.

Tito strengthened his political power base in Jugoslavia by obtaining absolute control over the fragmented opposition and by filling all the important government posts with his men. As the Communist group gained power the chances of a restoration of the monarchy faded. At last politically secure in his own country, the Jugoslav leader made his play for the disputed territories. Repeated statements that 'our brothers in Istria, in Slovenia and in Carinthia will be liberated' alarmed the British Foreign Office who saw in them clear indications that Tito intended to seize any neighbouring regions in which there was a tie of blood to any racial group in the Republic. The cries for annexation of Carinthia were taken up by 'Radio Free Austria', a propaganda instrument of the Soviets, which announced that the liberty-loving peoples of Austria endorsed 'Jugoslavia's just claims to the province of

Carinthia'. Concurrently, the JANL began an active recruiting drive among the Carinthian Slovenes. To further aid the war of nerves against Austria Tito raised an Austrian battalion of partisans, but although the unit did fight in battle and did lose men, its role was primarily political; to demonstrate that Austrian soldiers in the armies of Freedom, also recognized the validity of Jugoslav claims. Complementing the military Front there was also a political cat's-paw organization, the Austrian Freedom Front, which, not surprisingly, supported the territorial claims. These two, fake organizations were to enter Carinthia. The politicians would organize the rigged ballot and the Austrian battalions (by now there were four on establishment) would crush any opposition. In order that this swindle should work it was vital to gain time; to prevent the British Army from entering Carinthia and to obstruct their advance from Italy into Austria.

Intelligence sources provided Alexander, Churchill and the British Foreign Office with details of the growing threat. Diplomatic channels were used to advise Tito against precipitate action, but he was in no mood to retreat although he did make an attempt at conciliation and offered Alexander a Force of 200,000 soldiers to be employed in the battles for the Alpine Redoubt. With the war won they would then go on to form part of the Allied forces of occupation. The sinister implications of the Jugoslav offer were appreciated by the Foreign Office whose attitude is reflected in this extract of a memorandum dated 12 March 1945.

'We are likely to have enough trouble with Jugoslav forces in Venezia Giulia and with irregular Slovene formations in the Klagenfurt area without adding to our difficulties by assisting in the introduction of 100,000 Jugoslav Regulars into the Austrian mountains . . . it had been generally agreed, at the insistence of the Soviet government, that no minor allies will be invited to share with the three major Powers in the occupation of Austria. Tito's request on this head will, therefore, easily be turned down.'

The Foreign Office and the military commanders were aware of Jugoslav intentions and were determined to prevent them by emphasizing in Eighth Army's battle plan the need for crack units to advance at speed into Trieste, Istria and southern Austria.

Accounts of the end of the war in Jugoslavia extend, therefore, into the areas bordering that country and are treated in the following pages at several levels, military, political and genocidal.

The opening movements in the final offensive by the JANL were made by the newly formed Fourth Army whose first task it was to break the German Front between the River Una and the Adriatic Sea. The second phase of the offensive was to mount an energetic, two-pronged drive to strike across Istria towards Italy and to enter Austria from the south-west. The timing of Fourth Army's offensive was co-ordinated with Anglo-American operations in Italy, in a first move intended to draw German reserves from Italy towards themselves. German Intelligence sources, interpreting the signs of an imminent offensive, forecast that the main Jugoslav blow would fall on 10 April. In the event they were two days out in their calculations, but the predicted area was the correct one.

Erich Koerner, formerly Major on the Staff of Army Group 'E' and seconded to 97th Corps, was at Corps HQ in Mustar during those last eventful weeks.

'By the end of April our forces were dangerously overstretched and Corps Order of Battle included units whose men could not be considered as reliable soldiers. For example, the 41st Infantry Division was made up of a great number of men who had been military criminals, guilty of such serious crimes as desertion. How could one repose confidence in such men? The 237th Division was made up of men over the normal military age, while in complete contrast, the 188th Mountain Division was neither a Division in strength nor a Mountain one in equipment and training, but was a miscellaneous assortment of recruits lacking any kind of battle experience.'

The 97th Corps did in fact put up a good showing, but was pinned to the ground by several Partisan divisions while others by-passed it and raced for the prizes which Tito wanted. On 1 May elements of the Jugoslav Fourth Army entered Trieste, Gorizia and Tolmein, while others began to close in upon Carinthia. The German front in North-West Jugoslavia was torn open and through the gap poured the partisan forces.

The German Army units stood, like rocks in a maelstrom, trying to block the Red tide. Then came a blow which shattered all their hopes. The German Army Group holding Italy surrendered, uncovering the right flank and allowing British Eighth Army to come up out of Italy and head across Istria and into Austria. The news of the capitulation of Army Group 'C' came as a terrible shock to the commanders of Army Group 'E' in Jugoslavia.

'We had not been advised that negotiations were in progress and when the capitulation came, suddenly we had nobody covering our right flank. The situation had other, more political, considerations, namely, were we of Army Group 'E' bound by the surrender in Italy? If we were then further resistance to the Jugoslavs could be interpreted as breaking the armistice conditions. If we were not so bound, how were we to act against those British and American troops who were crossing our Army Group boundary line in north-eastern Italy?'

Loehr decided on his own initiative that his forces would not be bound by the surrender in Italy, but would continue to fight on. Militarily he had no other choice for any capitulation on his part would expose Army Group South to the danger of being outflanked and it was only the fighting ability of that Army Group that was providing the shield behind which his men could escape into Austria. In front of him was the JANL which could scent victory; on the right flank was nothing but a gap in Istria through which the British Eighth Army was moving. Loehr could not surrender and endanger Army Group South, but he could negotiate with his enemies for his Army Group to withdraw out of Jugoslav territory and back into Austria. He also had to consider those allies who had served with the German armies. He could not simply abandon them. Of prime concern were the Croats whose men had been loyal comrades in arms, but who would be treated as traitors if they fell into partisan hands. Loehr asked the Croat leaders whether they would surrender to their political and racial enemies or retreat into Austria with the rest of his Army Group. Unanimously, the Croat Council decided that the whole nation would go with the Germans. The consequences of that decision will be recounted later in this Section.

Throughout the rainy days of that first week of May, Loehr's formations moved back, step by step towards reception areas in Klagenfurt, Völkermarkt and Marburg which the thoroughly professional Field Marshal had had prepared for them. With that retrograde movement under way, the Army Group Commander began to negotiate with the senior commanders of the JANL. He sent General Felmy of 34th Corps to talk to the British, and De Angelis of 2nd Panzer Army went to treat with the Soviets.

The German Army's Intelligence Service which dealt with Foreign Armies (East) had issued its assessment on 15 April, and reported that the Western Allies would soon join forces with the Germans and would march against the Communists. This lie inspired the men of Loehr's Army Group to continue the now hopeless struggle and urgently to attempt to reach Austria where the conjunction with the Anglo-American armies would be made. The German formations in Jugoslavia were in a parlous state. Radio announcements and bulletins made it clear that Germany had been totally occupied by the Allies. Hitler was dead and there was no supply system from the Reich to the field armies. How long could the Army Group live from its reserves of food and ammunition? Already the fuel situation was so critical that seven out of ten motor vehicles had been destroyed and of the remainder two out of three were drawn by oxen. Only such vital vehicles as ambulances had enough petrol.

Partisan attacks increased and the evacuation of Army Group 'E' out of Jugoslavia is one of the tragic acts in history. If one considers it as a painting, every human emotion is depicted on the canvas. One sees small bands of men who know that their lives are forfeit. They lie in scrape holes in the mud waiting for the partisans to attack. 'They're coming!' The words pass from man to man along the Company line. At first there is nothing to be seen and then in lines, in waves and in groups the guerrillas swing forward. Every second German soldier is taken from the firing line to form a Reserve Group. 'Open fire at 100 metres. Make every shot tell.' The warning is plain enough. There is no reserve ammunition. Once the bullets have been used up it will be a matter of bayonets and knives.

The partisan formation floods over the short, spring grass. Their first ranks cross the 100-metre line and are met with bursts of fire which tear gaps in the partisan ranks, but still they come on. The machine-guns traverse along the lines of the Reds and many drop, cut down like corn. The guerrillas close their ranks as they near the German line, closing up and closing up again to form a human wedge that will smash through the German front. Behind that line the German reserve group is kept behind low earth walls, hidden from sight.

To the German soldiers in the firing line, to load, aim and fire is an automatic routine. Then at last, when the partisan lines are less than 30 metres distant the German defenders stand up. A last look round to see who is still fighting and then the desperation of close-quarter combat. Panzer-fausts detonate in front of the closing partisans. Rockets explode, blowing bodies to pieces. Hand-grenades burst, a vicious burst of machine pistol fire cuts down a Red group more aggressive than the others. Then the contest is hand to hand and the force of the partisan wedge drives it through the German line. Once through, and the guerrillas charge forward only to recoil as suddenly out of the ground the German reserves stand up and at point-blank range cut down the exultant Jugoslavs. The survivors of the guerrilla waves recede and flee. It is over for the time being, but they'll come back again, and again and again. Today, tomorrow and on every succeeding day until the German group is dispersed or captured or its members are dead.

There was an unreality to life. The war was nearly over. In Italy there had been the surrender of Army Group 'C' and it was rumoured that a general and unconditional surrender would soon come into effect. If it did how would it affect the formations deep inside Jugoslavia? Then came another rumour that the Jugoslavs were allowing the Army Group to pull out and had placed a time limit on this withdrawal; it had to be completed by 15 May. All German troops must evacuate Jugoslav territory by that time. It was a straw eagerly grasped at, but the next series of partisan attacks showed it to have been just another latrine rumour. In hate-filled despair the Germans marched towards the River Mur, in southern Austria, which formed the frontier.

On 6 May the JANL Fourth Army along the Adriatic forced the German 97th Corps to surrender. That inexperienced formation had hoped to reach Austria by adopting the German Army tactic of a 'moving pocket', in which fighting units protect the core of Service units and the wounded. The 97th Corps 'pocket' fought its way, beating off wave after wave of partisan attacks, but after five long days and nights of battle it halted, exhausted and beaten. The Corps Commander signed the instrument of surrender and with the passing of 97 Corps the whole of north-western Jugoslavia was liberated. Now there was time to prepare the ground for the political struggle, together with other JANL units which were employed in Istria on political exercises, usually painting up pro-Jugoslav slogans to create the impression that the territory was solidly for Tito and the Party.

In that first week of May, in the province of Carinthia, the Austrians needed to organize for the future, but this activity would be political and would exclude the military. In Vienna the provisional government set up by the Soviets and recognized only by them, had nevertheless established itself and had sent out feelers to other liberated areas of Austria. In Carinthia, an underground organization already existed and this, although Left inclined, was not Communist-dominated as was the Soviet-backed Austrian Freedom Front. Politically the time was ripe for the Carinthian group to take over the government from Gauleiter Rainer who, like Ueberreither of Graz, was determined to fight on. At a battle conference held in Graz on 6 May, Rainer learned from Kesselring that the war was ending and that any attempt to continue hostilities in his Gau would be both a political and a military folly.

The Carinthian group knew that power was passing from the military and the Party into their hands, but they were uncertain of how they should act and telegraphed for advice from Sir George Franckenstein who had been, before the Anschluss, the Austrian Ambassador in London and who was in exile there. Sir George's reply stressed that the Allied troops entering Carinthia must be met by democrats from the Resistance and not, under any circumstances, by Nazi leaders wishing to make a good impression. This advice prompted the democratic group to act against Rainer who promptly relinquished his office. Carinthia became the first of the Austrian provinces to declare for the provisional government in Vienna. Had they known of the politico–military movements which were taking place across the border with Jugoslavia their enthusiasm might have been tinged with concern, for a secret telegram to London sent by the British Ambassador in Belgrade held disturbing news. He wrote, 'A Jugoslav Division is under orders to move into Austria and to take Klagenfurt.' Tito's planned *fait accompli* was in operation.

Alexander, advised by Churchill of this new concern, ordered Eighth Army to speed-up its drive into Austria. The British divisions thrust forward, but en route met German detachments which did not accept that the surrender in Italy included them and sought to delay the advance. A short, fierce series of fire fights destroyed these last-ditch fanatics and the 78th and 6th Armoured Divisions roared up to the frontier.

'It was a marvellous feeling to be entering Germany – well, the Third Reich. We were all thankful that the Germans had not held the mountains in strength. Why they had not, I do not know. Perhaps it was the armistice with us in Italy that had weakened them on the ground. I don't know. All I do know is that if they had put up a strong defence it would have taken us years to fight our way through.

We crossed the border and had a modest celebration. Two plaques: one for 6th Armoured and the other for ourselves were nailed onto the frontier pole. Immediately inside Austria there was a big hotel. We pulled up outside it, went in and ordered beer. It was good stuff and we toasted the end of the war. In my truck there were only four left who had come out with the battalion to Africa. All the others were gone; dead or wounded. We drank to absent friends and then pushed on.'

Concerned at the news that the Jugoslavs had crossed the Carinthian border, and made aware of the need to be first on the ground, British V Corps ordered its units to take Villach and to press on at first light on 8 May. Commanding Officers were told they were to drop off groups so as to occupy every village and to do this even if the Jugoslav troops were already in occupation. The partisan army was to be treated correctly but distantly because they were trespassing on our territory.

The 8 May was a day of frantic activity in Jugoslavia and in Carinthia. In Klagenfurt, the provincial capital, the committee members making up the local government were aware that two military forces were moving towards Carinthia. The JANL formations coming up from the south now had on their establishment four battalions of Austrian communists who would seek to impose a government of Tito's choice through a rigged election, while from the west Eighth Army was coming, and it was not known whether the British were coming as liberators or as conquerors. One Austrian expressed his opinion: 'Even if the British are harsh, at least one day they will leave Austria. It does not matter how accommodating the Jugoslavs may be to us, they will be with us for ever. The choice is clear. It is essential to do everything to speed the British entry.'

The civilian committee's questions on the attitude of the military to any possible unrest or partisan activity by Austrian guerrilla groups became suddenly redundant. A porter entered the conference room and announced that the British had reached Klagenfurt. Then came telephone calls to say that the advance guard of the partisan army was fast approaching the city. It had been a close-run thing. Three hours only separated the tanks of 6th Armoured Division from the reconnaissance cars of Tito's leading troops.

During my service in Austria I worked in Civil Censorship and recall, almost verbatim, two letters dealing with Carinthia.

Today I witnessed the arrival of English troops into Klagenfurt. They are all handsome, bronzed young men dressed in short trousers. About midday some of them in the main square lit little fires over which they made tea and they sat there not at all self-conscious, eating and drinking. The English eat white bread on which they spread butter and then they lay on top of the bread and butter slices of tinned meat. They seem to lack for nothing and seemed quite happy although they did not talk to us. They behaved as if we civilians were not there and strolled about without their guns which they left in their unguarded trucks.

Officers can be recognized by the coloured neckscarves they wear and there is in the English army an absence of Prussian saluting and heel-clicking. The soldiers I saw looked more like people on a holiday excursion than soldiers at war.'

Another letter was more concerned with politics:

There was an announcement on the radio yesterday (8 May), that the Nazis are out. Since that announcement there has been no other news on the radio, but there has been a great deal of yodelling and the singing of Austrian folk-songs. It is as if everybody is trying to prove what a loyal Austrian he is. So we have no news, no weather reports, nothing of importance or of interest – just everlasting yodelling.'

In the short period of time between the arrival of Eighth Army into Klagenfurt and that of the Jugoslavs, the British troops had occupied most of the important buildings and areas of the town. The JANL baulked by this speedy move then went out to occupy the villages and hamlets, but they

Above: on the outskirts of
Mauthen on 7 May 1945, a patrol
of the 56th Reconnaissance
Regiment, belonging to 78th
Division, is met by Dr Meinlander,
Burgermeister of Mauthen, and
asked to drive with all speed to
Klagenfurt. **Right:** the
battle-hardened, but smartly
turned out men of the Eighth
Army made a vivid contrast with
the partisans of Tito's army.
Klagenfurt main square, May
1945.

lacked transport and could only move at a marching pace. The British had transport and moved quickly so that when Tito's dusty patrols marched in they found outside the principal buildings fully armed sentries, immaculate in khaki drill. In some of the chief towns of the province, since the war had not officially ended, there were also German military police and sentries guarding their own unit headquarters. It was not unusual in those first days of the occupation to see German and British police on point duty directing traffic.

The speed with which V Corps had advanced into Carinthia had foiled the Jugoslav intention to seize the province by *coup de main*, but the problem remained of how to convince Tito that his JANL units should leave Austria. This was a very delicate problem, for the British lines of communication to Italy ran through or near to territory controlled by the Jugoslavs and one false move might provoke the guerrillas into cutting the British road and rail links.

The British were not the only ones with the need to negotiate with caution. Loehr's hope of extricating his Army Group intact had achieved nothing. The leaders of the JANL were deliberately delaying a settlement of the move, waiting until their forces had arrived in strength and outnumbered the Germans. Then they could insist upon compliance with any demand. They knew that the war in Europe was nearly over and if they could delay negotiations until the capitulation had come into force the whole of Army Group 'E', some 400,000 men, would be their prisoners.

It will be recalled that under the terms of the surrender all military movement was to end during 9 May. The deadline imposed was one that Loehr's men could never meet unless they began to move immediately towards Austria. The Army Group Commander turned a deaf ear to the entreaties of his subordinates to break off the talks and order the Army Group to fight its way through, and to continue the fight even after the deadline had passed. Loehr refused to give an order that might make his men outlaws through a contravention of the armistice conditions, but gave his Generals operational freedom to act as they thought fit, an offer which several of them took. Those escaping units used commando tactics and guerrilla skills to pass through the JANL ring and, in a war to the knife, attacked and destroyed any Jugoslav groups which tried to obstruct or to delay them. Such ruthlessness was not confined to the Germans alone. One German regiment which had been surrounded, then capitulated, and even before the unit had been completely disarmed partisan murder squads began to shoot the unit officers. Anticipating that this might be the fate of them all, the regiment closed ranks and fought with bitter determination until it had carved its way across the Mur and into Austria.

Had Loehr known of the treatment which his formations would endure as prisoners of war he might have been more bold. German military histories as well as personal accounts are filled with stories of summary executions. At Pola, for example, German naval and army officers were rounded up, lined up on the sea mole and killed by machine-gun fire. Following that massacre, other officers captured in Pola were flung into the sea with their feet weighted with iron. Partisan justice was harsh and public, and to avoid torture hundreds committed suicide; not just officers, who realized that the braid on their shoulder-straps was a death sentence, but rank and file who suspected that some reason would be found to kill them, too. For those men a bullet in the brain was quicker than being beaten to death and less painful than being burned alive. Death was present everywhere. The racial hatreds between Slav and Teuton touched new depths in those first weeks of May.

While Army Group 'E' was in a state of dissolution, the British were alarmed at Tito's refusal to withdraw his men from Carinthia. The reason he advanced for this trespass was that the German armies had invaded Jugoslavia out of Austria in 1941, and that he was simply pursuing the enemy back into that territory. The Jugoslav leader had issued a deliberate challenge which had to be confronted. Logically, it was not possible for Carinthia to be occupied by two armies, particularly if they had diametrically opposing views as to how the occupation was to be conducted. Relations between Eighth Army and the JANL deteriorated to a dangerous low. Churchill determined to resolve the dilemma by asking President Truman to state the US position on forcible annexations and went so far as to warn the President that there would be no future for Europe if Tito succeeded in his demands and actions. Truman's answer was that no territorial demands brought about by force would be countenanced. Churchill, now assured of American political support, then asked Alexander how his troops would feel about a new war. The Commander-in-Chief discussed with his Army commanders whether in the event of hostilities between Jugoslavia and the Western Allies their soldiers could be relied upon to fight against their former ally. Alexander's telegrams to the Prime Minister stated, 'My soldiers will obey orders, but I doubt whether they will fight against Tito with as much enthusiasm as they did against the hated Germans.'

The troops in Italy were put on full alert and then to ensure that the Anglo-American force had sufficient strength, Truman issued orders and soon eighteen US divisions were in position to support Fifth and Eighth Armies. The prospect of war with Jugoslavia was now very real. The crisis point was fast approaching. Plans were prepared for an assault landing from the sea against Jugoslav-held Istria. RAF and American bomber groups were briefed. The Western Allies were prepared to act, but the final, most important factor before they moved was to determine the attitude of the Soviet Union. Would Stalin support his loyal satellite to the point of war, or advise Tito to give way? Stalin advised the Jugoslav leader to withdraw his forces, but Tito did not immediately comply. Instead of a clear decision he offered to place his forces in Austria under British command. While this non-reply was being studied in London the JANL formations put on marches and ceremonial parades. They soon found themselves outclassed by a British Army whose service had been a mixture of bitter fighting and ceremonial 'bullshit'. In a contest of one-upmanship if the Jugoslavs paraded a battalion of tattered brigands, on the following day, the British paraded the Brigade of Guards. A march past of partisan armoured cars would be followed by a review of a British Tank Brigade in which every vehicle gleamed and glistened in the sun. If a Jugoslav military band paraded it would be upstaged by the massed pipes of the Argylls and the Irish Brigade. These were all 'hearts and minds' operations, fought out with 'bullshit' instead of bullets. Against Eighth Army's experience the JANL had no chance. The partisans admitted defeat on parade ground skills and tried fly-posting of Austrian villages with notices proclaiming that Carinthia now lay under Jugoslav military administration. British patrols removed these announcements and inevitably tension grew. In Klagenfurt there was one particularly dramatic incident. JANL troops had acted provocatively and when British troops ordered them to leave had brought up two light tanks.

'There had been an English tank positioned outside the Landhaus since the English arrived. The Jugoslav soldiers were very excited and when their two dusty tanks arrived they began to cheer. An English officer went across and spoke to the Titoist commander. It was clear that an argument had developed.

The English officer stopped talking, turned round, climbed onto his tank and disappeared inside it. He reappeared and stood up in the turret. I can see him now, with earphones on and a microphone round his throat. He spoke into this and very slowly the gun on the English tank, which had been pointing up towards the sky, began to lower and then the turret began to turn towards the first Jugoslav vehicle. There was an absolute silence. The gun was brought right down and was aimed directly at the Jugoslavs. Suddenly the partisans started their tank engines and drove out of the square. We Austrians went wild and we all applauded as if it had been an entertainment. Looking back I realize how naive we all were. A war might have broken out in that square on that day.'

The British Government refused to take Tito's men under Eighth Army command and he accepted Stalin's advice not to jeopardize the fragile peace. On 18 May, the JANL units left Klagenfurt singing their partisan songs and moved back across the Mur, the southern boundary of Austria. As Tito's men left by one road there arrived in Carinthia, by other roads, those formations of Army Group 'E' which had managed to cross the border before the deadline expired. Among the stream of troops and carts were the mounted divisions of Pannwitz's Cossack Corps who were allowed to camp temporarily in the fields outside Klagenfurt before moving off to Lienz in East Tyrol. Still held south of the Mur were the German formations, the Croats and the other national groups.

When the proud glitter of victory is tarnished by random, individual acts of cruelty against a defenceless and vanquished enemy, such deeds reduce the man who commits them, but when cruelty is organized and directed at governmental level the whole nation is diminished. Western nations do not usually know a passion so compelling as to produce a blood feud, but such things are a feature of Balkan life and so great has been their influence that they have been known to weaken national unity on behalf of the narrow interests of race or political creed.

Above: Tito's partisans march through Klagenfurt on their way back out of Carinthia. **Right:** on 5 May 1945, the Chetniks, Jugoslav anti-Communist partisans, who had surrendered to the British Army in southern Austria, were disarmed. At this parade, the flags of the united nations were carried by a colour party; the Chetniks believed themselves to be on the same side as the Allies. Very soon after this parade, the Chetniks were handed back to the Jugoslav Communist Government.

In this context we pass from battlefields of valour to other fields on which national revenge and racial retribution were taken against the enemies of the people. There were so many considered by the Communist regime of Jugoslavia to be its foes. The Croats and the Slovenes, both of whom had declared themselves independent of the central government; the Chetniks, the royalist partisans, Montenigrins, Bosnians and others who stood condemned in the eyes of Tito's supporters. It is the terrible fate of the surrendered German soldiers and of those Jugoslavian national groups which concludes the story of the last days of the war on the south-eastern section of the Southern Front.

In those first days of May, Tito's forces were exultant. Victory was assured and the day of retribution was at hand. The Croats and Slovenes finally surrendered and the genocide began, but the story of the horrors committed against their own peoples comes later. First we deal with the Jugoslav treatment of the German soldiers who had hoped to escape into Austria, but who were taken by the JANL. In the first blind rush of hate against the former occupiers of their homeland, partisan murder groups carried out summary executions of any German they thought merited death. After that first frantic blood-letting the survivors of Army Group 'E' were force-marched around Jugoslavia in a trek that was calculated to debase and torture them.

The full story of the 'murder march' through Jugoslavia, as it was called by its victims, will now never be told. So many of those who began it did not live to complete it. Many of those who experienced its horror were so deeply affected that they died a few years later. The 'murder march', the 'starvation march', the 'march of hate' – it is known by these and other names – was called by the Jugoslav Government the 'march of expiation'. It was a 2,000-kilometre trek by starving German prisoners across the length and breadth of Jugoslavia and was intended as a vivid demonstration of how the partisans had humbled and brought low the mighty German Army.

When writing a book based to a very large extent on personal recollections of events which occurred more than four decades earlier, one must be prepared for exaggeration, for loss of detail and, in some cases, pure invention to make the story conform to the end result. The stories I was told of the 'murder march' tallied so well with one another that I could only conclude that either a huge propaganda deception was being practised or that my informants were telling the truth. I have selected elements from a number of stories told to me and combined them to furnish a single narrative covering all the main points.

'When the surrender came into force my regiment was among those around Laibach in Lower Steiermark. For our first days as prisoners we were fed with food drawn from German Army stores. There were sufficient rations and these were distributed and cooked in the routine way. It was during the third or fourth day of

our captivity when things deteriorated. Our officers were taken away and then our senior NCOs. We were, of course, unarmed and all weapons had been handed in at the time of the surrender. We were, therefore, defenceless against the viciousness of the attacks which then began. Late one morning groups of partisans began to assemble and then, as if by signal, they rushed us. They stole everything. It was clear that medals, watches, pens – any personal possession in fact would be taken, but we had not expected them to steal clothing; boots, socks, hats, even spectacles. They took anything that they fancied. Some of our soldiers were reduced to just underpants and a shirt.

We were marched away to a central concentration point where a number of units had already been gathered. Almost as soon as our group arrived the whole column was ordered to march. Until we learned better we stayed at the back of the column hoping that way to avoid being beaten by the guards or being physically assaulted by the villagers and townspeople. We soon learned that those at the rear always have to march much more quickly than those at the front. I do not know why this is, but it is a fact. Also of importance was that those at the rear get fed last and worst. Then, too, the time that those at the rear spend at rest is limited by the impatience of the guards to be on their way. Also at the rear of the column you are subjected to attacks by hooligans and riff-raff.

Within days we were organized and had a rota worked out. We introduced a column discipline, that is to say, we prisoners decided on a daily basis which unit would lead the column and which would tail it. That way each group led or tailed the column during some period of the march, and remember, none of us knew where the march would end; indeed, whether the march would end. It was the uncertainty that was so bad.'

There were women on the march, nursing sisters and telegraphists from signals units.

'There were several hundred women in our group – we were the sexual toys of the guards or of any peasant who fancied a German girl. On more than one occasion our guards lent us out as temporary gifts to soldiers of the Red Army and to Bulgarian units which were serving in Jugoslavia. It was not long before we had all learned the whore's trick of pretending to enjoy it. That way the man climaxes more quickly whereas resistance prolongs their pleasure because sadists delight in causing fear and overcoming resistance. There were some girls who used their bodies as barter objects – to have a single protector and thus avoid being raped by a number of men. I never saw such a thing work. The guards did not need to be protective towards us. They had a couple of hundred young females to choose from and the bodies of the girls were available at any time. It was fortunate that the Jugoslav soldiers were very young and quite unsophisticated so that they were not in search of, shall we call them unusual practices. Then too, they had a primitive fear of menstrual blood and it was usual for us to show them any bloodied undergarment to convince them that we were unclean. Of course this only worked about every other fortnight. You could not cheat more frequently with the same guard. Funnily it was not always the pretty girls who were raped most frequently, but those who were mature, or even buxom.'

Men and women suffered a common fate. If they fell out from the column they were shot where they lay. A samaritan who tried to help the victim would also be shot. Dysentery accompanied the column. Dysentery marched with the prisoners and there were no medical treatments to stop the spread of the disease, nor was there anything that could be given to diminish the pain.

'It was a very hot May and it seemed to me that clouds of blue-bottles and green-bottles accompanied our march. Those who had dysentery were caked with it – there was no opportunity to wash soiled clothing or stinking bodies. Flies flew above the slow trudging columns and settled in droves whenever a rest was granted. We were all lousy, of course, and the fear of lice-borne diseases was very strong.'

The torture of the trek lasted for two months. In the first weeks a daily norm of 50 kilometres per day was set and maintained. The German prisoners at that time were fit and strong young men who were accustomed to marching long distances. But soon dysentery, starvation and beatings reduced the march norm to 20 kilometres and any attempt to raise it too high left piles of dead prisoners lying in groups along the side of the road. The partisan guards were changed every fifth or sixth day so that those who dealt out the beatings were never too tired to flog and those who lusted after the German girls did not wear themselves out. The wounded were shown no consideration. They too had to march. If they could go no farther they were told to kneel down and were shot. In the early days the other prisoners carried their wounded comrades on makeshift stretchers, but by the middle period of the march the prisoners were no longer able to carry those who fell out.

'The farther we marched the more severe did our hardships become. We were deep in the Balkans where life had always been cheap and living was harsh enough even for the civilian population in peace-time. We humiliated and stinking prisoners were accounted less tham dogs. Imagine how hard things were for us. The remnants of our clothing were stolen from us by peasants whose own clothing was in a worse state than even our lousy rags and tatters. Many of those civilians took a perverse delight in refusing us water. They would make us beg for a drink. It is my firm conviction that only our hatred for all of our torturers kept us alive. We were determined that this scum would not defeat us morally. We knew somehow and believed it with absolute conviction that the Reds would not kill us all – although they killed a great many. But if only one of us survived the world would learn one day of what the Jugoslavs had done to us. How naive we were. When we did at last get home, I was lucky and was released at the end of 1946, I got back to my home in the Rhineland that was now part of America – it was in the US zone of occupation. Nobody wanted to know of what I had suffered in Jugoslavia. We all suffered, is what I was told.

It is strange how the mind works. When the column reached Slovenia it was not so pleasurable to sleep out in the open as it had been in the dry southern regions of Bosnia. Slovenia was damp and cold. In Bosnia it had been warm at night and if you are warm hunger seems less acute, somehow.'

In that part of Jugoslavia which had once been Austria, in a region where the Slav farmers had been savagely dispossessed by the Nazis, the German prisoners were set to work on reconstruction. This all-embracing term covered every form of physical labour from ordinary farm work to clearing cesspits or being used as cattle to pull the ploughs. The work was hard, the hours were long and the farmers not only vindictive but also keen to denounce any slight infringement by a prisoner in order to demonstrate their own loyalty to Tito and the revolution. Two things kept the surviving prisoners sane; one was the fact that the area of their captivity had once been Austrian and showed it in architecture and in its husbandry, evidence of the Catholic and German influences. The prisoners felt at home in a German niveau. The second factor was that the food, too, although simple and unsophisticated, was German and neither Slav nor Bosnian.

The total number who died on the hunger march or as prisoners of the Jugoslavs will never be known. The Soviets and, possibly the Jugoslavs too, inflate or reduce figures to accord to some propaganda point. It is certain, however, that more than 60 per cent of those who surrendered on or about 8 May, were dead before the year was out.

Not all atrocities committed in those days were simple murders. Some of them were decisions, taken 'of necessity', but which condemned thousands to death or to imprisonment. Across the border in Austria, the British Army, acting under orders from its government, was preparing to dispatch the Cossack peoples back to Russia. While the populations of western Europe and America were still glowing with the euphoria of the new-won peace, in southern Austria and in Jugoslavia thousands of Cossack men, women and children were delivered up to bestial horrors. The Cossack Corps was officered by Germans of whom the Cavalry General von Pannwitz was the senior. Under his command were the 1st and 2nd Cossack Divisions, drawn from peoples from the Don, from Siberia, from Kuban and from smaller communities. All had volunteered to serve with the German Army and all had been on anti-partisan operations against the JANL. That was their crime.

On 8 May it was ordered that from the time of the surrender all movement was to halt, but Pannwitz knew that to comply with this would entail the destruction of his men. At 23.00 hrs the regiments were ordered to saddle up and they rode out from their encampments to the west of Varasdin on a ride to freedom. With the Cossack cavalry travelled their wives and families, riding in a great number of open carts, for this was less a military operation than a migration. Such a movement could not go unnoticed; nor could it go unchallenged and the partisan attacks came in upon the mass of Horse. In the darkness of the night the sudden flash and detonation of grenades, mortar bombs and machine-gun fire split the column again and again. In that dark night, those who lost touch with the main body were taken by the guerrillas and tortured to death.

The frequency and weight of the JANL attacks weakened the 2nd Cossack Division which made only slow progress and was involved in fierce battles with the partisans. The 1st Division was more fortunate and passed so

These Cossacks had fought with the Germans against the Soviet system and came up into Austria out of Jugoslavia, where they had formed part of Pannwitz's force. The whole corps surrendered in the Klagenfurt area, and were eventually forcibly repatriated to Russia, where most of them were either murdered or imprisoned for decades. **Above:** they surrender their arms, under British supervision. **Below:** their farewell parade; note that the rank and file are dressed in German uniforms.

quickly into Austria that at dawn on 9 May, British military outposts outside Völkermarkt saw the horsemen riding out of the mist. After a few hours' rest and time to concentrate the scattered Squadrons, the whole Division paraded for inspection by the Corps Commander and local British commanders. In elegant precision the Sotnias wheeled into line and passed the saluting base at the trot and then at the charge. It was their farewell to a way of life and those who witnessed that parade were moved by the emotion of the moment. At noon the regiments laid down their arms and rode to St Veit where they were joined two days later by the survivors of the 2nd Division. There Pannwitz's Corps camped, but the dullness of prison life ended abruptly when on 28 May, in accordance with a direct order from London, the process of handing over the Cossacks to the butchers of the KGB began. It was a political decision and the soldiers who had to carry out the action detested those in London who forced them to cram families into cattle-trucks and to send them to certain death.

The reports I heard and read at the time troubled me. In November 1945, when I returned to England on leave, I spoke of these things. The reactions of my listeners varied between 'Serves them right; they fought on the wrong side', 'We British do not betray people', down to the contemptuous, 'So what?'

The Germans were soldiers and became prisoners of war. The Cossacks chose to fight for Hitler and paid the price of making a wrong decision. What can one say of the Jugoslav ethnic groups except that they deceived themselves. The cruelty of self-deception is that the victim himself remains unaware of his blindness. How could the Slovene leaders have been so naive as to believe that their declaration of independence from Jugoslavia would ever be accepted by Tito's government?

The national parliament in Slovenia had declared for independence during the night of 3 May and invited King Peter to return and to rule over them. The defence force of the newly declared state numbered 12,000, together with other non-Slovene units: three regiments of Serbian riflemen and a few Chetnik groups. Against that puny force the JANL sent in fourteen infantry divisions. Soon the Slovenes had been driven out of their capital, Ljubljana, and into the frontier area between Austria and Jugoslavia. At Unterbergen the refugees were halted by units of the British Army whose first order was that the Slovenes were to lay down their arms. The mass of unarmed people, between 25,000 and 30,000 in number, camped in open fields outside Klagenfurt, waiting to learn what was to become of them. They had not long to wait. By deception about 1,500 were chosen. Believing that they were being taken to Italy the group boarded trains at Maria Elend and at that station some idea of their fate was given to them. A priest was beaten to death on the platform. The refugees were headed for a martyrdom road which took them from Maria Elend through starvation camps to the deep and silent woodlands of Kocevje. There, in clearings, the 1,500 were put to death. Officers and priests were shackled and either clubbed to death or buried alive. From the time of the first fusillade there sounded in the wild forests of

Kocevje the chanting of a requiem for the dead, a singing which no machine-gun fire could silence. The last Slovene group was led out to die and in a spirit of defiance one of the condemned shouted the conviction that even today inspires the Slovene exiles: 'You swine did not defeat us. We were betrayed into your hands.'

The Slovene women were raped repeatedly. Killing aroused some partisans sexually and they used the wives and daughters of their enemies to appease their inflamed appetites.

From that first massacre one man escaped and returned to Klagenfurt where the great mass of Slovenes still awaited transport to the destination which they had been assured was Italy. The survivor told his story but was not believed. Who would give credence to such horror? Thus assured by their leaders other Slovene groups left the fields of Klagenfurt for a journey that would end in unmarked graves in the thick forests of northern Jugoslavia.

By far the largest movement of population was the migration of the Croats. The German Government had supported the separation of Croatia from the other States of Jugoslavia and had encouraged the new nation to form military and air force units, many of which had fought alongside their German comrades in Russia. In Jugoslavia three Croat divisions, with some German specialist battalions, were employed on anti-partisan operations in the mountains. German reports on the Croat units praise their loyalty and bravery. 'They were the best soldiers I ever met' is a phrase frequently expressed.

Early in 1945 it was clear that an independent Croatia had no future and plans were made to evacuate the entire nation into Austria. In numbers it was a movement of more than half a million people. On 6 May the Croat civilians shielded by their soldiers, moved back. The war ended. The deadline for movement passed, but still the Croats continued their march until on 15 May, the trek had reached the southern bank of the River Drau. Had reached, but could not cross because the northern bank was held by a Bulgarian division with orders to bar the way until Marshal Tolbhukin gave authority. Unwilling to wait and even more unwilling to surrender their weapons, which was the second Bulgar demand, the Croats moved towards the small market town of Bleiburg where their forces were already battling against the 51st Partisan Division. The Croat Guard Regiment and the army's paratroop battalion as well as other units were put into action, and in a hard-fought battle cleared the road to Bleiburg. Some idea of how bitter the fighting had been can be gained from the fact that partisan losses exceeded 80 per cent. These terrible casualties were the result of the partisans' abandoning their standard guerrilla tactics and sweeping forward in successive lines of infantry, advancing shoulder to shoulder in the wasteful 'wave' tactics taken from the Red Army's Infantry Training Manual. To use such primitive and suicidal methods against skilled, professional and hate-filled men could only have one result – a blood-bath. At the end of the day it seemed as if the road to Bleiburg was finally open, but then a new enemy appeared. Patrols from British Eighth Army, moving out of Italy, were blocking the road forward.

There was no other choice for the Croats now. Behind them was the JANL. Across the Drau the Bulgarians and in front of them the British.

The Croat leaders offered to surrender to Eighth Army. The British officer regretted, but his orders were that the Croats could not pass over into Austria but had to be handed over to the Jugoslavs. He assured the Croat leaders they need have no fears. The Tito government subscribed fully to international agreements governing prisoners of war. Regrettably, he had to impose a time limit. The leaders had 50 minutes in which to accept his demands and disarm their forces. If they did not he would have to join with his Jugoslav allies and force the Croats to comply.

The JANL commander issued his own ultimatum. Compliance with a quarter of an hour or his men would open fire. At 16.00 hrs on 15 May 1945, the sufferings of the Croats began. They may have been politically naive in expecting to remain free, but they knew now with terrible certainty the fate that faced them all. Fathers ended the lives of their wives and children rather than have them subjected to partisan torture and imprisonment. Some groups of men, armed and unarmed, determined to fight on and tried to force their way through the ring of enemies that enclosed them. Elsewhere the mass of white flags showed that most of the nation had accepted the bitterness of defeat.

The march into the interior of Jugoslavia began. Few finished it. On the road between Bleiburg and Marburg, a short distance – not more than 100 kilometres – 110,000 (one hundred and ten thousand) Croats were murdered in the first few days. The survivors were herded together and then underwent the torment of a month-long march eastwards to the Roumanian frontier and then southwards to the border with Greece. Those who came through that ordeal were very few indeed; as was intended. If one measures war casualties as a proportion of the total population, the Croats are among those at the top of that grisly table. More than a quarter of a million men of the Croat nation had already fallen in battle before the emigration began. Following the partisan 'victory' at Bleiburg, as it was hailed by the Tito government, nearly 200,000 more were killed. It was a fearful blood-letting – a butchery of which the West knew nothing and cared less. They'd fought on the wrong side. Serves them right! In the name of allied solidarity, in the name of democracy and in the name of freedom, a quarter of a million Croats were killed.

Nowhere in this terrible tale of rape and murder is compassion for the victim to be found; no understanding of the aspirations of the Croats or forgiveness for their transgressions. No. They were Croats, Slovenes, or Bosnians and they died. At one place near Marburg – the Ponje mountains – the dead were shot at the edges of huge pits, group after group after group. Those who were shot first died fully clothed, but complaints from local civilians watching the butchery that this was a waste of clothing produced the order that the victims should die naked or in their underclothes. And so, in the vast meadowland at the foot of the mountain, the Croats were brought out in batches, were forced to kneel on the edge of the pit, looking down at the twitching bodies of their compatriots, aware that they would soon form the next layer of bleeding flesh. What is the point in recounting horror after horror? With repetition the senses dull, and slaughter, even that of children and women, becomes just another thought that is quickly put out of mind. Then one reads that tanks and bulldozers had to be brought in and driven, day after day, across the death pits, and horror returns. When bodies putrefy the gases inside them inflate and when such numbers are involved the inflation is powerful enough to cause the earth to move, to open and to uncover the bodies. So tanks had to be brought in to drive across the pits forcing the twitching dead down and the vehicles continued this gruesome task until the gases had finally dissipated and the protesting soil no longer heaved.

Massacres and death marches marked the final end of the Jugoslav war. For weeks the guns had been silent throughout most of Europe. On the south-western sector, in Italy, it had ended on 2 May. The focus of our attention switches now to the Italian peninsula, but first mention must be made of the role of the partisans in both Jugoslavia and Italy. I do not judge whether one man is a patriot or a murderer when he fights in a partisan force. What is important is what those hungry, badly clothed and ill-armed men achieved against a skilled, ruthless and heavily armed enemy. To link the narrative between Jugoslavia, where the partisans by their own efforts won victory, and Italy, where they achieved so much, is this account by Major Arthur Farrand Radley, MBE, who served with partisan groups in the area of north-east Italy and north-west Jugoslavia.

'I was Captain Thorley, a British Liaison Officer for the Special Operations Executive with the Italian Partisan Division 'Nino Nannetti', on the Pian di Cansiglio, a high plateau, thirty miles north of Venice. Through my binoculars I could pick out a great white German hospital ship in the harbour, glistening in the clear evening light.

Although I was called Thorley by the SOE as a nom de guerre, I was immediately Captain Arturo to my hosts who proudly sewed this in the red scarf which I wore.

I had flown in not long before in a Lysander aircraft and it was incredible that fascinating flight over the German-occupied coast to the east of Venice in the evening light when the enemy on the ground was too preoccupied to send up a fighter or to plug us with flak. We even had an air strip picked out in hand-lit flares – and all this right in the middle of German-occupied territory.

How had I ever got into this? Three years in Malta on half rations and daily blitzing before volunteering for SOE at the call for people who were 'not musclebound'. I was originally selected for the Resistance in Austria but the only British officer in that area was caught. One operation with the SOE in France and now here I was with this Leftish outfit in Italy. They were less interested in winning the war for the gallant Allies than in settling their own scores with the Fascists. But so long as they fought Germans that was all right by us at the time. They had had a hard winter doing just that.

Now the intention was to plan for the last stage of the war in Italy and to communicate that plan to SOE HQ in Siena. We radioed the details back. The Nino Nannetti group intended to occupy a set area and to mop up any demoralized Germans before 'liberating' the area from Fascist aggression. It needs little imagination to understand what that meant.

All that was needed was a signal from base and this came when it was clear that Kesselring was ready to negotiate. Our partisans did what they said they would do and more than 8,000 Germans surrendered to them in a moving ceremony in the main square of Montaner, a small village. The local band played Bandiere Rossa, the 'Red Flag' and more than a thousand vehicles were handed over and left in a vast column strung right along the main road, a real prize and legitimate booty after all that had been suffered.

Then things went wrong. We had assumed that Eighth Army would have been alerted by our SOE base about our particular operation and that official attacks would be withheld. Not a bit of it. Hours before we could raise them on one of our regular scheduled transmissions, the RAF came over and shot up all the lorries in the transport column. We were not very popular with the partisans after that.

Life, however, was for the living, and we all filed down the mountain path into Vittorio Veneto and took over the best hotel. My room still bore the nameplate 'Oberst Muller – Chef'. There was also in the hotel the office of the DAF (Deutsche Arbeits Front) which the British assumed had been reserved for the Desert Air Force. Colonel Muller gave himself up to the 17/21 Lancers, but refused to hand over his revolver, claiming that the Geneva Convention of 1929 and the Hague Regulations entitled him to retain it. The Adjutant of 17/21st was of a different opinion and relieved him of it.

The 17/21 was the spearhead of Eighth Army and was followed by the Guards Brigade hotfoot for Trieste. Then came my own unit and the Military Government, headed by a Territorial Brigadier, John Dunlop, who astonished the locals by an impassioned speech in fluent Italian. His Deputy, Alex Wilkinson, was to be my boss in the Military Government of the Austrian Province of Styria where, after a unique chapter in post-war relationships, he got the Grand Gold Medal of the Province and I the Grand – possibly the only occasion of an enemy Power thus honouring its occupiers.

Back in Vittorio Veneto it was an odd situation. Our war was over but the war in Europe was not yet. The New Zealanders were ordered to dash along the motorway and take Venice. They crossed the main A road to the north-west and saw a lot of chaps wearing the wrong uniform. These were the German 91st Light Infantry Division (Hermann Goering) also with orders to get the Hell out of it all. What was there to do? Simple. Salute mutually and carry on. When the Kiwis got to Venice they found our 'Nino Nannetti' boys in full possession, so much so that when I got there myself I was met by our own gondola and escorted to our own Palazzo on the Grand Canal; the Volpi.

Our British team were the first into the top hotel, the Daniele (later to be requisitioned at half a crown per night all in.) I took part in a victory ceremony in St Mark's Square and witnessed the unique exploit of Popski's Private Army (an Eighth Army band of irregulars led by Lieutenant-Colonel Vladimir Peniakov, a

White Russian based on Cairo) in penetrating an area where there were no vehicles. His amphibious Jeeps waddled ashore from the Lagoon, did six laps of honour and waddled back.

And what of VE-Day itself? As I said before, 8 May was an irrelevance to us in Italy; we had already won OUR WAR. But VE-Day did call for a celebration and we radioed our base asking for provender to fuel a Partisan Victory Banquet. They sent us a plane-load of corned beef. On VE-Day itself I was at Treviso aerodrome saluting the US Army Air Force Colonel and signing for one plane and one load of bully, while he and his crew beat it for the fleshpots of Venice.

To the partisans the war didn't end with VE-Day. It was just the beginning of their war against the Fascists. The cartoonist Jon of the newspaper 'Eighth Army News' excelled himself in portraying a partisan literally armed to the teeth (clenching a stiletto and overwhelmed by weapons of all sorts) confronted by the Two Types who ask him, 'I say, old man, haven't you heard the jolly old guerra is finito?' Well, for me it wasn't quite. I had a spell at Eighth Army HQ – on the Staff – and so on into Austria, my original destination.

When I left Italy it had been sunny; just as I crossed over the border it started to rain. I thought of Manchester, where I had been born and knew that the war really was over and that I was at home.

In 1968 I went back to Montaner. It was midday and the sun was boiling hot. In the main square where the Germans had surrendered in 1945 there was an old crone carrying a bundle of washing. Suddenly the 'Red Flag' blared out loud and clear, just as it had when we sang it more than twenty years before. Was this some extra-sensory perception trick? Not a bit of it; just a loudspeaker van round the corner campaigning for the Senate elections.'

7
ITALY

Only days before the war ended in Italy, Mussolini, the fascist dictator, was murdered by being shot to death. Details of how the body of the former leader had then been publicly exhibited to the fury of a mob which had once acclaimed him, as 'Duce' were given to Hitler. He insisted that when the time came his own body must be incinerated until nothing identifiable remained for the Soviet enemy to display for the gaze of the vulgar masses.

Mussolini, Clara Petacci, his mistress, together with a number of ministers from the fallen fascist government, had joined a German Army column which was near Lake Como, travelling through territory held by the 52nd Garibaldi Brigade of partisans. The guerrillas had set up a barricade across the road along which the convoy would have to pass, under normal circumstances a foolhardy, not to say suicidal, enterprise. So badly had German control been eroded towards the end of April that Major Kritz, the convoy commander, did not use his armoured car to smash through the barricade, nor did he attack the partisans despite his superior fire power and numbers. Instead, obedient to partisan hand signals, Kritz ordered the convoy to halt at the barricade. The Italian fascists inside the trucks were convinced that they were about to be betrayed and opened fire, an action which produced a partisan response. Their volley of shots was ragged but effective enough, and a white handkerchief waved through the observation slit of the armoured car showed that the convoy had given up the fight.

Major Kritz was quite charming. All he wanted was to return home, the war was nearly over – it was 26 April. There was no need for any more killing and he would like, please, from the commander of the 52nd Garibaldi Brigade the promise of safe conduct. A partisan search of the lorries found the fascist ministers who were dragged out. Mussolini, dressed in a German Army greatcoat and steel helmet, was identified by Count Bellini delle Stelle, the Brigade Commander, who advised the Partisan Committee of National Liberation that the former Duce was under arrest. Two days later a murder squad arrived to take custody of the fascists. The ministers were butchered and then, at the gates of a villa near Mezzegra, the Duce and his mistress were shot. In Milan there was the obscenity of a public display of all the murdered victims, hanged upside down by their feet from the iron girders of a petrol station. This atrocity was both photographed and filmed. Mussolini had come full circle; from accession of power to death in the dust – and all within twenty-three years.

By the time that the Duce's violated corpse had been cut down and buried, Major Kritz and his convoy had arrived back in Germany. Did the Major, in later years, remember with remorse the allies of his country whom he had abandoned to be slaughtered by his country's enemies?

The death of the former Italian Duce was only one factor in the confusion of intrigue and of national and international politics set against a background of battle which marked the end of the war in Italy. At national level the political state of Italy was chaotic. There was an Allied-imposed government in the south. This had succeeded Mussolini's dictatorship, but it was a government with little power. In the north the Duce had ruled over a government, just as powerless, which had been set up by the Nazis. The most active political force was the partisan movement, whose national committee was almost totally Communist-dominated and which was determined to seize power from the nominally democratic government, using force if necessary.

At the level of international politics Italy's democratic government was faced with territorial demands from neighbouring countries; from Jugoslavia which laid claim to Fiume, Trieste and the Istrian peninsula, as well as from Austria which demanded the return of the province of South Tyrol.

On the military level there were four huge armies; two German and two Allied which faced one another south of the Po. Should these be once again locked in battle, there was the probability that the fertile and industrially rich northern provinces of Italy would be destroyed in the fighting. To prevent this and to bring about a quick end to the war, secret negotiations and intrigues were conducted between many sorts of principals and at differing levels of power. From the complicated mass of meetings and assignations only those of importance will be described in the course of this narrative.

To set the scene for the drama which produced the first capitulation of a complete German Army Group and a whole theatre of operations, it is enough to say that the Anglo-Americans had invaded the mainland of Italy during September 1943. The optimistic hope that the US Fifth and the British Eighth Armies could quickly occupy the whole peninsula, was dashed when Hitler decided to defend it. Nineteen months of bitter fighting brought the Allied armies almost to the River Po. It seemed that only a few Apennine peaks prevented Fifth Army from advancing into the Plain of Lombardy and that a succession of river barriers was all that held back the divisions of Eighth Army. One final offensive might well bring victory and in the New Year General Mark Clark planned this battle. He was well aware that it would be no easy-won success, for his battle-hardened troops would be opposed by the equally veteran divisions of German Tenth and Fourteenth Armies, which had been pushed back relentlessly, but which were neither defeated nor demoralized. Those armies would continue to defend their positions tenaciously and with confidence, for behind them there were the Alps, a mighty shield of mountains into whose fastnesses Army Group 'C' would withdraw and from within which it would continue to defend the Fatherland.

The Alps played a significant part in the military thinking of both sides, and to understand the last days of the war, not merely in Italy but also in Germany, it must be recalled that by the end of April 1945, the largest piece of territory still administered by the Third Reich encompassed the western half of Czechoslovakia, almost the whole of Austria west of Vienna, northern Italy and Jugoslavia and a small part of southern Germany. Within that shrinking area lay the most mountainous regions of central Europe. Western Intelligence officers noted with concern that great masses of the German armed forces were being pushed by Allied pressure into territory which favoured the defenders; that is the Germans – rather than the attackers – the Eastern and Western Allies.

The slow, Allied advance up the Italian peninsula had demonstrated that the soldiers of an army which held the high ground could delay for months the advance of a superior enemy force. Cassino, early on in the campaign, had frustrated the drive on Rome for almost six months and during the autumn offensive of 1944, the Eighth Army's 'Gothic Line' operation was blocked by the Gebirgsjäger of 100th Regiment who held the crucial Monte Gemmano. The staunch defence put up by those German mountain troops wrecked the timetable of an offensive which had been intended to 'reach Bologna in two days, Venice in four and Vienna in a week'. In the spring of 1945 both Allied armies were still miles short of Bologna. The Apennines and a firm German defence had beaten them. How then could the Allies expect to fare as, in their northward drive they encountered the Alps on whose high ground were battle-hardened and determined defenders?

It was, therefore, important for the Allies to destroy Army Group 'C' in the Po Valley before its divisions could reach the mountains. Speed was crucial to that plan; speed to delay the German withdrawal into the Alps and this delay could only be brought about by mobilizing all the Italian partisan units and by incorporating them as an important element in the Allied battle plan. Some of the guerrilla forces would be unleashed in the rear of the German armies to attack, to intercept and delay the enemy. Other groups would set out to seize the high ground before the Germans reached it. The enemy, if he had escaped the anticipated débacle south of the Po, would not be able to escape through the Brenner Pass and would be brought to the final battle in the Alpine foothills, trapped against those mountains in which he had hoped to find refuge. So much for the Allied intentions.

The commander of Army Group 'C' was aware of an imminent Anglo-American spring offensive. If this followed the normal pattern it would be made by both Allied armies moving ponderously forward. By mounting strong rearguards the German commanders could hold the Allies at successive river lines, particularly the Po while the divisions of Tenth and Fourteenth Armies moved across the Plain of Lombardy and into the mountains. The fear that struck a chill into the hearts of the German commanders was exactly that which the Allied High Command had planned; that there would be a mass uprising of the partisans and that they might capture the high ground.

It was unthinkable that senior commanders of the German Army should treat with bandits, for that was how the guerrillas were seen by orthodox military officers, but they might pre-empt a partisan uprising by negotiating with the most senior Allied leaders for Army Group 'C' to withdraw out of Italy and back into Reich territory. In truth such an idea, treacherous in that last spring of the war, had progressed past the concept stage and delicate negotiations had already begun. Months earlier, the German Ambassador to Italy, Rahn and the Cardinal Archbishop of Milan, Schuster, had met and as a direct result Rahn had begun to discuss with US Intelligence officers in neutral Switzerland, plans to save the German armies and northern Italy from being destroyed. The talks had continued throughout the winter, but now, with the approach of spring, they became urgent.

Thus, all the political and military threads that make up the story of the last campaign are laid out, except for one – and this has the most profound effect of all, for it can be said that it altered the course of European post-war history. This factor, based on the Alps, was a propaganda triumph for Josef Goebbels. He proclaimed that there existed in the mountainous areas of southern Germany, of Austria and of northern Italy, a fortress complex into which Hitler and his associates would withdraw. In this specially constructed and outfitted bastion they would hold out, for years if necessary, and out of this they and a well-equipped army of élite troops would erupt to win back Germany and to achieve a German victory. Since the Alpine Redoubt, as it was called, affected Allied policy so deeply, let us study how the story began, how it developed and how it became accepted so completely that it nearly split the East-West alliance.

In the autumn of 1944, stories began to circulate in Switzerland that the Nazis had set up a vast military complex in the mountains of southern Germany and Austria. The origin of these stories cannot be positively determined, but they probably stemmed from Goebbels. Agents of the SD, the SS Intelligence Department, picked up the tale and forwarded it to Gauleiter Hofer of Tyrol, together with American reactions. During November 1944, in an attitude of self-praise he sent a report to Martin Bormann, the tenor of which was that US experts had forecast unacceptably high casualty figures would result from the fighting to overcome this final bastion of the Nazis. Hofer's report included the other American fears that 'East-West tension will become visible if the war drags on too long.' This situation could be exploited by the Nazis who should seek to open negotiations with the West at the expense of the Soviet Union. Hofer urged that a defence redoubt be set up in the German/Austrian mountainous regions similar to that which already existed in the Italian/Austrian area, i.e., in his own Gau. One sector of this southern redoubt Hofer had merely strengthened – a fact which he did not feel it necessary to include in his report. This strengthened segment he had modestly entitled 'The Hofer Line'. For a northern redoubt he urged that masses of food, ammunition and military supplies be stored, underground factories be built to produce necessary weapons and aircraft. To preserve secrecy and to reduce the number of unproductive mouths all civilians, particularly foreigners, would have to be moved out of the redoubt area and replaced by American and British prisoners of war whose presence should deter Allied air raids. The garrison of the redoubt would have to be made up of élite military units, backed by 30,000 men of the Standschützen, local defence units which were the Tyrolean equivalent of the Volkssturm. The redoubt would also nourish the German partisan movement, Wehrwolf for, to quote Hofer, '. . .the eyes of all German activists will be directed, full of hope, towards the defiantly resisting redoubt. German men will be attracted to help their comrades and thus there will be a stream of reinforcement to the garrison . . .' Poor Gauleiter Hofer firmly believed that the massive undertakings which he had proposed could all be carried out and, despite all evidence to the contrary, he was confident that Germany could still win the war.

A professional appraisal was that of General von Hengl who presented a report soon after he was first ordered to command of the redoubt garrison. His chief conclusion was that the military units in the area were completely inadequate. No Army divisions had been transferred to the mountains. Instead there had flooded in a miscellany of civilian ministries and agencies as well as Luftwaffe ground staff. In a post-war report he stated that the strength of his corps during the period from 1 to 5 April was 30,000 men. 'After capitulation I had 38,000 in my billeting area, most of whom were members of military agencies and 90 per cent of whom were non-combatant. The Army reached the Alps in fragmented groups . . . the prerequisites for guerrilla warfare were lacking . . . there was a lack of labour forces, materials, weapons and ammunition.' The report then went on to analyze the claims made in the Gauleiter's report. 'Viewed soberly there were many false assumptions. Fortifications could not be built high up in the mountains during late autumn and winter . . . Time, distance and transport difficulties made it impossible to establish a new armament industry underground . . . the few roads and railways in the valleys would have been rendered useless through enemy air raids and it would have been impossible to transport and to store in bomb-proof shelters the machinery, raw materials, provisions and combat material to stand a long siege . . . I do not believe that the Alpine Redoubt would have had a pronounced effect upon the resistance by Germans to the armies of occupation, nor would serious quarrels have arisen between the Allies because of a prolongation of the war. The Allies would always have united their efforts at the expense of Germany. In any case,' von Hengl's report concluded, 'in modern warfare high mountains, deficient in roads and influenced by the seasons are utterly unsuited as bases for operations . . . The Alpine Redoubt existed merely on paper . . . It was a slogan . . .'

Von Hengl was able to dismiss the Redoubt as a slogan, not only because he had been in the area, but because he viewed the options and proposals objectively as a soldier and not subjectively as a Party politician. He analysed the Gauleiter's proposals and found the premise faulty. There was no chance of success. How different were von Hengl's conclusions from those of the Americans who despite access to superior Intelligence sources, nevertheless accepted the Goebbels myth *in toto*. They did not check the frightening claims; they checked nothing and, consequently, accepted that the Redoubt existed in all its horror. Goebbels' propaganda campaign may have had a secondary intention; to stiffen the resolve of the German people and in that the Propaganda Minister succeeded. The prime intent, to frighten the Allies was likewise achieved. To give substance to the outline story of an Alpine fortress Goebbels wrote about Hofer's recommendations as if they were already operational. Thus, according to Goebbels, food stocks were already piled, underground factories were in full production, the élite units garrisoning the Alpine Redoubt were in action and, here he added his own special refinement; in the vast caverns of the Alpine complex, German scientists were working to produce *THE* secret weapon which would ensure a German victory.

Allied Intelligence-gathering sources garnered the terrifying details that were published in the German Press or reported over the German radio. How successfully Goebbels' tall tales hoodwinked the Allies can be seen in the key sentences of an Intelligence summary produced for Supreme Headquarters Allied Expeditionary Forces (SHAEF) on 11 March 1945, that is only sixty days before the war ended.

'Accumulated information and photographic evidence make possible a more definite estimate of the progress of plans for the 'Last Ditch Stand'.

German defence policy is to safeguard the Alpine Zone . . . Defences continue to be constructed in depth in the south, through the Black Forest to Lake Constance and from the Hungarian frontier to the west of Graz . . . In Italy . . . defence lines are built up in the foothills of the Italian Alps.

The results of air reconnaissance show at least twenty sites of recent underground activity as well as numerous natural caves, mainly in the region of Golling, Feldkirch, Kufstein and Berchtesgaden . . . accommodation for stores and personnel. The existence of several underground factories has also been confirmed. It thus appears that ground reports of extensive preparations for the accommodation of the German Maquis-to-be are not unfounded. As regards actual numbers of troops, stores and weapons . . . evidence indicates considerable numbers of SS and specially chosen units are engaged on some type of defence activity at the most vital strategic points . . . The most important ministries and personalities are established within the Redoubt area . . . while Hitler, Goering, Himmler and other notables are said to be in the process of withdrawing to the mountain stronghold.'

American psychologists announced that their understanding of Hitler's mentality indicated that he would entrench himself in an Alpine fortress from which he would continue the war. They were, therefore, prepared to accept the Goebbels legends.

Hitler received Hofer's November memorandum during April 1945, and he ordered that the Gauleiter's plans be put into immediate effect. It is hard to credit that the German leader believed it possible, at that stage of the war, to set up factories out of nothing, to stockpile food and fuel, to concentrate airforce squadrons and, presumably, to build the airstrips from which the aircraft could operate. Hitler must have known of the critical fuel shortage and of the decline in the German explosives and propellants industries. Did he not see the reports? Did he not believe them, or had he not drawn the correct conclusions from the facts that were laid before him? There is another possibility. By April Hitler had decided to remain in Berlin and thus whether there was a redoubt or not was of little consequence to him. He may, however, have been prepared to take part in a propaganda charade. The situation begs the question. Hitler may have been either misinformed or he may have misunderstood the situation. But how could trained Intelligence officers with superior knowledge have believed in so obvious a fiction as Goebbels' Redoubt?

The conventional Intelligence agencies of SHAEF, backed by ULTRA, checked against radio intercepts and the interrogation of prisoners and confirmed by a network of agents inside Germany, would surely have brought to light earlier than the last months of the war, the existence of any prepared redoubt. Logic must have convinced the US officers that the fortress was a fantasy. Allied sources knew the location and strength of every major German formation. Yet Intelligence officers believed reports that crack units were moving into the Alpine fortress area. Did those officers ever ask themselves who these could be? Among the finest fighting formations on the German War Establishment, were the SS and the Paratroops. Allied Intelligence sources knew that all the Germanic SS Divisions were on the Eastern Front, that the greatest number of paratroop divisions were facing Montgomery or were in Italy. They knew that the Mountain divisions were mainly in Norway and the far North. Who then could these other élite units be who were moving in to garrison the Redoubt? Captured German General officers denied under interrogation any knowledge of the redoubt; nevertheless, the Americans persisted in the belief that it did exist and for that reason did not think it necessary to check the location of the reported underground factories or the situation of the fortifications.

It may well be that the US Intelligence officers, having failed to forecast the Ardennes offensive in December, overreacted to Goebbels' stories and convinced themselves that the redoubt did exist because they wished to believe it. Supremely confident in their own assessments and appreciations, they made reports to Eisenhower which caused him to divert southwards his main thrust towards Berlin. That change in direction will be dealt with more fully in the section of this book which deals with the campaign in the west.

The growing acceptance of stories of 'the last-ditch fortress' were sufficient impetus to bring the Americans back to discuss the German surrender offer. Both sides were now very eager for a solution although each for a different reason. The Americans were anxious to destroy the defensive complex they thought existed, and felt this were best achieved by removing Tenth and Fourteenth Armies from the German order of battle. The senior German commanders were aware of an increase during the last months of 1944 and the first months of 1945, of both the scale and weight of partisan operations. They saw with anxiety that some areas of northern Italy had passed out of German control, and in bandit-infested areas (the German term for regions held by the partisans) German convoys had to be large enough to be able to defeat guerrilla attack. The fear of a spread of partisan activity made it vital for the German leaders to obtain an agreement.

It was not the leaders alone who were aware of the shift in Italian attitudes. For the German rank and file there was the knowledge that it was no longer safe to go out alone. Gunther Schroeder, Grenadier in the 29th Division, was convalescing in a suburb of Milan.

'We were conscious of the fact that civilian attitudes towards us had changed. As late as the summer of 1944 we had been welcome nearly everywhere in northern Italy, although I must admit there were certain areas in most cities where no German soldier went. I was hit during an air raid about 11 December and spent two months in hospital and as a convalescent. When I was mobile again and allowed out of hospital, I could feel the change in attitude. Nobody spoke to us. In bars we were not served until last. In the towns gangs of rowdies pushed us off pavements. Officers lectured us on not showing aggression to the Italians. Why we took our arms about with us in town if there was no intention of using them, seemed to me to be just stupid.

I was not in Italy during the last weeks of the war. My wound re-opened and I was evacuated to Innsbruck, but from what I have heard the provocative behaviour of the Italian youths led to clashes that had to be hushed up.'

Despite the provocation the German authorities did not dare to take reprisals against the civil population for this might have led later to a charge of war crimes. Such a possibility inhibited many German officers who would once have acted with ruthless efficiency to put down the partisan 'rabble'.

The secret negotiations of the autumn of 1944 made little progress, but with the war now being fought on German soil, it was clear during the early months of 1945 that the war's end was in sight. At this point when mutual fears – that of the Americans of an Alpine Redoubt and that of the Germans of being trapped by the partisans – lent fresh impetus to the negotiations. Rahn, the German Ambassador, brought into the discussions SS General Wolff, the Police Commissioner for Italy and, thus, one of a very small group of men who held the power to make binding decisions. The assiduous SD had learned during February 1945 that Dulles, the American Head of Intelligence, was in Switzerland with the German officers he had come to meet. Word of the proposed discussions reached the Head of the SD, Kaltenbrunner. Surprisingly, he did not have Wolff and the others arrested for high treason, but used their channels of contact to make his own attempts at negotiating a peace settlement. He failed.

The first meeting between Dulles, heading a party of Allied military commanders, and the German delegation led by Wolff, took place in Lugano on 19 March, but broke down because the Allied party did not have the power to halt the now imminent spring offensive. The dates and timing of major operations had to be agreed by all the Allies and the agreed details were binding. This was the principal, but not the only reason for the breakdown in negotiations. When talks resumed the German team introduced other demands, the naiveness of which were astonishing.

The surrender of Army Group 'C', which had been agreed in principle, should neither be announced nor come into effect until after Berlin had fallen, so that history would not condemn the negotiators as having betrayed Hitler. That their soldiers would be killed in a prolongation of the fighting was, seemingly, of less concern to them than that their honour should not be seen to be tarnished. The German team further insisted that Allied troops in Italy should not enter Austria or Germany because other German Army Groups, which had not yet given up the struggle, were still fighting the Russians. Another demand was that Army Group 'C' should maintain law and order in its own area of Command and thus avoid an Allied military occupation. It is no wonder that negotiations failed. Wolff brought in Colonel General von Viettinghof, the Army Group Commander, to add his influence to the now urgent discussions. A crisis meeting of the German principals was held at Roccaro on 22 April. The Allied offensive in Italy was now in full swing so that there was an urgency to the discussions for the German fears were being realized. The partisans had risen *en masse*. Wolff was entrusted with the negotiations, including a request to General Sir Harold Alexander that he accept the German Army Group surrender.

It was mandatory that Alexander, Supreme Commander in the Mediterranean Theatre, inform his political masters – both in the west and in the east – of important developments in his theatre of operations. Dutifully, Alexander reported to the Russians that the Germans had made peace overtures and was shocked by the violence of their response. Goebbels and his agents had spread thoroughly, continuously and convincingly the lie that the Western Allies would, sooner or later, join forces with the Germans and march against the Russians. Alexander's report seemed in Stalin's eyes to confirm that this was happening. Not only had the Propaganda Doctor influenced the course of Western strategy by the story of the Alpine Redoubt, but he had scored a second victory and had divided the Allies in the moment of their triumph.

In fact, Alexander's report came at an excellent time for the Red Generalissimo. There was bad blood between himself and the Western politicians following the Yalta conference. As a result of Alexander's dutiful note he, Stalin, could accuse the Western leaders of treachery. The fact that talks at this time and the surrender of any German Army Group might speed the Allied armies to victory were irrelevancies to Stalin. Convinced by his own xenophobia that the Allies were preparing to march against him, his orders to the Red Army commanders on the southern sectors of the Eastern Front resulted in the Austrian population of those areas being conscripted to dig trenches whose parapets faced westwards, the direction from which any Anglo-American attack would come. Stunned by the bitter Soviet reaction, Eisenhower ordered that all surrender or armistice talks be stopped.

This order shattered the Germans, but Alexander's statesmanlike views prevailed upon the Allied Supreme Commander and Eisenhower allowed the Italian talks to reopen. A surrender was agreed upon – this time without terms – and two German officers flew to Caserta to complete the negotiations. The delay had produced a rapid deterioration in the German military and political situation, so that there existed in northern Italy a state of armed insurrection. The partisan bands had come down from the hills into the major cities and, joined by those elements in the population which were determined to demonstrate their new-found loyalty to democracy, entered into pitched battles with German units. The critical situation in the great Italian cities of the north could be avoided by simply evacuating them. There remained the greater danger of the rural guerrillas seizing the Brenner. To prevent this, Wolff and von Viettinghoff opened new negotiations with partisan groups in the South Tyrol. A meeting was arranged in Bolzano and the German commanders effectively handed over control of the South Tyrol to the Italian irregulars. To quote Gauleiter Hofer: 'The administration of the province was handed over to the Italian terrorist groups and the local (i.e., Austrian) security units were disbanded . . . Italian terrorists had forced their way' – and, by implication, had gained power – 'into a fundamentally German area.' Hofer was less concerned that the fighting should end than that the region should remain in Austrian control.

Hitler had decreed, in the event of the Allied armies dividing the Reich into a northern and a southern zone, that Field Marshal Kesselring should be the Supreme Commander South. In this capacity Kesselring was furious when he learned of the surrender offer. His reaction was to dismiss von Vietinghoff as Army Group Commander and Wolff as Chief of the SS and Police in Italy. The removal from office of these men at that time produced a confusion which was further obscured when Kesselring's new appointees were arrested by those whom they had come to replace. With the announcement of Hitler's death the position reverted and both Wolff and von Vietinghoff were reinstated. Their actions and those of other commanders show clearly that discipline and the command structure were breaking down.

Some officers acted not merely on their own initiative but very often in their own best personal interests. Gauleiter Hofer, who had been rather obscured in the negotiations of the immediate past, was still convinced that he had a role to play and in a radio broadcast on 2 May, forbade the destruction of any bridges in the Tyrol, an order which Kesselring quickly countermanded with the order that the Gauleiter was not to interfere in military affairs. The signals that had passed between Supreme Commander South and Hofer were picked up by officers of the American Seventh Army, who were baffled by the complexities of this in-fighting. On 3 May, representatives from Seventh Army met Hofer and asked him whether he or Kesselring held the power. To demonstrate that the authority was his, the Gauleiter ordered the evacuation and destruction of all artillery positions around Innsbruck. His obvious keenness to ingratiate himself with the Americans produced from them a demand that he make another radio broadcast informing the people of Tyrol that the war was ending and that they would be occupied by the US forces. The Americans, still fearing an Alpine Redoubt, were convinced that the capture of its principal city, Innsbruck, would destroy this last bastion.

With this meeting between the officers of the US Army and Gauleiter Hofer we have come just a little too far northwards and a little too quickly in time. Let us, then, go back in distance to the Apennines, and in time to the second week of April when the Allies offensive in northern Italy opened.

The Allied plan for the final offensive in Italy anticipated that Army Group 'C' would either stand and fight, seeking to delay the Allied advance at each river line, or else it would retreat without coming to battle. In the event of the latter option, Army Group 'C' would then occupy and defend the strong river line positions with rested and properly equipped troops. The assessment by Intelligence officers was that the Germans would stand and fight south of the Po. If this assessment of the enemy intentions were accurate there glittered the prospect of destroying the enemy's thirty divisions.

General Mark Clark's plan had three phases: to deceive the enemy as to the sector in which the main blow would fall; to destroy the German forces in battles south of the Po; and then to enter into a battle of pursuit, north-west into France, north through the Brenner Pass into Austria and north-east into Istria and thence to eastern Austria.

Colonel General von Vietinghoff, anticipating an Allied spring offensive, had requested that his armies be allowed to withdraw across the Po and to defend that waterway from the northern bank with a firm front, with rested troops, assured lines of communication and with the Alps behind them into which they could withdraw. As Allied planners had anticipated, Hitler refused authority for the armies to withdraw and by his refusal condemned them to destruction.

Mark Clark's battle opened with a drive by Eighth Army's four Corps, from east to west, V, II (Polish), X and XIII. We shall cover the actions of only a few units from the infantry divisions of Eighth Army, the soldiers of which were shown the array of 'Funnies' that they would use during the offensive, among which were flame-throwing vehicles (Wasps) and Fantails (amphibious, tracked personnel carriers). Massive air support from heavy bombers down to rocket-firing Typhoons and Hurricanes, was promised.

Eighth Army's battle plan was for an advance across the Senio, then to establish bridgeheads on the River Santerno out of which the Polish II Corps would swing towards Bologna. The 78th British Infantry Division would then force its way through the Argenta Gap, a 4-mile wide strip of land between Lake Comacchio and the marshes of the River Reno. Out of that gap would erupt the mass of Eighth Army's assault divisions to hold and to destroy the enemy in the flat lands of the Po.

On 9 April huge bomber formations roared over the British front, heading northwards to destroy tactical targets behind the River Senio. On the ground the British infantry along the river were pulled back for a distance of some four hundred metres. Then with a violent barrage unparalleled since El Alamein, Eighth Army's massed artillery opened fire. North of the river from the front line along the bank to reserve positions, kilometres in the rear, was a mass of smoke and explosions. During that terrible, four hour long bombardment the British battalions closed up to the river again and launched their assault boats into the disturbed waters. It was a quick crossing and the barrage had been long and destructive, but as the assault boats touched the northern bank the battered but undefeated German Grenadiers manned machine-guns and mortars, firing and firing until their resistance was smashed in hand-to-hand fighting.

That was the pattern of operations in the early days of the offensive. Advances would be halted suddenly at some water barrier; a river, a canal or else by floods which were produced deliberately to impede the advance. Each barrier would have to be forced before the advance could roll again. Lake Comacchio, an extensive but shallow piece of water, had been extended by deliberate flooding. Reaching inland and just to the east of Argenta the saturated land presented, so the Germans believed, an impassable barrier. The Intelligence details which were essential if a successful passage across the floods were to be achieved, were scanty until the partisans learned that the local German commander had a passion for eels. His supplier, a fisherman sympathetic to the guerrillas, was encouraged to use his eyes. The details he noted came back to Eighth Army Intelligence and the attack against the Germans came in from an unexpected direction. They may have been surprised when the giant, troop-carrying, amphibious Fantails lumbered out of the smoke-screen, but they were not cowed. Their OPs brought down a defensive fire which crashed among the armoured vehicles. Bazooka teams worked their way forward and determined anti-tank gun fire forced the British infantry out of their carriers to fight dismounted.

The part played by a Brigade of the Queen's Regiment during the last weeks of the war is typical of the hard slog undertaken by the Allied soldiers fighting, as they were, against the lie of the land. Day after day the understrength infantry companies went in against the grenadiers and paras of the German rearguard. Farm buildings, crossroads and ditches were places which, the Queen's had learned in years of battle, had to be crossed very quickly. The artillery of an army that is falling back can afford to be lavish in its supporting fire, for the more ammunition that is fired off the less there is to carry back. The German gunners, aware that a short way down the road there would be another shell dump, did not stint themselves against good targets like spearhead units foolish enough to halt at a crossroads for a discussion. The first confusion that accompanies a sudden, unexpected and furious bombardment was exploited by Panzerfaust teams who would work their way forward through the close country and select a target. A Sherman would brew up or else infantrymen would erupt over the sides of a stricken Fantail. There would be the urgent cries 'stretcher-bearers, stretcher-bearers' and the grey-faced wounded would be recovered and laid on the lush, spring grass. This was all part of a typical day of battle for the infantry and nobody bothered to look at the sprawled body of the Panzerfaust man lying on that same lush grass. So fast was the pace of the advance that there were times when the shells which crashed round an attacking battalion were not from enemy guns aiming accurately, but from the attackers' own guns. Accidents do happen, but the realization that British artillery and British aircraft had caused the casualties somehow made the losses harder to accept.

'Things went from bad to worse on one particular day. The tanks that should have supported us didn't arrive so we led off without them. The whole area was a massive, big swamp and we sloshed through water that was chest high in places. I could remember stories of infantrymen like ourselves being wounded and drowning in the mud of Passchendaele. And we were wading through water that was four feet deep. I didn't like the thought at all.

I can't remember exactly where we were. I think we were moving towards the Benningnante river. After some time we got onto a bit of dry ground, some sort of low hill, I suppose and from there the attack proper started. That sloshing about in the water had only been the approach march. At 'O' Group we had been told that a barrage fired by unbelievable masses of artillery would support our battalion assault. Well, the shit certainly flew overhead all right, but some of it fell among us. Our own shells. There weren't many of them. It was probably only one gun that had got the range wrong, but that doolalli gun was on our Platoon front, of course. Then Ted stonked us with some 88s. The Company Commander did something about them. He got onto TAC and almost immediately the RAF came down. We got little trouble from Ted's gunners after that, but some of the Hurricanes thought we were the target. As our officers told us, mistakes do happen. Why we were given recognition panels to mark our positions, I'll never know for the pilots ignored them completely. They bombed behind the triangles, that is they bombed on our side of the line, and not in front of the triangles, that is on Ted's side of the line. Yet with all the bombing from our own aeroplanes and with all the shells that fell short, we did not lose many men; but the loss of each of them was resented.'

The Argenta Gap had been pierced. Ahead of the Queen's Brigade of 56th Infantry Division lay one river barrier after another as they struggled towards the Po. Some of those water barriers were bounded. At others, Wasps had to burn out the enemy before a crossing could be made. In other places, it was a formal affair of gun barrages, tank support, rocket-firing Typhoons screaming down and all the intricacy of a set-piece battle.

For the Germans the spring offensive had begun disastrously. Mark Clark's plan had caught the German armies deployed incorrectly and the alternate punches by Eighth Army on the right and by Fifth Army on the left had given von Vietinghoff's men no respite. Despite the courage and endurance of the Grenadier rearguards, Tenth and Fourteenth Armies were soon in full retreat. Those formations now nearing the Po were caught up in a chaos of motor vehicles, carts, guns and marching columns, all making for the few bridges which spanned the river or the ferries which crossed it. In some places the speed of the British advance brought Eighth Army's gunners forward so quickly that they could fire upon and smash the German columns as they struggled back. In this situation some German commanders held back the heavy weapons and vehicles so that the soldiers could cross and where time ran out the heavy equipment was simply abandoned. What could have been, in January or February, a planned and orderly withdrawal was, in the last weeks of the war, a total rout.

The unit commanders of 1st Para Corps were called to a battlefield conference during 23 April. Heidrich, the Corps Commander, related how little had been prepared for the withdrawal of the divisions across the Po and how even that little that had been accomplished had been destroyed during Allied air raids. Orders were issued that the Corps would make its passage during the night of 24 April. Any trucks that could not be ferried across would be burned but ever a practical man, the Corps Commander, gave orders that the tyres should be removed first. They would be used as supporting rings for those of his men who could not swim. Only ambulances filled with wounded were to be given absolute priority of movement; everything else had to rely upon the initiative of the unit commanders.

'We were a group of paras, part of a force drawn chiefly from 994th Grenadier Regiment. As members of Corps Defence Battalion we moved from Il Bosco near Felonica, the Corps HQ, and took up position in open country. We had learned that to occupy a house or a building was an error. The Jabos (fighter-bombers) might not see individual soldiers hiding in ditches, but they could identify a defended house and make it a target.

It was a lovely spring morning, that of 24 April. All night long there had been movement as bodies of troops passed through our positions heading for the river. We were told that ferries would operate until first light and then all movement would halt until last light. Any units still left on the south bank would stay there all day, would hold their ground and prepare for defence. The reason was clear. Allied aircraft would operate at sun-up and would attack any target like a large raft crossing the water. Our bridgehead at Felonica was quite strong in men. In addition to those, like us and the 994th, who had been detailed to stay as a rearguard, there were all those others who had not crossed during the night. Some of those units were anti-tank detachments and their guns were soon in position at crossroads. We also had Nebelwerfer detachments, Panzer and some Engineer units, all still well-equipped. We all worked to strengthen the bridgehead even though we knew we would not have to hold it for long.

Columns of black smoke were rising all around us. The rearguard units were destroying the soft-skin vehicles. Some of these were filled with stores so that we did not go short of anything to eat or to drink. We lay there all day. The enemy Air Force must have been busy on other sectors for they did not trouble us. Late in the afternoon a mist came up and began to thicken and under this cover the whole area came alive and rafts were launched, were filled with troops and rowed across. Traffic was flowing again across the Po.'

Towards evening, enemy artillery fire began to fall in our positions, but it was not aimed fire but was searching the ground. We stayed in position and then out of the mist came the first enemy tanks. Our Pak opened fire – the gunners had plenty of ammunition – and a little battle ensued. Those guns of our heavy artillery which had crossed the Po and were now in position on the north bank, joined in and their accurate fire forced the enemy tanks to pull back.

Right: an Italian partisan machine-gunner during the battle to liberate Bologna, 21 April 1945. That day the Poles captured the city, and the Allied commanders entered Bologna on 22nd. **Below:** senior commanders salute as the Allied national anthems are played.

We were not troubled again. I was on what must have been one of the last patrols south of the Po. We did a quick sweep along the bridgehead perimeter but met no enemy troops. It was about 4 in the morning when the time came for our Company to pull out. The guns on the northern bank and the heavy machine-guns put up a barrage to cover our pull-out. Before we left we blew up the usable tanks and guns on our sector and then crossed the river. The Po seemed to be as wide as an ocean, but once on the north bank there was a hot meal waiting for us and trucks took us to where the Corps HQ was located. Now we had a wide river as a defence in front of us. We could hold such a position for a long time – or so we thought.'

The 167th Brigade of 56th Division crossed the Po ahead of the Queen's Brigade, but as the Queen's moved towards the river there was often bitter fighting against German units still trying to escape the Allied drive. Despite the stiff battles there was a feeling among the forward elements of Eighth Army that the enemy front was giving way. There was a confidence in the air as the battalions and divisions streamed across the Po in pursuit of the German armies.

'The whole Eighth Army seemed to be on a huge swan, streaming out across the plain. On our way up to the Po there was loot galore. I'd never seen anything like it. Our tanks had to push Ted's lorries into ditches to clear them from the road. We felt that the enemy was losing his grip. In the old days he would have booby-trapped that lot. Now it was scarper time.'

Roads leading up the line were indeed choked with trucks, tanks and every sort of vehicle, but these were British vehicles all advancing and all filled with soldiers aware that the operation was going well.

'As we drove over the Po there were many who remembered the old First Army days in Tunisia when the Luftwaffe held the whip hand. Now the measure of our victory was that not even one German plane was seen during our advance. Our columns were packed bumper to bumper. If the Luftwaffe had had any strength it would have been used against such marvellous and comparatively easy targets as we made. But we were not attacked – not once.'

The Fifth Army's campaign can be seen as a contest between II and IV US Corps, and the unit we shall follow is the 88th ('Clover Leaf') Division of II Corps. The Corps task was to capture Montrumici, a mountain considered to be of such importance to the German defences that it was garrisoned by 8th Gebirgs Division. Corps attack opened on 14 April under an air assault as heavy as that which supported Eighth Army, and a barrage of 75,000 shells. The infantry regiments of 8th Gebirgs Division were not shaken by the noise and fury of the bombing or the bombardment. Instead, backed by their gunners they engulfed in a storm of fire the attacking US infantry struggling up the slopes. Despite this fury, Montrumici was taken by the 88th on the second day of battle and the advance was carried forward to Monte Adone, the division's second objective. For the men of 88th Division everything they longed for as infantrymen lay just beyond Monte Adone. Every infantry unit in the Allied armies had been told of 'the last hill before the plains', that fabled point from which they would be on the high ground dominating the enemy who would be made to suffer what the Allied infantry had had to endure.

For the 'Clover Leaf' Division that point was the peak of Monte Adone. In furious assault they stormed it and then flooded down towards the valley of the Po. The hard crust of the German defence line on the Fifth Army front had been broken, but the advance by the six divisions of II Corps, moving in line abreast towards the river, was no easy task. Opposition ranging in scale from single snipers to batteries of heavy artillery and the staunch defence of a determined rearguard slowed the Corps drive. The 88th sent its infantry regiments leap-frogging forward in continual assault. They bypassed Bologna to the west and headed northwards through Cravalcore and Mirandola to Poggio Rusco, a few miles south of the Po. The roads forward were crammed with abandoned enemy material and the 88th's own bridging equipment was held in traffic jams caused by the clogged roads. When the 88th reached the river, the first men of the division clambered across on the girders of a blown bridge to reach the northern bank. The Rangers established a small bridgehead into which other battalions, sailing across in anything that would float, then concentrated. When at last lorries were across the Po, the impatient 88th resumed the advance, no longer heading due north but eastwards towards a new objective – Verona.

On the Adriatic side of Italy the 2/7th Battalion of the Queen's Brigade lost their last man killed in action on the 27th, in one of those fierce fire fights which marked that final week. By midday the battalion had crossed the Adige and by last light the leading company was fifteen miles beyond it. Did the Queen's men know as they crossed the swift-flowing Adige, the significance of their passage? In the first verse of the German national anthem the demand is made for a Fatherland that stretches from the Baltic to the Adige (in German the Etsch). In their swift passage the Queen's had crossed the emotional frontier of Germany. Of far greater importance to the Germans at that time was that their defence line along the Adige had been made redundant by that crossing, and the Queen's drove forward and passed artillery positions fitted with guns which lacked the crews to man them for the gunners were still a long way south, trapped in the crush of the German retreat.

The change of direction by 88th Division took it along Highway 12, a road that was one of the principal escape routes for Tenth Army's formations pulling back in exhausting foot marches from the Po. In that sector there were now the 1st and 4th Para, veterans of the fighting at Cassino, at Anzio and the Gothic Line. Their line of retreat had taken them diagonally from the Eighth Army side to face the Americans. Their attempts to halt the 88th were disastrous. The Para battalions were overrolled and dispersed. When the first units of 88th entered Verona on the night of 25 April, they had not only cut the lateral links between the German forces, but even more importantly a principal escape route to the Brenner. Mark Clark may not have succeeded in destroying Army Group 'C' south of the Po, but it was now very likely that the bulk of the enemy force would be trapped and destroyed before it could reach the safety of the mountains.

US armoured regiments poured forward over the newly erected Po bridges to beat down the growing opposition to Fifth Army's advance. The American advance was now slowed by the narrow, serpentine roads which gave every advantage to the staunch defenders. Each village on Highway 12 had to be captured individually and some, the old Tyrolean town of Vicenza, is a good example, had to be fought for in house-to-house battles. The 88th crossed the Adige on 28 April. The American advance from Verona to Vicenza took the division squarely across the German lines of communication. This is a frightening situation for an army in retreat, but not every German unit was alarmed at this possible threat. A great many were firm in resolve, rock hard in defence and audacious in assault. When such aggressive detachments found the Vicenza road cut and their way forward barred, they reacted as they had been taught; they attacked. Out of the woods bordering the mountain roads extended lines of Grenadiers broke cover and advanced at a jogtrot across Alpine meadows already coloured with spring flowers. German gunners manning the ubiquitous 88, swung their pieces into action against such easy targets as US soft-skin vehicle columns. Other American units which had travelled for miles along deserted roads suddenly bumped into opposition: snipers, mortars and even Panzerfaust fired by some determined resister. This type of small action was standard fare to the infantry, but there were occasions when even the normally non-combatant divisional 'tail units' were caught up in such little flurries of action. One detachment of cooks was fired on and went into action. They forced the surrender of sixty-six Germans, thirty Fascist officers and most of an Italian Fascist militia battalion. But it was not always the Americans that were surprised. Some German units marching up the road were overtaken and shot to pieces by Sherman tanks which were roaring on towards the next objective.

Situations like these, described in military communiqués as 'fluid', were operations by small detachments fighting an infantry war at its basic level, and in the course of such fighting the 88th came out of Verona and into Vicenza. There – and the hearts of the infantry fell – on the left side of the road were the foothills of another mountain range, the highest and most difficult mountains in Europe – the Alps. The time that the Allied infantry had spent on the flat lands had been very short, but also full of action. Now it would soon be back to fighting for a single mountain top and scrambling up rock faces.

Despite the Allied successes, despite the fast advances and the signs of victory, the numbers of prisoners taken was not significantly higher during the first ten days of the offensive than during any other major operation. On 29 April, however, the German commanders realized that escape through the Alpine routes was almost impossible. It was from that time onwards that the

Above: the first British-constructed bridge across the Po, at Occhiobello, 27 April 1945. **Below:** eager Italian civilians crowd around an American mobile news unit in Vicenza, shortly after the liberation of the city by the US Fifth Army.

numbers of men surrendering rose to flood proportions. Troops surrendered not as individuals but in organized bodies. South of the Po the 148th Division and the Italian Fascist Bersaglieri Division, trapped by US forces and the partisans, gave up the struggle. On that day too, the German/Italian Army of the Liguria, under the command of Marshal Graziani, signed an armistice. It is indicative of the way in which Fifth Army was splitting the German Front that the Chief of Staff of Graziani's Army had had no contact with the Ligurian Army for more than two days.

Indicative also of the state of German discipline was the refusal of the Commander of 75 Corps, Schlemmer, to surrender because of the personal oath of allegiance which he had sworn to Hitler. His was the last organized German force in north-western Italy to surrender. His Corps was concentrated to the north-west of Turin, and his refusal to end the fighting might have ended in tragedy. The US IV Corps received orders to destroy this obstinate German unit and made obvious and ostentatious preparations to carry out its orders; not only did they have the power to do it, but also the inclination. The announcement of the death of Adolf Hitler allowed Schlemmer to surrender without compromising his honour, and with the surrender of 75 Corps the last German opposition in north-west Italy came to an end.

Back on Eighth Army side the swan was now really on. This was it. Every man in Eighth Army's divisions realized, with a sense of wonderment – this was IT. The Eighth had the bastards on the run; they were offering less and less resistance and they were moving back at the double. A major part of 155th Division surrendered to the Queen's. Lined up by the sides of the road, their immaculate officers wearing gloves and with the rank and file carrying full equipment, the Grenadiers waited with uncomplaining patience until someone took charge and led them off into captivity and out of the war. Signposts on the Queen's line of advance showed names made familiar as household words: Padua, Verona, Venezia. The 2/7th Battalion was selected to be the first to enter Venice, the Pearl of the Adriatic. There was not, as many old soldiers believed, a race between the Londoners and the New Zealanders as to who would take the city. The Kiwi Division had been given a far more important task. It was to drive at top speed for Trieste where the Jugoslav Army seemed intent upon occupying the whole of the Istrian peninsula. The New Zealand Division was to put out a cordon of units to halt the Jugoslav drive to the west.

To speed the New Zealanders, all other military traffic was ordered off the road. The Queen's sat and watched as the Kiwi trucks drove at top speed up the highway. When the last had vanished from sight, the Queen's mounted up and rolled on towards and into Venice. The 88th Division struck that afternoon of 28 April, against the determined and battle-hardened paras who had withdrawn diagonally across Italy from the Eighth Army Front to that of Fifth Army. The élite paras had lost the greatest part of their heavy equipment south of the Po, but the depleted battalions had gathered what they needed from the abandoned vehicles and weapons dumps left along the

Above: the German garrisons on the islands of Venice surrendered to the 2nd New Zealand Division on 29 April 1945. Here they march down to boats waiting to take them to prison camp. **Below:** the victors pose for souvenir photographs in a gondola, 30 April 1945.

roadsides. They had been in battle for days and their battalions were down to Company strength, but those very few men achieved results out of all proportion to their numbers. The 88th did not bother to fight down this determined opposition, but bypassed it, leaving the German paras to be rounded up by other units. The 'Clover Leaf' Division had had orders to reach Bolzano quickly and were determined to allow nothing and nobody to stop them. One regiment of the 88th headed for Bolzano via Feltre while a second drove towards the same objective via Borgo and Trento. Then new battle orders were received. For 2 May, a newer but more distant target was named. This was to be the final objective. The Division was ordered to reach Innsbruck via the Brenner Pass. As Bill Morgan of 351st Infantry Regiment expressed it:

'I should love to have met the john who thought that one up for us. We were a spearhead division and high in morale, so it was obviously a job for us. But we had been losing men and those who were left were getting very tired. Then we were told we were to advance through the Brenner Pass and take out Innsbruck. We all knew that the Brenner was the German Army's lifeline and that the Tedeschi would not sit idly by as we cut it. The Brenner is about twelve miles long and goes through the mountains. There was only one road and God knows what Kraut troops there were ready to oppose us. It shook me the casual way in which it was put to us. The 88th will penetrate the Brenner with the objective of capturing Innsbruck. I would love to meet the Staff Colonel who picked that one out of the hat for us.'

In the event the battle order was unnecessary. Those political moves which have already been described had brought the war in Italy to a close. The whole spring offensive it might be claimed, had been unnecessary. Of course the soldiers were not told of the secret negotiations. From quite high up in the military hierarchy down to the lowest level, each and every fighting man had gone into the battle determined to break out of the imprisoning Apennines or from behind the constricting rivers and to smash the Germans. They were told nothing of negotiations or of armistice offers.

The Queen's Brigade, now firmly billeted in Venice, were not all charmed with the city they had captured.

'So this was Venice. We all thought it a dump. The gondoliers put up their prices immediately. They must have thought we earned as much as the Yanks. I had heard a lot about this so-called beautiful city. To me it was a waterlogged dump smelling of damp and drains. Nor did the Eyties there like us. The main square was filled with little tables and chairs and on every chair, all day long, there was either some old woman dripping with pearls or some well-dressed nancy-boy in a silk shirt and ponced-up hair. We had been out since well before Alamein and on those bloody chairs in the main square of Venice were the people whom we had sweated to liberate. They didn't want to be liberated. They told us so. And the waiters hated our guts, too, because we weren't like the pre-war British. I, myself, preferred the Venice Lido. It was a nice bit of seaside, although even there you got the old dears and the poofs. It struck me that the war had been fought to make the world safe for nancy-boys and queers to live in.'

On 2 May came the news that the war in Italy had ended. The Queen's, the senior English Regiment of Foot, celebrated with a Thanksgiving Parade and in the fashion of that élite regiment achieved an immaculate turnout. Down in Naples the military celebrations were few and discipline was very tight. All Allied units in the Naples city area were confined to barracks. Those in authority feared that a mixture of excited civilians and the military on a night so charged with emotion and fuelled with vino, might cause the soldiers or the locals to think it a good thing to celebrate the end of five years of fighting with street battles. So the Allied troops whose efforts had brought victory and freedom were held confined while the civilians celebrated.

The first that the 88th Division knew of the ending of the war came when a German delegation approached the forward units of 351st Regiment. The German para officer who came in under a flag of truce reported that fighting had ended at 14.00 hrs and that under the terms of the armistice all units were to hold their positions until further orders came through. Such news needed to be checked, but as is usual in desperate situations, all the radios were malfunctioning. The 351st could not raise Corps by radio to confirm the German statements. It was a bizarre situation when radios that could not contact Corps, just a few miles down the road, could receive loud and clear, BBC bulletins from London announcing that it was all over in Italy. Not until 3 May, twenty-two hours after the fighting had ended officially, were all the units of II Corps advised of the fact. The 88th Division was given one last mission. It was to send a regiment through the Brenner Pass, and at 10.51 hrs on 4 May the first units gained touch with 411th Regiment of 103rd Division of US Seventh Army, at Sterzing. A vast Allied battle line – for it must be remembered that the war in Germany was continuing – extended from the Baltic to the Plain of Lombardy. The Allied forces in Italy had been the first to gain the total capitulation of an entire German Army Group. It was a fitting climax to thirty-two months of battle for the men who had opened the Second Front in Italy.

To the New Zealanders up in Istria the end of one war seemed to be leading straight into another, and this one would be fought against an army which had been an ally. It was a bewildering time for soldiers, as yesterday's allies became tomorrow's possible enemies. The New Zealanders were too thin on the ground to hold the entire region and needed a back-up force. The Queen's Brigade was moved to a sector between Gradisca and the River Isonzo where the Companies faced the bitter veterans of Tito's army who demanded and believed they were entitled to the territory. In the section of this book that deals with Jugoslavia, we saw how Tito's armies mounted a two-pronged drive: northwards into Austria and north-westwards into Istria. Just as the British 78th Infantry and 6th Armoured Divisions had baulked Jugoslav intentions in Kärnten, so did the 2nd New Zealand and 56th (London) Divisions hold back the partisans from Trieste and out of much of the Istrian peninsula. The British formations flung out a thin line of infantrymen, who dug in and waited. Behind the rifles, other divisional units occupied every village and town in the peninsula, forming in each an island of

Above and below: the capitulation of German forces comes into effect in Milan; SS troops leave to the shouts and threats of the Italian population. Opposite page: the grand parade of Italian partisans in Milan on 6 May 1945. It was addressed by their commander, General Cadorna, just released from Milan prison.

British phlegm against Jugoslav propaganda and confrontation. The order had come down that Tito's men were not to be allowed to advance westwards and occupy the province in a fait accompli. And so the British and New Zealand infantry held firm until Tito restrained the provocative behaviour of his men. The tumult and the shouting died away. The partisans became friendly again – just as they had been at the war's end. Their crudely-made Union Jacks reappeared on walls in Jugoslav territory, and the British units went back to restoring native civil life to normality in areas devastated by war. Trieste and the peninsula did remain in British hands – but it had been a close run race.

Meanwhile, behind the thin British outpost line that was facing the partisans, the 6th Armoured and the 78th Infantry Divisions moved towards Austria and began the task of searching for, rounding-up and disarming enemy troops.

You can guess how we felt. We had been told that Ted had signed an absolute surrender on 2 May. Yet here we were on 6 May still patrolling up in the mountains. We didn't lose any men, but we might have done so and that's what upset us. We were supposed to be at peace and yet we were still on a war footing. Some Jerries who came in as deserters that day told our Intelligence Officer that their officers had said the Italian surrender did not apply to them. They were not in the Army Group which had surrendered in Italy. It was all a mystery to me; one lot

*had jacked it in, the other lot hadn't. All I know is that you could still get killed in
the last knockings of a war that was supposed to be over.'*

The end of the war on the Fifth Army front produced the situation where
Army Group 'C' still administered its units. German officers and NCOs were
still in command, discipline was still maintained and the Germans retained
their personal weapons. Isolated within this mass of armed and hostile
veteran enemies were small groups of US troops who had turned from
fighting to organizing the reception of this huge number of prisoners. The
situation was tense for it was still possible that the Germans might take up the
war again to support those other armies which were still battling on the
Eastern and Western Fronts.

In the Bolzano region of South Tyrol the atmosphere was made worse by
SS General Wolff's bizarre behaviour. He was still at liberty and at work in
his luxuriously appointed headquarters building which was guarded by SS
military police. On 6 May there was a mild challenge to his authority when
the Tactical Headquarters of the US 88th Division entered Bolzano and
looked about for billets and office accommodation. The American suggestion
that it should take over Wolff's HQ was turned down, but he did 'permit' the
88th HQ to use one of his sub-offices. This easy victory encouraged other
German units in the belief that' the Americans could be ignored, and soon
many of them had begun to act in a way that went beyond non-cooperation
to become insubordination and insolence. One German unit actually held a
parade to decorate its Grenadiers with medals. The protests of ordinary US

Above left: armour of the New Zealand Division enters Trieste on 2 May 1945, where tension ran high during the weeks following the end of the war. **Left:** in the area held by 56th London Division, preparations were put in hand to prevent the Jugoslavs seizing the Trieste area by force of arms. Here, men of 167th Brigade of the 56th Division dig defensive positions, while a party of Jugoslav troops stroll nearby. **Right:** Tito also made claims on the southern provinces of Austria; here, British soldiers tear down a poster proclaiming the area to be Jugoslav.

soldiers at this surprising leniency were answered by statements that this form of handling had been ordered by higher authority. Against a background of covert passive resistance, work began on removing to prison camps the units of Army Group 'C'. Then came a fresh order. A distinction would be drawn between the enemy soldiers who had been taken in battle and who were, therefore, prisoners of war, and those who had been ordered to cease fighting as a result of the general surrender. These latter were 'Surrendered Enemy Personnel'. Under the terms of the Geneva Convention a victorious army did not have to feed soldiers who surrendered in an armistice. They and their upkeep became the responsibility of the civil power, in this case the Allied Military Government which would feed them from food stocks held in German Army depots. It was a neat ploy and one which made Fifth Army's task more manageable. There followed a tightening-up of control within the 88th Division area. Those SEPs who had been allowed to walk about in the town and to use the bars and cafés were confined to barracks or camp areas. All trucks were removed from German formations and concentrated in huge vehicle parks.

SS units continued their policy of ignoring the orders of anybody but their own commanders, but their turn came with the appointment as Town Major of Bolzano of Colonel Fry of the 88th. He first established the identity of all the SS units in the town, their strength and their locations. Next he formed and led an 88th Battle Group. The first raid was on Wolff's private villa. Colonel Fry and his group arrived during a party to celebrate the SS General's birthday. Wolff and his guests, the senior officers of Army Group 'C' were all arrested. Frau Wolff, no doubt dismayed at this sudden and dramatic upset to her domestic arrangements, was foolish enough to threaten Colonel Fry with a complaint to his superiors. She, too was taken. In another raid two thousand men of Wolff's HQ Staff were imprisoned. A search of the SS General's villa showed what a thrifty man he had been. He had been saving for a rainy day and to such good effect that he had amassed a fortune in excess of four million pounds as well as a collection of rare coins, formerly the property of the King. This short, sharp action placed the Americans firmly in control and the raids were followed by others.

With the local German units confined and awaiting imprisonment, the 88th Division's infantry could concentrate on operations designed to clear the mess left over from the war. In the Tyrol were concentrated displaced persons, war criminals, men on the run and the flotsam and jetsam of many military bodies. Now that the Americans had shown that they were in charge information on caches of loot stolen from half the countries of Europe were brought in by local people anxious to be on good terms with the conquerors. More than twenty tons of gold were found in the caves and caverns of South Tyrol and brought into Bolzano, together with jewellery and works of art of every description. With that round-up the military tasks of the US 88th Division were completed. The warriors now had to make place for the administrators who would endeavour to return the people and treasures presently located in the Tyrol back to their own countries and owners.

The BBC bulletins which the 88th had picked up on their radios had also been received by the units of Eighth Army. There was little excitement in the billets of the infantry battalions of the combat divisions, but a general feeling of relaxation followed by an awareness of how tired they were. Men sat quietly drinking and smoking; not talking much but remembering and seeing in their minds the mates who hadn't made it. There seemed to be so many of them, a procession filling the mind with pictures from past battles. What the morrow would bring was of little importance for whatever happened it would not be a day of battle.

During 8 May, while bonfires burned in Britain to celebrate VE-Day, the 6th Battalion The Queen's Own Royal West Kent Regiment, moved across the border and into Austria, to the province of Carinthia and, specifically, to the little town of Greifenburg. The well-worn but serviceable 3-tonners of the battalion made slow progress as they drove eastwards through the mass of enemy vehicles, marching columns and string of panje carts all heading westwards away from Jugoslavia and the vengeance of the partisans.

Representatives of most of the races of Europe had flowed into Austria. Some were there as political prisoners. There were columns of Allied prisoners of war still being forced-marched across the shrinking Reich; displaced persons, slave workers and refugees who had fled before the Red Army, all were to be found in Austria in those days. To those masses was added a new element. Not only the military columns of Loehr's Army Group 'E', but those others who, in the harsh judgement of post-war revenge would be considered as traitors to their homeland. These were, principally, the Cossack and Croatian peoples. The task of 78th Division, of 6th Armoured Division and of the other units of Eighth Army had changed abruptly from combat duties to those of administrators.

'I do not think that anybody can comprehend the problems that we faced. Quite suddenly we had to administer the lives of thousands of bewildered people whose languages we could not speak. Who among us at that time spoke Russian, let alone Cossack? None of us spoke Croatian, nor Georgian and none of those for whose welfare we were now responsible, spoke English. We were forced to use German Army interpreters who may, or may not, have given our orders accurately or relayed to us correctly the requests made by the refugees.

Imagine the problem of feeding, watering, caring for and ministering to over thirty thousand people as well as their cattle. Latrines, camp guards, permits, requisitions, measles, anti-louse spraying – the problems of a small market town suddenly dumped into the laps of a handful of soldiers who only days before had had their time filled with battle patrols, DF fire, bridge-building and killing the enemy. The AMGOT officers came up into Austria once the difficulties with the Jugoslavs had been sorted out, but for the first weeks it was a military problem exclusively and an absolute nightmare.'

If for those in authority the immediate post-war weeks were fraught with one sort of complication, it was also a period no less uncertain and difficult for the rank and file. Many of those in command were professional soldiers;

soldiering was what they wanted to do. The conscript mass of the army wanted nothing more than to relax before going home to demobilization. They wanted to enjoy the victory which they had won, unwinding from the years of battle, in a lovely country like Austria. A great many of the men in the British divisions had not been home for years. The 78th had been in action since November 1942 and the 46th, as well as 6th Armoured, since the spring of 1943. But instead of the rest they had anticipated, there were refugees to sort out and guards to find for the many camps that had been set up as well as patrols in the mountains to look for those isolated and desperate men for whom the shooting war had not ended with the signing of pieces of paper. There was the ever-present awareness that there might yet be some group determined to fight and to die for Volk, Führer und Vaterland. The knowledge that it was still possible to be killed was a sobering thought which made men extra-careful. There was the realization that any house might harbour an anti-tank team; a ditch might conceal a bazooka team. The other Allied armies had the right idea – bash the Jerries. When an American armoured column moved along a road, any house not flying a white flag was deemed to be an enemy one and was fired at. If a single shot were loosed off at a US column the village was bombed from the air. The economical French used guns instead of aircraft, but the result was the same. The Red Army used terror tactics to ensure there was no opposition to them. Only the British pushed slowly forward committing no unnecesary acts of violence.

In those last days a British recce group heading into the eastern Tyrol had a unique meeting. The detachment, after clearing Lienz, drove slowly into the dusty main square of the village of Hinterbichl on the morning of 8 May, and must have been surprised at their reception. Mounted in Greyhound scout cars, weapons loaded, cocked and trained, the crews, alert for signs of trouble, saw a number of boys, some of whom were in Hitler Youth uniform while the others – the majority – were wearing leather shorts and Steirer jackets. The machine-guns on the Greyhound cars swung towards the group of youngsters who, although frightened, stood their ground. The commanders standing in the vehicle turrets could see no weapons and jumped down from the turrets. When they were quite close the leader of the boys turned to face them, lifted his arms and the Vienna Boys' Choir began to sing *God save the King*. The Eighth Army had made contact with one of the national treasures of Austria.

PART THREE
THE WESTERN FRONT

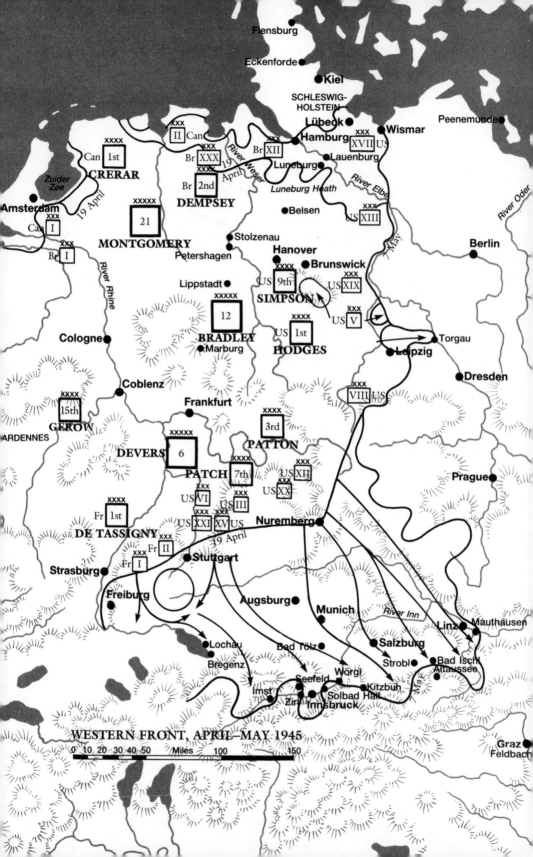

Flensburg

Eckenforde

Kiel

SCHLESWIG-
HOLSTEIN

Lübeck

Hamburg   Wismar   Peenemunde

xxxx
Can 1st

CRERAR

xxx
II Can

xxx
Br XXX
19

Br 2nd

DEMPSEY

River Weser

xxx
Br XII

Lauenburg

xxx
XVII US

Luneburg

River Elbe

Luneburg Heath

Belsen

xxx
US XIII

Berlin

Zuider
Zee

Amsterdam

xxx
Can I

xxx
Br I

19 April

River Rhine

xxxxx

21

MONTGOMERY

Stolzenau

Petershagen

Hanover

Brunswick

xxxx
US 9th

SIMPSON

xxx
US XIX

xxx
US V

Leipzig

Torgau

Lippstadt

xxxxx

12

BRADLEY

Marburg

xxxx
US 1st

HODGES

Cologne

Coblenz

Frankfurt

xxx
VIII US

Dresden

xxxx
15th

GEROW

ARDENNES

xxxxx

6

DEVERS

PATCH

xxxx
3rd

PATTON

Prague

xxxx
7th

xxx
US XII

xxx
US XX

Nuremberg

xxx
US VI

xxx
US III

xxxx
Fr 1st

DE TASSIGNY

xxx
US XXI

xxx
XV US

19 April

xxx
Fr II

Strasburg

xxx
Fr I

Stuttgart

Freiburg

Augsburg   Munich

River Inn

Linz   Mauthausen

Lochau

Bregenz

Bad Tölz

Salzburg

Strobl

Bad Ischl
Altaussee

Seefeld   Wörgl

Kitzbüh

Imst   Zirl Solbad Hall
Innsbruck

WESTERN FRONT, APRIL–MAY 1945

0 10 20 30 40 50   Miles   100   150

Graz
Feldbach

When the Western Allies landed in Normandy on 6 June 1944, it was clear
that the defeat of the Third Reich was certain, although there were setbacks
to the Allied progress through France, Belgium and Holland, culminating in
the German counter-offensive in the Ardennes – the Battle of the Bulge.

With that offensive crushed, the Western Allies drove to the banks of the
Rhine and crossed that river on 23 March. The next objective was the
German industrial area of the Ruhr, and the pincer arms of First and Ninth
American Armies closed at Lippstadt on Easter Sunday, 1 April. Through
that encirclement the industrial heart of the Reich was separated from the
body, and the whole of German Army Group 'B' was trapped. The battle to
reduce the pocket lasted just over two weeks and when it ended the Army
Group Commander, Field Marshal Model, was dead. He had shot himself
rather than surrender. Twenty-four General officers and an Admiral decided
not to follow the same lonely path and they led into captivity 325,000
soldiers and a further 100,000 men of the Flak batteries which had guarded
the Ruhr.

From 16 April, when the great encirclement battle around the Ruhr ended,
no cohesive German battle line existed in the west. Within days Allied
military power ruled between the North Sea and the River Elbe. From the
Normandy beaches to the borders of Czechoslovakia there was no firm
German Front facing the Western Allies. There were certainly a number of
major German formations, but each was now fighting for itself. The Army
Groups were almost autonomous. This is not to say that fighting had ended.
On the contrary, the battle was the more fanatical for its being engaged by
dedicated individuals or by small groups of convinced National Socialists.
There was no longer the move and sweep of armies, but merely isolated units
retreating eastwards towards – nothing, for at their backs stood the Red
Army. The viciousness of the fighting of the last weeks of the war was the
product of National Socialist indoctrination of the Hitler Youth to whom a
life given to destroy an enemy tank was not a waste but a shining example of
heroism. In the west, as in the east, the Hitler Youth formed anti-tank teams
or Wehrwolf groups seeking to stop or slow down the Allied advances across
the Fatherland.

The claim made earlier that all Europe was free from the Channel to the
Elbe is one that requires qualification. The whole of central Germany was
certainly conquered, but there were in the north of Holland and along the
Baltic coast strong armies as yet undefeated, just as in the South of Germany
there were even more powerful enemy forces which were pulling back into
Bavaria and Austria, those regions in which the Alpine Redoubt was thought
to be centred. Finally, among those places not yet reconquered were ports
along the Channel coast which were still garrisoned by German troops, the
Channel Islands, as well as Norway in which there was still an army of
occupation.

The shadow of the Alpine Redoubt hung over all military decisions and it
is necesary, I feel, to restate briefly that the strategy of the Anglo-American
armies was changed by the fear of that mythical fortress. It had always been

accepted by the Western Allies that the capture of Berlin was the principal target. In the opinion of all the Allies the city was the brain and heart of the Nazi system; the breeding-ground of Prussian militarism; the cradle of the Junker mentality. Berlin had, therefore, a particular military attraction. In Eisenhower's directive, issued during the last week of March, which set out future operations to bring the European war to a close, no mention was made of that city. At some time Eisenhower had decided not to head for Berlin. Whether he had listened to advice or whether the decision was entirely his own is uncertain, but to him, Berlin was certainly no longer the great prize it had once been.

The British Army, under Montgomery, certainly expected to continue their advance from Hanover to the Reich capital. On Montgomery's right wing, Simpson's Ninth US Army, firmly believed that it had been selected to make the final assault. Omar Bradley, however, was convinced that an all-out attack against Berlin would cost the US Army dear. He calculated that the Americans might well lose one hundred thousand men – and for what? For a mass of buildings with all the attendant problems of an urban population and within the foreseeable future the Americans would have to leave the city anyway; for it was in the Soviet Zone. Why, Bradley asked, pay a heavy price for a prestige objective which would be held for a matter of months only? It was a plausible argument, particularly since the Red Army on the Oder was only forty miles away from Berlin, and the nearest Allied unit was nearly 200 miles distant.

It may also be that the fears of an Alpine Redoubt were too strong to ignore. Certainly the directives from the individual US Armies' Intelligence groups all stressed the Redoubt. Eisenhower's next action was completely out of character. He advised Stalin that the main thrust by the Western Allies would be aimed at bisecting Germany. This would mean a drive upon Leipzig (about 100 miles to the south of Berlin) and, with Germany divided, the main forces under his command would swing southwards to attack the Alpine Redoubt. In making this decision, Eisenhower acted without having consulted his Allies or obtained from the Combined Chiefs of Staff the authorization that was required.

With hindsight it is easy to criticize Eisenhower for his decision to turn south, but one must consider the Intelligence advice he was given, the political pressures to which he was subjected and the military situation as he saw it. His most senior Intelligence officers all assured him that the Redoubt was a fact and that it was being constantly reinforced by élite troops. How could he dispute the advice of experts who had been trained in Intelligence and whose opinion it was that the Redoubt posed a very serious threat to the Allied right flank? Politically, too, the European campaign was considered by a great many Americans to be less important than the Pacific Theatre of Operations and that Japan was the more deadly enemy that should be destroyed first.

To placate those voices, the policy makers urged Eisenhower to produce a quick ending to the European war. This meant not letting his armies become involved in a long-drawn-out campaign to surround and to starve out the Redoubt. Instead it should be excised by a swift military operation. The Supreme Commander was himself convinced that the emphasis in Germany had moved from the north to the south. Berlin had become a cypher and it was the destruction of the still vast German field armies which was the more important goal. His experts had forecast a steadily increasing strength of the enemy forces pulling back into Germany and Austria where the Redoubt was thought to be located. It must be a greater advantage, so the Supreme Commander reasoned, to advance eastwards to meet the Russians in Central Germany and by that junction halt the flow of enemy forces from the north of Germany into the South. Then the armies of his southern wing would strike down into Austria to prevent the German forces from the Eastern Front moving westwards into the mountains of the Redoubt.

On all those grounds it made sense to Eisenhower to issue the necessary orders that changed the thrust line of his armies. There was bitter opposition. Those who saw through the smoke and chaos of the immediate battle were aware that the end of the Third Reich was imminent and that combat would soon be replaced by politics. To those who could see that far, Berlin was no empty cypher but a very important prize. The British were horrified at Eisenhower's decision. They could see that Berlin, Vienna and Prague would all soon become towns of the vast Russian empire. Stalin, too, realized the worth of those cities and the political power that would be his if he took them and held them. Only the Americans with their gaze fixed on the Pacific were hostile to the British proposals and ignored any British warnings about the Soviet threat. The die was cast. Berlin was no longer the principal objective and Montgomery's Army Group no longer had the principal role of striking the Nazi beast to death in its lair. Instead it was reduced to the role of flank guard to Omar Bradley's armies.

With the advances detailed below, we enter into the last round; a time when the concentration camps were overrun, the time when isolated groups of young and fanatical children and old men of the Volkssturm sought to achieve what vast and well-organized formations had not done – to halt the advance of the Allied armoured divisions. It was the time of formal ceremonies at which German officers at various levels of command signed instruments of surrender. The accounts detailed below will not record at length conditions in the camps nor will they describe the major acts of surrender at Luneburg Heath, at Reims or in Berlin. Those events are already well documented. Instead the emphasis will be on local surrenders which brought home to German commanders the depth of their Army's defeat. After such ceremonies there would be no chance for the Junkers to proclaim again the myth that they were stabbed in the back.

The story of the final battles on the Western Front begins in the north of Germany, where Montgomery's 21st Army Group (First Canadian and Second British Armies) are fighting in the northernmost provinces of Holland and Germany. To the south of British Second Army is Ninth American, under Simpson, which had formed part of Montgomery's Army

Group from the time of the Ardennes offensive to the first week of April when it reverted to Bradley's 12th Army Group. Below Bradley's armies are those of Devers's 6th Army Group (First French and Seventh US Armies). Theirs is the task of cutting through the Alpine Redoubt and particularly into Western Austria, where a great mass of German units has concentrated and into which VIPs, prisoners of the Germans, have been evacuated. Also in that area, foreign governments still loyal to Hitler have exiled themselves, and in the caves of the region are located the looted treasures of most of Europe.

Before the events of the last weeks in the Baltic regions of northern Germany are described, we must consider those last outposts of German military power, the fortress ports along the Channel coast and the garrison in Norway. Hitler's decision to turn certain ports in the Channel Islands and on the west coast of France into fortresses, was made in response to Admiral Krancke's telegram which contained the following paragraph:

'It is absolutely essential that the most important harbours on the south and west coast are denied to the enemy for the longest possible time . . . in order to slow down the flow of supplies and reinforcements to him . . . The Navy will support the defence of the fortresses and the fortress areas through the use of all available naval forces and when these are lost the weapons and the men are to be used in the defence of the landward perimeters.'

Although many of the fortress ports were captured quite quickly, La Rochelle, Saint Nazaire, Lorient and Dunkirk held out until the end of the war. The last to surrender was Dunkirk and the German perimeter around the area was reinforced by the garrisons of Nieuport and Ostend. The Germans may have been shut in, but the garrison proved its aggressive abilities when in the dawn of 5 April, Rear-Admiral Frisius opened Operation 'Blücher'. This was little more than a raid, but it was so unexpected and so powerful that British Headquarters, in a moment of panic, ordered the bridges surrounding Dunkirk to be blown up. Then a counter-attack, supported by rocket-firing aircraft was launched, but it was not possible to dislodge the pugnacious Germans from their brand-new front-line positions.

Frisius knew very well how close was the war's end and signalled the Navy High Command (OKM) to establish whether his forces were included in the armistice which had been signed at Luneburg. Montgomery had demanded that they should be, but the only response from OKM to Frisius was that he would be informed verbally. Assured by radio that his forces were excluded from the surrender at Luneburg, Frisius was able to reject the terms offered him. He was concerned about his military honour; if he held out until the general surrender the Allies could not claim to have defeated his forces. It came about as he wished and when Frisius signed the surrender document the war was indeed ended. The last 'fortress' along the Atlantic Wall had surrendered.

In Norway the German garrison was made up chiefly of units of 20th Gebirgs Army, a Force that had been involved in the retreat from Finland.

Right: Rear-Admiral Frisius, German commander of the surrounded port of Dunkirk, reads the surrender conditions, 9 May 1945.

To support the crumbling fronts in the east and west, a succession of the divisions in Norway set out for Denmark. When the last transport left during Easter 1945, only 2nd and 7th Gebirgs Divisions remained to form the army of occupation, backed by a few miscellaneous detachments from the Navy and the Luftwaffe. A plan for the invasion of Norway by Swedish troops was made redundant by the German capitulation, and the occupation ended without the blood-letting which had marred the liberation of other countries. A dear friend of mine, Major Jim Harvey, was sent to Norway to arrange the evacuation of the German forces there. On the Narvik docks he had watched, impassively, the shattered Luftwaffe and Naval units as they embarked. Those units were unremarkable; grey men who shuffled along, despair on every face. But then came a distinct change. The first battalion of the Gebirgs Divisions came into sight and swung, singing, down the road towards the jetty. Jim Harvey was deeply moved. Passing before him he saw not the soldiers of a defeated army, but the sort of men that he had led in desperate battles around Ypres and on the Somme. Young, confident and self-possessed, the Gebirgs Divisions swung past Jim Harvey and he stood there choked with emotion; with memories of soldiers whose officer he had once been. These Gebirgsjäger were men whom he would have been proud to lead into battle for in them he recognized comrades in arms. The German Army in Norway went home and with their last minor pieces taken from the board, let us now consider what had once been the German Western Front, and in particular the area along the Baltic.

Running on a line from West Holland to a point around Hamburg and Schleswig-Holstein were small enclaves of territory in which the German war flag still flew and which were invested by British and Canadian divisions. Among the British formations were some that had first won their reputations in Africa, Sicily and Italy. The 7th Armoured, 51st Highland and 50th Tyne Tees Divisions had also been in the van of the battle from D-Day onwards, but by this phase of the war Britain's manpower shortage had affected the flow of infantry replacements and battalions were amalgamated and even divisions had been broken up. The 50th Tyne Tees, one of the four best divisions of the British Army, had suffered that fate and its battalions had been sent as reinforcements to other formations. It is with the British Army that this account opens; an army whose infantry battalions might not be either as numerous or as strong in men as once they were, but still an army numbering more than a million men. All were aware that they were on the last lap – Montgomery had told them so, and many believed that he was infallible. Some, however, resented his use of sporting metaphors when applied to war:

'What sickened me was not so much his going on about God being with us. It was much more the idea that the war was some sort of great sporting contest in which it was pretty rotten luck to get yourself killed. Perhaps he had forgotten that war kills people. It isn't rotten luck – it is what happens in war. I resented this 'knock em for six' attitude that he had used in the desert and which had passed right down through the army so that even our officers talked like it. My father in the Great War, resented the idea that the newspapers tried to spread of jolly Tommies fighting the Germans as if they were terriers killing rats and I resented it, in my war, when the crusade we were supposed to be fighting was cheapened into some sort of Test Match.'

While from the west, Allied armies swept towards the Elbe, drove southwards towards Austria and northwards to the Baltic, and while in the German capital Hitler was preparing to drown the Red Army in a sea of blood, in the far north of Germany the Supreme Commander North, Admiral Doenitz, was preparing to take up his duties. On 21 April he had met Hitler in a Berlin that was certain to be encircled within days, and by the 23rd he had organized a committee to help him carry out his new and onerous tasks.

A series of meetings was arranged between Doenitz and the Party's political leaders of northern Germany. At one of these conferences he ordered Kaufmann, Gauleiter of Hamburg, not to surrender the city for, not only Hamburg, but all the ports of Schleswig-Holstein were the principal debarkation points for the refugees from the East. It was the Admiral's task, as he saw it, to lead Germany towards the inevitable capitulation with as much dignity as could be managed, with as many concessions as could be obtained from the victorious Allies and with minimal bloodshed and chaos.

Consider then the Admiral's feelings when he learned that the Reichs-führer SS, Heinrich Himmler, had arrived in Lübeck together with a very large number of uncompromising SS men, and that the Reichsführer expected to become the next leader of the Third Reich. Such a group would be dangerous to the future of Germany. Himmler must be neutralized, but the meeting between the Admiral and the SS Commander was indecisive. Then came a telegram from the Berlin bunker naming Doenitz as Hitler's successor. The course was clear. A cease-fire with the evacuation of as many as possible, both civil and military, from the east. Doenitz produced the telegram at a second meeting with Himmler and it reduced the Reichsführer from a demanding braggart to a mere cipher. He asked to be named as Second-in-Command, but this Doenitz rejected with the brutally cold remark, 'I cannot use you in the present situation.' Armed with the power that came from a second telegram announcing Hitler's death, the Admiral first dismissed the former Foreign Minister, von Ribbentrop, and then distanced himself from all those who were Old Guard Nazis.

The most important of the conferences held immediately after the death of Hitler was that attended by all those who held political and military power in the shrinking area of the Third Reich. Among these were Schoerner, whose Army Group was defending Czechoslovakia; Frank, the Reichs Protector of Bohemia; Seyss-Inquart, the Overlord in Holland; Lindemann, the General Officer Commanding in Denmark; and Terboven, the political leader in Norway. In clear terms Doenitz laid out the situation in which Germany was placed and expressed the intention to end the war with the minimum of casualties. The problem causing him the deepest concern was that of the refugees in the east whom he hoped to transport to the west. To achieve this aim the ports in Schleswig-Holstein had to remain in German hands and this was likely to prove difficult because the advance by British Second Army had brought its divisions to the borders of the province. The way to prevent a British advance was to offer a surrender and to prolong the negotiations. During the time which would be gained, the German Navy's convoys could ply between the embarkation and debarkation points.

Plans for the capitulation were already drawn up and Doenitz ordered that these be put into operation. Admiral von Friedeburg was sent to Montgomery's Headquarters to open negotiations and that move marked the beginning of a week of surrenders and capitulations which ended with the ceremony in Berlin on 8 May and which, officially, ended the war.

8

THE BALTIC SECTOR: HAMBURG

When the British Army returned to north-west Europe on 6 June 1944 after an interval of almost four years, its position in the Allied battle line was on the left flank. Following the breakout from the Normandy beach-head and the pursuit through France, Belgium and Holland, the Canadians moved to the extreme left wing. It was in that disposition, with Second British Army deployed between First Canadian and Ninth US Armies, that Montgomery's 21st Army Group crossed the Rhine and advanced towards the River Elbe. The Canadian Army was ordered to collaborate with British XXX Corps in the destruction of the German forces between the River Weser and the Zuider Zee. Thereafter, the Canadians were to liberate Holland.

Straube's II Para Corps, which was holding the line of the Elbe-Hunte Canal, put up resistance so determined that the Canadians had to be massively reinforced by the Polish Armoured Division and 3rd British Infantry Division. Slow progress was made, but with the capture of Oldenburg the campaign in north Holland was effectively ended. In the west of the country, however, the German Commander-in-Chief, von Blaskowitz, blew breaches in the Zuider Zee dykes and the inundations halted the Canadian operations. The armies faced each other across the water barrier, completely immobilized. The whole of western Holland was now totally cut off from supplies and to relieve the famine situation British and American bombers dropped foodstuffs and clothing instead of bombs.

'At that time I was still only a schoolboy and, of course, knew nothing of the organization and planning that had gone into the airdrops. As I understand it now, General Crerar (the Canadian Army Commander) and von Blaskowitz, had agreed on dropping sites and also agreed that the German Flak would not fire on the Allied aircraft. Despite this I have been told that some aircraft were lost through engine failure. Those men died to free Dutch children and we shall never forget them.

As a boy-scout I was ordered to a drop zone to help stand guard over the food that had been dropped. Our underground organization arranged for the distribution to individual communities and they distributed the rations on a per caput basis. Tea and coffee were the two most welcome things and there were foodstuffs quite new to us like powdered eggs, potato flour, dried minced beef and milk. For the men there were cigarettes and for the children there were chocolate and boiled sweets. These things compensated for the fact that we were still not free, but at last we knew that soon we would be free again.'

British Second Army, under Dempsey, held a thrust line that was directed north-east towards the Baltic. On Second Army's right flank, VIII Corps had earlier crossed the Weser against fanatical opposition by 12th SS Panzer

Grenadier Training Battalion. Their attacks against the Rifle Brigade bridgehead at Petershagen had been totally aggressive, but more than anything their sniping had been masterly and, according to Rifle Brigade reports, their defensive tactics were exceptional for recruits lacking any former combat experience.

'Most of our casualties were due to sniper fire and in most cases the killing shot was put through an eye. Those blokes were shit-hot snipers.'

From the other side, a Sergeant of the 12th SS describes the battle for Stolzenau:

'I was a Sergeant Instructor in the battalion. My own service had been with the Leibstandarte in Russia. Usual decorations, Iron Cross, Infantry Assault, Close Combat, wound badge in silver. I lined my platoon along the railway embankment. This stands about twenty feet above the ground between the River Weser and the village of Leese. The first British probes were easily repulsed – our field of fire was excellent. We could see every movement that the Tommies made. I had my mortars behind the railway embankment with the Reserve Sections and three, tripod-mounted MG 42s firing on fixed lines. The battalion had ammunition enough. We had been ordered to hold to the last. We did not know it then but there was a V2 assembly plant about two kilometres behind the railway line, just north of Leese, and it was our task to hold until the civilian scientists had got away.'

The Commando Brigade that had come up in support of 11th Armoured Division, attacked Leese in a frontal assault from Stolzenau while armour coming up from the south, at Stolzenau, outflanked the German line and forced the 12th Battalion back to the next line of defence, the River Aller. British VIII Corps bounced that, too, and drove towards the great Steinhuder Meer, so distinctive a landmark that the Luftwaffe used it as a concentration point for its fighter defence squadrons. During that week some of the Corps units reached Belsen, the first concentration camp of great size to have been liberated by Second Army. Experience of other smaller camps, which had been overrun in the advance from the Rhine, together with hints from 1st Para Army HQ that there was typhus in the camp, still did not prepare the British officers and men for the horrors they encountered. So terrible was the chaos at that time that the SS authorities in charge of Belsen had no idea of how many inmates there were in the main camp, Camp 1. The figures supplied to the senior British officer by the SS was 40,000, but this took no account of the ten thousand dead who were lying in the open, in the huts or even under the floorboards of some huts.

Appendix 'O' to Chapter VII of Second Army History deals extensively with the Belsen camp and the following extracts are taken from it.

'Disease of all kinds was rife and in a vast number of cases it was difficult to tell which condition predominated – whether it was typhus, starvation, tubercle or a combination of all three, which was responsible for the shattered wrecks of human beings who formed the majority of the inmates . . .

It was impossible to gauge the daily rate of new cases (of illness) as so many, if too weak to call for help, received neither food nor treatment . . . Conditions in the huts were indescribable. Rooms and passages were crowded with both living and dead; only by entering the huts could the real horrors be appreciated . . . the appalling sanitary conditions in which excreta from those too weak to move or help themselves fouled the rooms or trickled through from upper bunks to those below . . . Latrines were practically non-existent and what there were were consisted simply of a bare pole over a deep trench without any screening . . .

There had been no water for about a week owing to damage by shell fire to the electrical pumping equipment on which the system depended. Food was of poor quality and the number of meals varied from one to three per day. During the last days (of German control) the entire rations issued were one bowl of soup per person on each of four days and once only a loaf of black bread, divided between several people . . . There was no shortage of food stocks from which supplies could have been drawn . . . Red Cross boxes were found containing tinned milk, soups, meats, etc., which had been sent by Jewish societies for Jews; these had been stolen by the guards and . . . nothing had been distributed.'

As a first step the British Army sealed the camp using men from one of the batteries of 63 Anti-Tank Regiment. A Field Hygiene Section was sent in by 11th Armoured Division and 27 water carts supplied fresh water in place of the camp's infected supplies. So bad had been the mismanagement of the prisoners that during the first few days of British control, 548 of the inmates died in a single day. But within a short time the British Army had the situation in hand. The typhus-ridden were isolated; diets were provided to ensure that the camp inmates did not die from over-eating, the dead were buried and the area was disinfected.

Meanwhile the British advance had been drawing closer towards the great Hanseatic port of Hamburg which, since 15 April had been under the control of Major-General Wolz, the city's battle commander. To him, as to all the other commanders had gone the uncompromising Führer Order – hold to the last. In the case of Hamburg there was some sense in that death-dealing order. As we have seen from the Chapter on Kurland, the German Navy was running a rescue operation bringing back into the Fatherland those hopeless, freezing refugees who waited on the open beaches and docks for the boats to come. A premature surrender of Hamburg would involve also that of Schleswig-Holstein, and it was from the ports and harbours of that region that the rescue convoys were operating.

General Wolz had a scratch Force to help him carry out Hitler's order. The usual outer casing of Volkssturm battalions, the mustard-keen Hitler Youth with their Panzerfausts, surrounding a small core of the city's garrison regiment, some Flak batteries, Lieutenant-Commander Cremer's close-combat tank destruction unit drawn from U-boat volunteers, and the remnants of some SS units, including a group from 12th Training Battalion. Unusual among Germany's Gauleiter, most of whom were very keen on fighting to the last drop of everybody else's blood, Gauleiter Kaufmann of

Hamburg was very keen to surrender the city and had telegraphed Doenitz asking for authority to do this. The Admiral refused the request and pointed out that to do so would sacrifice the seven million Germans in the east who were expecting to be shipped to the west. Instead of a surrender Doenitz ordered a most energetic defence.

From the military he got it. The miscellaneous collection of units assembled under Wolz, made aware by unit orders of the day of the vital importance of delaying the British capture of Hamburg, went into action with such determination and verve that Cremer's men won for themselves a mention in one of the last OKW communiqués: 'In a supplement to the High Command Communiqué of 25 April it is also stated that a battle group commanded by Lieutenant-Commander Cremer . . . destroyed 24 enemy tanks and other armoured fighting vehicles within two days . . .'

Hamburg was a major city and the unexpectedly severe resistance at its south-western approaches put up by the Hitler Youth and the U-boat men, raised apprehensions by Second Army that the enemy might have to be taken out street by street, house by house. The British therefore ran down the scale of operations opposite the city to patrols and local attacks while building up strength for an all-out assault. In the event it was not necessary. As April died, the political scene changed with Hitler's death and the rapid advance of the US armies into the rump of the Fatherland. In the east, too, the last embarkation points were being overrun by the Red Army. The great mass of the seven million whose fate had concerned Doenitz so much, were now part of the population of the Soviet Empire. There was now no point in fighting for Hamburg and Wolz was ordered to arrange its surrender. The end of the war was not far off and the only remaining questions were, who would have the authority to carry out the surrender of the German Armed Forces and, whether those forces would obey the orders? It was a time of local surrenders and parleys, but for 21st Army Group the beginning of the end for Germany came with the proceedings to surrender the city of Hamburg. Throughout 2 May, Wolz had been in touch with the principal British formation facing the city, 7th Armoured Division, and it was agreed that elements from the British Army would enter the city at 13.00 hrs on 3 May.

The Queen's Regiment, one of the infantry formations of 7th Armoured, had once had men serving who remembered the battle of El Alamein and the opening days of the campaign in Italy, but now, after nearly a year of battle in north-west Europe, those still with the battalions who wore the ribbon of the Africa Star were very few indeed. As the numbers of the veterans reduced so did the numbers of those fresh to battle increase. But it was not always those unused to battle who were tricked by the enemy. In the latter days of April a patrol from a Queen's battalion struck an enemy group whose members promptly waved white handkerchiefs. The British moved forward to disarm the Germans and were shot down by a pair of machine-guns hidden by bushes. The wounded survivors were convinced that the enemy troops had been from the SS. Certainly the remnants of the 12th Battalion were in the area. On the 28th those men had made a well-executed, almost classic infantry attack, using field craft and the tactics of fire and movement with exceptional skill.

'They moved like weasels in and out of cover in a flash, working their way forward. It was when they came in for the charge that we were able to clobber them fair and square. A lot of them were dropped; the rest vanished.'

The Queen's regimental history reported 60 of the enemy battalion dead and another 70 taken prisoner. It was due payment for the treachery of abusing the white flag. Shortly after breakfast on the following morning there occurred one of those lunatic meetings which cause one to question the sanity of the Germans. The forward line of Queen's sentries reported the approach of a group of three men, two officers and a civilian. This was obviously the group that had been expected to come in to meet General Lynne, commanding 7th Armoured, and agree the final surrender terms. It was not. The 7th Armoured Divisional Intelligence Officer had no chance to discuss anything with his opposite numbers. The civilian swept them aside, buttonholed the DIO and in tones ranging from pleading to demanding, declared that his Company, the Phoenix Rubber Works, should be spared from further damage. The fighting should be made to bypass it and, of course, it should not be bombarded. That the British Second Army might have to unleash its terrible force to take Hamburg was of little concern to the Herr Direktor; what was of importance was that the battle should very kindly be diverted past his property.

When Wolz and his delegation did arrive they were passed on by General Lynne to General Dempsey of Second Army at his Headquarters at Luneburg who soon established that an even greater surrender was imminent. Blumentritt's Army Group, which included the Hamburg sector, had offered to surrender and arrangements had been made to meet British staff officers on the Lauenburg road, at 10.00 hrs on 3 May. This was not the end. The surrender of all the German forces facing 21st Army Group was now likely, and in view of the discussions at the most senior level, Blumentritt withdrew. Wolz surrendered Hamburg and the Queen's, tank mounted, rolled across the two great iron bridges into the city. Over the city's Town Hall, the Adjutant of 1st/5th Battalion raised the regimental flag. El Alamein had been the end of the beginning; the surrender of Hamburg was the beginning of the end. It was a glorious day.

Just outside the city we were crashing along in our Greyhound armoured cars, for all I know it may have been one of the suburbs of Hamburg. We shot round a corner and there in front of us was a large barracks. On the barrack-square stood a whole brigade drawn up by battalions. At the head of the parade stood the officers, immaculately dressed, full decorations, gloves, highly polished jackboots, a really marvellous turn-out. We pulled up and I jumped down. I was a sergeant at the time. My Squadron Commander joined me and we walked towards the parade. There was a series of commands and they all came to attention. Through an interpreter we were asked whether we were sufficiently high in rank to accept the

Above: citizens of Hamburg resort to water from a fire hydrant; the tremendous bomb damage inflicted on the city had caused many homes to lose their water supply. Below: among the first tasks of the British Army entering Hamburg was to ensure the maintenance of law and order. For this they used the existing German forces. Here, British military policemen issue instructions; 3 May 1945.

surrender. My Captain said he was and with complete nonchalance ordered that all arms be collected, that the troops remain confined to barracks and that a white flag be hoisted over the buildings. Arrangements would be put in hand to transfer the unit to a prisoner-of-war camp. A British prisoner-of-war camp?, he was asked, and when he said yes, there was relief on the Germans' faces. They had all feared that we would hand them over to the Russians.

It obviously irked the Germans. There they were drawn-up on parade looking absolutely pukka, putting on their last parade and the only audience they had were some scruffy swaddies from the British Army whose Sergeant and Officer looked like a pair of overalled motor mechanics. You could feel the disappointment. They had expected at least that Dempsey or Horrocks or some high ranking brass hat would have honoured the occasion. As it was it was a sergeant and a subaltern officer. How frustrating for them.'

Another memory of Hamburg from one of the first unit to enter the city:

'I must say I had expected to see a city completely flattened. We had all heard about the bombing raids and we'd seen other places that really were as flat as a pancake. So I was surprised to see so many buildings still standing. Just after we crossed the big bridge that leads into the city from the railway station the tank I was on stopped. There was a British soldier – he turned out to have been a prisoner of war – wearing a top hat and playing a wind-up gramophone. He was blind drunk but quite happy. Whenever I think of Hamburg I think of that swaddie in an empty street playing the record, Moonlight on the Alster.'

The Second Army Report of Operations describes in very sober words the events of those exciting days:

'Meanwhile conversations were held at the Headquarters of 21st Army Group with the delegation headed by General Admiral von Friedeburg. He stated that he had arrived from Keitel to negotiate surrender of the German forces (in the North) to Field Marshal Montgomery. He stated that they were extremely worried about their soldiers and the valuable people being savaged by the Russians. He further requested the passage of civilian refugees moving back from the Russian sectors to safety through our lines, stating that he had been trying to get the population fleeing from the Russians back into Schleswig-Holstein. He added that a considerable number had already been moved into that province, that conditions were fairly chaotic and that food would last for only fourteen days.

The General Admiral suggested that, to allow the occupation to keep pace with the enormous administrative tasks, Second Army should agree to advance bound by bound. This would give the Germans time to organize their administration and to hand over something workable.

The Commander of 21st Army Group stated that under no circumstances would he agree and that first of all von Friedeburg must surrender. After that it would be the duty of the staffs to work out the most suitable ways and means of enforcing the act.'

Above: fully-armed German military police direct British military convoys as the advance is taken into the province of Schleswig, 3/4 May 1945.
Above right: suspected saboteurs of the Hitler Youth, captured by elements of 7th Armoured Division near the Elbe, are searched. Pulling down their trousers is a simple way of ensuring their immobility.
For some, suicide was the only way out of the trap. **Left:** Heinrich Himmler. **Right:** von Friedeburg. Both had taken poison.

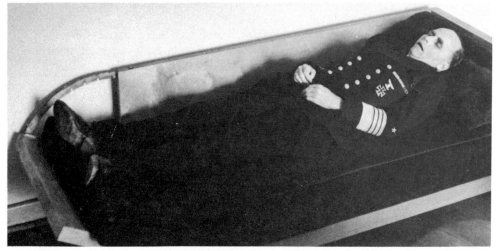

It must have been a moment of glorious triumph for Montgomery. He could, with the full knowledge of a job well done ask, when the German representatives first arrived, 'Who are these men and what do they want?'

The Commander-in-Chief 21st Army Group made it very clear that in the event of the German delegation not returning by 19.00 hrs he would commence very rapid operations against them. Von Friedeburg, in reply to a question, said that he was fairly well-informed of the war situation, but when he was shown Montgomery's battle map and realized the hopeless position in which the German forces were placed, he burst into tears. The surrender document was signed at 18.20 hrs on 4 May and was followed by the signal, 'Local German surrender signed by the Commander-in-Chief 21st Army Group and German representatives today. All offensive operations will be cancelled forthwith and all troops will be ordered to cease fire at 08.00 hrs 5 May.'

On 5 May the situation in which the German forces was placed can only be best described as chaotic. In addition to the units facing Second Army there were others seeking asylum in the west by disengaging from the Russians and offering to surrender to the British. There were masses of refugees who had been brought in from the east as well as fragments of a great miscellany of military units that had also been evacuated by sea from East Prussia, from Kurland and the other few remaining Baltic ports. In order to regularize the situation, Blumentritt's Army Group was ordered to produce an Order of Battle. It would be a difficult and tedious task to determine the regimental or divisional allegiance of those fragments, but the list would be vital when the time came to document the defeated German Army and pass it into prison camps. This process took just less than two weeks, by which time a roster existed enabling a proper system of dispatch to be implemented. Through the system and into special camps passed a procession of senior commanders, including the Luftwaffe's Field Marshal Milch, the Para Commanders Student and Meindl, Wisch and Steiner of the SS, as well as more than seventy-five other Commanders of General rank, and more than two hundred officers of Field rank who had held appointments in the OKW. The net was fine enough to trap even German officers and commanders disguised and equipped with excellently forged identity papers. The most senior of those caught was Heinrich Himmler, the Reichsführer SS and the German Police, overlord of the concentration camps. After wandering about Germany dressed as an army sergeant he was put into a Luneburg camp and under interrogation revealed his identity. A quick bite on a cyanide capsule, ten seconds of cramped agony and the Reichsführer was dead.

He was not the only one to die by his own hand. All over Germany members of the Nazi Party, senior officials and petty officials alike; mayors of small towns and others who feared that the war crimes laws would touch them, decided to end it all with a phial of cyanide or a quick bullet. Some took their wives and families with them; others died alone, sitting at their desks facing the photograph of the man for whose sake they were killing themselves. It was a time of signatures and suicides.

With the surrender of all the German forces facing Montgomery this account of the end of the war in the British sector closes. The tasks of administering the surrender of the German armies in the north and of caring for the refugees flooding in by sea from the east, were left to the so-called Doenitz government which would work under the supervision of an Allied control board.

It did seem, for a short time, as if Lindemann, the German Commander in Denmark, might cause problems for the British troops moving into that country, but Montgomery made it clear that he would tolerate no nonsense and the surrender of the German forces in that Kingdom was carried through at Command level without a hitch. At troop level the German rank and file seemed genuinely relieved that they had not been involved in a pointless battle – all that is except one SS detachment. This group refused to capitulate and took up positions in which they were prepared to fight and to die. The area of this defiance was that of 15th Scottish Division whose Commander was loath to send in his men against fanatics. In the divisional area there were units from the German Para Army that had contested the British advance and some of its detachments were put in to take out the reluctant SS.

Above: surrendered German military personnel marching through Copenhagen on their way back to Germany.

The military task was over. Already the teams of officers who had been recruited to carry out Operation 'Eclipse', the control of post-war Germany, had taken charge. Behind them would come, in time, the civilian experts of the Control Commission who would run each of the Allied zones, both in Germany and in Austria. But those administrations are outside the parameters of this book and we take leave of the British Army in Germany at Wismar, where battalions of the crack Parachute Regiment, veterans of Africa, of Sicily and of Arnhem, have gained touch with the equally veteran soldiers of the Red Army, victors of battles from East Prussia to the Baltic.

When the Americans landed on the beaches of Normandy on D-Day, they consisted only of Bradley's First Army, but this formation did not remain long in isolation. A rapid build-up through the Normandy beach-head and then the landing in southern France so swelled the American component of the Allied armies that it soon formed two complete Army Groups.

Bradley was the commander of 12th Army Group with Ninth (Simpson) and Third (Patton) Armies under his authority. The 6th Army Group, commanded by Devers, was made up of Seventh Army (Patch) and the First French Army (de Lattre de Tassigny). Flexibility was the keynote of Eisenhower's leadership and he did not hesitate to place US troops under British commanders where the military situation demanded it. It was a flexibility which had worked in Normandy and was applied again at a time of crisis in December 1944. During the offensive which has passed into history as the Battle of the Bulge, Simpson's Ninth Army was placed under the control of Field Marshal Montgomery, much to the chagrin of Omar Bradley whose frequent requests to the Supreme Commander for its return were not met until 3 April. In Eisenhower's opinion there was little point in strengthening Montgomery's Army Group after that date, for the Supreme Commander had already relegated to the British the task of guarding Bradley's left flank as his Army Group advanced eastwards into Germany.

The opening paragraphs of this section of the book have shown that the US operation which led to the encirclement and eventually to the destruction of the Ruhr pocket, tore the German front in the west wide open and that through that gaping breach poured the exultant troops of the American Army Groups. Ninth Army, under its dynamic Commander, Simpson, pushed quickly through central Germany, 'bounded' the River Weser and aligned itself to drive on the German capital, still confident that this was the SHAEF plan. No more than sixty miles separated the leading spearheads of Simpson's army from the city whose capture would mean the end of the war. But this was a prize not to be won by the Western Allies. On 15 April Omar Bradley asked Simpson to come to Army Group Headquarters, and without preamble or explanation issued the directive: Ninth Army was to halt on the Elbe; it was not to advance upon Berlin. Simpson asked, quite naturally, from whom this order came. Eisenhower, was the answer. Such an order was the Allied equivalent to a Führer Befehl which though unpleasant had to be

Above: the meeting of British and Soviet troops at Wismar, on the Baltic coast, 3 May 1945. **Below:** four days later at Wismar, Cossacks of the Red Army march past Field Marshal Montgomery during the British commander's visit to Marshal Rokossovsky.

obeyed. In accordance with the Supreme Commander's directive, when the Corps and Divisions of Ninth Army reached the river they halted there. And there they waited until days later the Red Army, urged on by its military and political leaders, opened the assault upon Berlin. This was not, as Stalin had assured Eisenhower, an offensive for which secondary forces would be used, but was instead an all-out drive by his best commanders and finest units to gain the political prize.

Thus, for Ninth Army, the war ended on the Elbe with the American formations halted and waiting until the Red Army reached the river. Only sixty miles of autobahn had stood between Simpson and the objective. 'No German force could have stopped us', commented one Staff officer bitter with disappointment. 'The only thing that stood between Ninth Army and Berlin was Eisenhower.'

Hodges' First Army, to the south of Simpson, advanced through the Plain of Saxony heading towards the Elbe against minimal opposition. The pace of this swift thrust threw the Soviets into a panic and Eisenhower ordered First Army to take up a 'halt' line on the River Mulda. Not until 25 April did the first elements of 69th US Infantry Division move towards the Elbe where contact was made with units of the Soviet 58th Guards Rifle Division at Torgau.

That meeting of the Red Army and the Americans bisected what remained of the Third Reich and as a result, Hitler's contingency plan came into operation. In the north Admiral Doenitz commanded, while in the south the task of leadership was undertaken by Field Marshal Kesselring. The end of the Reich was at hand.

The US Third Army, commanded by the flamboyant General George Patton, like its northern neighbour, First Army, raced eastwards through the gap torn in the German battle line. Opposition to its advance varied from minimal – a few random rifle shots or a Panzerfaust, to fanatical, where officer cadet units attacked in disciplined and skilful assaults.

Twelfth Corps is the unit of Third Army which we shall follow in this account, for it boasted of being the spearhead of Patton's force. Corps was spread facing both north-east and south-east. Among the formations facing south-eastward was the 11th Armoured Division and it was ordered to advance and make contact with the Red Army, whose arrival was thought to be imminent. On 26 April a tank group from the divisional 22 Tank Battalion and 41st Cavalry Recce Battalion crossed the border into Austria, the first Allied unit to do so from the west. Meanwhile the infantry Divisions of XII Corps that were facing north-eastwards were preparing to take up battle with the elements of the German Army pouring out of Czechoslovakia closely pursued by the Red Army.

The rapid advance by XII Corps was suddenly reduced to a crawl as snow, sleet and driving rain washed away the country road surfaces, for these had crumbled under their use by heavy armour. The speed of operations was brought down to the pace of an infantryman and the slowness of the advance allowed the enemy to regroup and to form a firm front facing the Americans. The advance although slowed did not halt and the south-eastern prong of the Corps captured Linz and, more horrifyingly for the men of 11th Armoured Division, the concentration camp at Mauthausen. Whereas the other horror camps had been hutted enclosures and, therefore, might have been seen as a temporary feature of National Socialist life, in Mauthausen the tall stone walls were several feet thick. This camp had obviously been planned to form a permanent part of the social fabric of the Third Reich. While the southern wing of Corps was driving into the Linz region, the 4th Armoured Division to the north had exploited the breaches which 5th and 90th Infantry Divisions had created in the Böhmerwald. Once through the hills of that extensive, dark and gloomy forest of Bohemia, the 4th Armoured drove fast again towards the objective Patton had assigned to it. Its task was to reach Golden Prague. It was the swift movement of an advanced reconnaissance group of 4th Armoured which delighted the Czechs with the prospect of liberation by the American Army. The euphoria vanished when the first group was not followed up by the rest of Patton's forces.

It was at this time that Patton became involved in rescuing one of Austria's living treasures; the Lippizaner stud. The famous Viennese riding school had been evacuated from the Austrian capital to Saint Martin, but most of the horses, six hundred and seventy in number, had been moved farther away from danger, eastwards to the village of Hostau in Bohemia. This region was still unconquered, a no man's land, towards which two Allied armies were advancing. To Colonel Podhajsky, Director of the School, the rescue of the Lippizaner was vital for there existed the danger that the Czechs or the Russians might seize the horses as war booty. Patton was invited to visit the school at Saint Martin where Podhajsky put on a full display to impress his guest. Patton, himself an excellent cavalryman, was impressed by the horsemanship, but could not understand how a nation at war could 'use the young and healthy men, of active service age, on nothing more than teaching the horses some clever tricks'. Nevertheless, he gave orders for a rescue mission to be undertaken. The Stud was again fortunate.

Colonel Reed, commanding 2nd Cavalry Group and entrusted with the rescue mission, was himself a passionate horseman and one who had trained for the Olympics. He sent Stewart of 42nd Recce Squadron to the Remount Depot in Hostau where the horses were quartered. Stewart returned days later riding a Lippizaner, his passage through the German lines assured through the authorization papers signed by a German General, another former cavalryman. Stewart then had the task of leading his unit back through the German lines to Hostau to bring out the horses and the 42nd was unlucky enough to strike an aggressive Volkssturm unit of Volksdeutsche and these had to be fought down. At Hostau the task began of preparing the animals for the short but perilous journey. The pregnant mares and the very young foals were loaded into trucks and the remaining horses were screened by the light armoured vehicles of the 42nd. There were objections by Czech partisans at the removal of this valuable property, but their protests were ignored; the operation had been authorized by Patton himself. These were not the only difficulties. German units, unaware that the rescue operation had also been authorized by their General, erected road-blocks and in one vicious little battle were totally destroyed. It was not all romance. On other sectors of the front the shooting war still went on and as late as 4 May, a German officer cadet unit ambushed and attacked a US recce detachment and inflicted unnecessary casualties.

Facing XII Corps was an enemy against whom it had fought in France – 11th Panzer Division – and it was to XII Corps that von Wietersheim, commanding the Panzer Division, intended to surrender. The following extract from a Third Army report shows clearly the confusion that existed on the German side during those last frantic days.

'Von Wietersheim had been superseded by Major-General von Buttlar, formerly of OKW, but Wietersheim decided to surrender the whole division, as he had considered doing for more than a month. He called a meeting of his ranking officers and informed them of his intention. When all present agreed with these plans, he again took charge of the Division. A Major Vogtmann was dispatched to the 90th US Infantry Division in order to negotiate. Firing ceased on 3 May at 14.00 hrs . . . Buttlar had been informed by messenger of the decision to surrender and that his group had been included in the terms.'

In those dying days of the Reich the roads were crowded with civilians and Allied prisoners of war whose guards had abandoned them. Slave workers, suddenly and mysteriously liberated, looked in their bewilderment for some responsible authority to tell them what to do. There were hordes of fearful Volksdeutsche seeking to pass out of the Sudetenland and into Germany proper. But of all the terrible sights of those dreadful days the one most remembered was the concentration camp people who were being marched westwards.

'At first we could not understand that this group, sitting apathetically on the roadside was any different from those other marching groups that we had passed. Then we heard over the air, "Did you see that Kraut shoot one of those civvies?" Our column stopped and some of the men went across to investigate. They came back and told us that the people at the roadside were political and racial prisoners. Medical aid was requested over the air and we pushed on. The route that those people had followed could be traced by the corpses lying along the road sides. Many of them, we were told, had been shot for falling out on the line of march. It was a sobering thought that a whole lot of those people in that concentration camp group would probably die within days because of the treatment they had suffered.'

Corps recce units first made contact with the Red Army on 8 May, when Troop A of 41st Cavalry Squadron advanced towards a battle between the Red Army's 7th Guards Division and an SS panzer formation. In the fluid situation of those last hours of the war in Bohemia, three major German formations, 2nd SS Panzer Corps, Eighth Army and the Cossack Army offered to surrender. Nor were these the only enemy units which preferred American captivity to durance vile under the Soviets. Faced with huge masses of prisoners, the Americans utilized surrendered German officers to transmit their instructions. It was a chaotic situation with the head of the surrendering German armies parleying with the US forces while 35 miles away the tail of the column, still in Prague, reported itself under attack by the Red Army and by Czech partisan forces.

The surrendering enemy forces were quickly separated into those units which had fought against the West and could be accepted as prisoners, and those who had battled against the Russians and who were, accordingly, passed over to the Red Army. Senior German officers were taken prisoner. In addition to von Wietersheim and von Buttlar of the 11th Panzer Division, a Press Release of XII Corps reported, 'Within twenty-four hours one Field Marshal and seven Generals paid unauthorized visits to the Headquarters of Corps. Six were prisoners and the other two, White Russians, sought terms of surrender.'

The German formations covered a vast area and with this view of literally square miles of prisoners the story of Third Army should come to its end. But the end was neither that quick nor that tidy. From a long time before VE-Day and lasting almost until the second week of June, Wehrwolf activity was reported to Army Headquarters. On 21 May sabotage was carried out against wires and poles of the civilian telephone system, reported 90th

Above: the end of the Wehrwolves. British paratroops serving with 11th Armoured Division gather round the body of a Wehrwolf who had been killed while trying to shoot a British serviceman, 5 May 1945. **Below:** only the slogans remain – 'Death to traitors!' – on the wall of a house in Horrem.

Division, and then a group of six US officers was fired on in the same area. A week later a divisional dump was set on fire and on 31 May three boys, the eldest of whom was only twelve, dynamited a bridge. There was an immediate and heavy clampdown which included a strict curfew and restriction upon civilian movement. These measures and a more severe handling of the parents of Wehrwolf who were caught – visiting the sins of the children upon the fathers – reduced and then finally halted Wehrwolf, the last flicker of resistance of an otherwise dead Third Reich. With the Wehrwolf activity ended, Third Army could say that its war was over.

Immediately below Patton's Third stood General Devers's 6th Army Group, made up of First French and Seventh US Armies, forming the Allied right wing. We have seen that some American armies had reached their 'halt' lines so that, for them, the shooting war was over. This was not the case for 6th Army Group whose formations were fighting their way through southern Germany towards Austria. The task of both armies was by swift, decisive action to take out that region in which it was believed the core of the Alpine Redoubt was located. This was to be a three-pronged operation. The French were to drive down from the area of Lake Constance and cut off the German forces defending the Austrian province of Vorarlberg. Seventh US Army was to thrust for Innsbruck, the putative capital of the Alpine Redoubt, while parts of Patton's Third Army, borrowed from Bradley for this operation, was to strike for Salzburg.

Only minimal resistance was encountered by the units of French 5th Armoured Division as they crossed from Germany into Austria on 29 April, and this seemed to accord with the leaflets which the soldiers had been given. The men had been told that Austria was a friendly country, but those first impressions were not to last and the advance guard ran into severe opposition as it approached the narrow causeway which separates Bregenz from Lochau. The causeway road was mined, barricaded and defended by batteries of 88mm guns. Against such opposition the French assaults could make no progress and casualties mounted. A stern ultimatum was issued; either resistance ceased or Bregenz would be razed. To prevent such a disaster Austrian and Swiss doctors met the French commanders and told them of the more than three thousand wounded who were in hospital in the town. Austrian partisan leaders, too, slipped along paths unguarded by German troops, to negotiate with the French, seeking to avert the destruction of their city. Lecoq, the French Commander, was adamant. He had no intention of taking casualties when with a single, furious bombardment he could destroy the opposition. Talks between the French military leaders and the Austrian partisan commanders continued for days, the French pointing out, with logic, that Bregenz could not be considered as an open town so long as it was defended by artillery and infantry. The final blow to the civilians came in the terse order from Berlin that the city must be held to the last. This directive from the Führer's Headquarters, in which the principal leaders, were now either dead or about to surrender, was a death-sentence. With a shocking lack of initative the partisan leaders made no further effort but allowed the military to continue its resistance. As a consequence the full force of the French assault fell upon the city. Fighter-bombers roared in, their aiming-point the Capuchin Abbey, which was believed to hold a large concentration of German reserves, and behind the fighters came the heavy bombers. Then the guns opened up a long and sustained barrage.

At this stage of the war the population of the Tyrol was almost exclusively female. All the men of military age were serving with the armed forces and there were no factories employing a large, male labour force. It was, therefore, upon the women of Tyrol that the fury of the bombing and the bombardment fell. Women dug out victims trapped in the shattered buildings, put out the fires and tended the wounded. When the bombers and the guns had done their work the French armour drove through one of Austria's oldest cities which was ablaze from end to end. Bregenz, which had survived nearly six years of war unscathed, had been smashed in a few short hours in the last two weeks of the war. White sheets and pillow-cases hung from damaged houses on the outskirts of the city and alongside these signs of surrender hung also the red/white/red flag of old Austria. Days later, in a formal ceremony of surrender, the keys of the town were offered to General de Lattre de Tassigny.

The senseless opposition which had caused Bregenz to be destroyed was repeated again and again at other towns and villages. It was the task of the German rearguard to hold back the French advance so as to allow troops to be sent to reinforce the front where Seventh US Army was making a strong effort. In such rearguard actions the civilians suffered most, both collectively and individually, and it was not uncommon for pilots to swoop down and machine-gun single Austrians on the roads.

'I was cycling to church. It was Sunday, the first Sunday in May, when a line of aircraft suddenly skidded sideways across the tops of the trees of a little wood and right over my head. I noticed that they did not have the usual black crosses on the wings. The aircraft swung round and circled over me – or so it seemed. By this time I was off the bicycle and was sheltering in a ditch. Those planes were so low that I could see the pilots looking down.

Suddenly, they flew low over me, only a few metres above the ground. I was terrified. I heard machine-gun fire and loud explosions. Somewhere ahead of me, I could not see where because the road curved, they had fired and bombed something. Whatever it was, it was burning. The planes screeched back down the road towards me and as the last one got near he fired his guns. He could only have been aiming at me. There was nothing else to shoot at anywhere near me.'

The German rearguard, often only in Company strength, occasionally consisting only of machine-gun groups, held the French advance through Vorarlberg and Tyrol so effectively that the Allies thought the region to be defended by whole Divisions of men and concentrated their own forces for a major assault. Fearful of the consequences which German resistance and

Allied determination would bring, Austrian partisans offered to guide the French through the German defensive positions and led the Alpine troops by secret paths and through waist-deep snow, over mountain peaks to cut off the German forces in Vorarlberg.

While some guerrilla groups offered assistance to the French, others carried out a form of passive resistance against the French. Vorarlberg and Tyrol were confronted with a choice of two occupying forces, the French or the Americans. The Americans had a reputation for generosity and they also had the best rations. The French were poor and that was a disadvantage, so far as the native population was concerned. The French, too, used Moroccan battalions and these were an alien and unknown quantity. The leaders of the Alpine provinces, therefore, did all in their power to ensure that the Americans arrived first and went so far as to blow up roads in order to slow the advance of de Tassigny's divisions.

To the east of the French, General Patch's Seventh Army was in action forcing its way through Bavaria and the mountain passes into Tyrol. The Army's three Corps had an important task to accomplish. They were to come round the eastern flank of the Alpine Redoubt and to sever the roads along which, so it was believed, reinforcements would come to nourish the mountain fortress. In common with most US assessments of possible German intentions, the Intelligence staff of Seventh Army wrote of the Alpine region as . . . 'the only truly defensible area left to the enemy . . .' and also forecast . . . 'a battle to the last man . . . by hundreds of thousands of fanatical German soldiers who would fight . . . on this last battlefield . . .' On 21 April the formations of Seventh Army opened the campaign against the Redoubt. Few of its men could have expected that within two weeks they would have driven through it.

'For weeks there had been stories of a last-ditch stand which the Nazi top brass would make. This fortress would be in the mountains that we were heading for. When you are infantry you do not move much out of your own sector so I can only say what happened on my regiment's front (100th US Infantry). Resistance varied. In some places we would be met by anxious women waving white cloths and there would be sheets hanging from every window, showing that they were all willing to surrender. At the next village there would be a group of fanatics who may have been only young kids but who were vicious killers. They often played "dead" when we passed them and then they would stand up and shoot us in the back.'

Some idea of the state of the German Army at that time is found in this succinct assessment in the US Intelligence Report dated 25 April. On the subject of First and Nineteenth German Armies, the writer reported . . . 'their numbers (1st and 19th) are little more than bookkeeping conveniences . . .' The report was based on intercepted enemy radio reports which spoke of a lack of co-ordinated orders and of thousands of soldiers who had left their units and who were to be encountered, dressed in civilian clothes as 'self-discharged veterans'. Of all the euphemisms that have been used to camouflage the harsh term 'deserter', this must be the most peculiar.

But there was no doubt about it. The solidity, the tenacity, the ferocity that had once been the marks of good German units were less frequently encountered. The German First Army was a shell, its Divisions averaging only 500 men each. The fragments of the SS who were to be found almost everywhere, still showed a rock-hard determination to resist; an élan in attack and exemplary combat skills. There were others made of less reliable material and as an example of the low-grade units in the German Order of Battle the US Intelligence report noted the Indian Legion,* concerning whose ability or willingness to fight, Hitler had once expressed himself very bluntly.

The French and American formations of Devers's Army Group had now entered Austria and found more frequent instances of those political moves that had begun to manifest themselves in southern Germany. In Austria, as in Bavaria, there were welcoming greetings from the civilian population and partisan activity *against* the Germans. In Augsburg, in Germany, the various resistance groups had presented a united front which forced the military commander to surrender the city, a move which caused the Deputy Gauleiter to commit suicide; one of a number in the town that week. In Munich a resistance organization which had been gathering strength throughout the war years, burst into open revolt during the night of 27/28 April. The liberation movement (the liberation of Catholic Bavaria from Protestant Prussia) was led by the Interpreter Company of 7th Military District. It is hard to think of a more unlikely group of revolutionaries than these, but their announcement of the Bavarian revolt and the death of Hitler – prematurely as it happened – frightened the High Command. It was a short-lived revolt – it died within a day – but it was a clear sign of the general disintegration.

While this military tragi-comedy was being played out over the air waves, the 45th US Division had struck trouble. The Munich SS Standarte, conscious of the significance to the Nazi ideology of that city, was determined to fight to the last. The battle was fought in the extensive park which surrounded the SS Academy, and was continued in its buildings and barracks. Upon 180th Regiment of US 45th Division fell the brunt of the most nerve-racking type of infantry warfare – house-to-house fighting. In the high, light and airy rooms of the college and in the SS dormitories, a bitter struggle ensued. Grenades and machine pistols were the chief weapons. The fighting flared and died, but then flared at some new point only to end and then to appear at a third and yet a fourth place. By the end of the day SS resistance within the buildings was weaker. Fearing to be outnumbered and trapped in a struggle within the Academy, the SS officers had thinned out their defence and had again taken up positions in the open grounds where their mens' greater proficiency in field craft would give them the advantage. This it did, but not enough to counter the US build-up of men and machines. By 1 May the whole area had been cleared and US Seventh Army was en route to Innsbruck.

*This was a unit made up of officers and men of the Indian Army who had been taken prisoner and subsequently subverted by the followers of Subash Chandra Bhose.

One of the entrances into Austria was the Fern Pass which was defended by the 14th Jäger Division.

'By evening the Division's strength had grown, but in an unplanned fashion and from the most surprising sources. We could not accept all the offers that were made. It took us a long time – a very long time – to convince one leader of a Reichsarbeitsdienst unit that his several hundred young men, most of whom were only 16 years old, could not be used. They were little boys, untrained and unarmed. Only the unit's permanent staff could be used, about a platoon strong. In contrast we received the headquarters detachment from the 'Atlantic Fortresses' group. This was about two Companies strong whose men may not have been trained in infantry warfare but who were U-boat men and, therefore, first-class material. The Imst region sent us a Volkssturm detachment, about 30 men and from both Corps and Army there was some artillery, another infantry Company out of Flak crews who had no guns and a further thirty officers from the General Reserve. Then there was a mortar platoon made up of Gebirgsjäger.

There were no field kitchens, wireless sets, tents or signals equipment. We had to run trucks to turn the generators so as to produce electricity to run the wireless sets. There were no maps, because of the snow which fell constantly there was the danger of avalanches, and we didn't know which were the danger spots. With this mixture of troops we had to defend what was perhaps the most important pass leading towards the Inn valley.'

The Austria into which Devers's Army Group fought its way presented an eccentric picture as the war drew to its close. It was a time of formal surrenders by Corps Commanders and also of fanatical resistance by common soldiers. It was a time of catching the few big fish, all of whom expected preferential treatment, and the imprisonment of the many who expected nothing. It was a time of suicides by those who chose to die rather than to live in a world from which their Führer had departed, and it was a time of rebirth, that of an independent Austria. It was a gloriously mad time. Some villages and towns where the locals burst into applause and showered kisses upon men of Seventh Army units, while a mile away in another hamlet bitter SS Wehrwolves mined roads or sniped at truck drivers.

'At the time I could not understand it, this resistance, this pointless resistance to our advance. The war was all over – our columns were spreading across the whole of Germany and Austria. We were irresistible. We could conquer the world; that was our glowing conviction. And the enemy had nothing. Yet he resisted and in some places with an implacable fanaticism. I know now what it was that animated the enemy although I didn't then, in 1945. The world of those children of the Hitler Youth was coming to an end. Soon there would be nothing left. No parades, no songs, no swastikas, no marching and no fighting for the Faith – for the belief in Hitler. The roof was falling in on those children's ideals. Denied the opportunity to be real soldiers, to wear a proper uniform and to fight as soldiers in a formal unit, those kids were determined to show us that they knew how to sacrifice themselves.

There was one boy whom we took prisoner. His rocket had hit my tank but had not exploded. I was livid that this snotty brat should endanger my life and I was out of that tank very quickly cuffing him about the head and shouting. When I let go of him he fell to the grass crying and saying something. I do not speak German but Abrahams, my sergeant did. What that child was saying was that he should have died for the Führer. The silly bastard was sorry that he had not been killed knocking out my tank.'

The farther the advance into Austria the more prominent became the signs of the Austrian Resistance Organization 'O5'. The first major contact between the Americans and O5 came at Innsbruck where units of the Austrian Resistance led by Karl Gruber had set out on 2 May to seize the Tyrolean capital city. This was a more difficult task than Gruber and his men had suspected for there were so many places that had to be seized and held and Gruber had only eighty-five men. There was also a strong SS presence to the east of the city which was acting as a nucleus for a great number of miscellaneous Nazi, para-military detachments. This strong Nazi battle group was moving rapidly up the Inn valley from Terfens and Solbad Hall towards the provincial capital.

Gruber's force, in good defensive positions, sought to hold back the advance of the SS columns and did this to such good effect that by nightfall the Nazi group was still some miles east of the city. The onset of darkness and the wintry weather forced an end to the battle and the Resistance leaders knew that the SS would not take up the struggle again until first light. This gave the O5 group the chance to clear the enemy at their backs. Leaving only a thin firing line facing the SS, the bulk of the group, by now reinforced by Austrian soldiers of the German Army, returned to the capital and captured those offices and installations which had not been taken during the afternoon. The first objective was the brain of the defence, the Army Headquarters on the Hungerberg. General Boeheims, the Commander of the whole German south-west Front, and his staff were taken prisoner and removed to the Klosterkaserne which the Resistance had also captured. With the brain gone the next objective was the voice; the radio station. By a ruse, the partisans pretended to be reinforcements, the station was seized, an announcer broadcast appeals to the Tyroleans urging them to join the uprising. Much of what was said over the radio was not at that time correct, but it served its purpose; it told the Tyrolean listeners that the Nazi period was ended:

'The hour of liberation has come. Offer no resistance to the Americans. Form a defence unit in every village (against the Nazis). Keep discipline and order. Raise the old Austrian or Tyrolean colours or a white flag. The armistice in the area of the south-western armies takes effect at 17.00 hrs. It includes the area of upper Italy to the Isonzo, Tyrol and Vorarlberg, ·Salzburg, parts of Carinthia and the Steiermark. Soldiers will remain with their units. Armbands are red/white/red. The Nazi salute is abolished. Salute by a hand to the peak of the cap. Signed by the Public Order Committee of the Austrian Resistance Party.'

The announcement was a deliberate falsehood to prevent further fighting. The leaders of the Austrian Resistance Organization knew that Tyrol formed part of Army Group 'G' and that force had not yet surrendered.

The response of the people of Tyrol to the partisan appeal was overwhelming. Thousands of volunteers came in, many of them armed and ready to take up battle. Each member was given the red/white/red armband and was enrolled into the national resistance organization. In a very pragmatic move all applicants were accepted even though it was known that some were Nazis who were turning their coats at the last minute. They would be dealt with when the time was right. Now, if they played their part in the forthcoming struggle, then they might redeem themselves.

From every house in the city the colours of old Austria flew in response to another broadcast asking the inhabitants to greet the American troops in a festive fashion. During the evening of 3 May, units of US 103rd Infantry Division advanced towards Innsbruck from Seefeld and Zirl, their columns guided by liaison officers from the 'O5' organization. In the evening one battalion of 409th Infantry Regiment was in the city, driving up the Maria Theresienstrasse in a blinding snow storm, but despite the bitter weather the streets were jammed with jubilant Tyroleans and the Americans could see in the day's dying light that The Star-Spangled Banner was fluttering over the Innsbruck town hall; raised by order of the Resistance.

The Americans were astonished by the warmth of the reception they received. Their orders were that they were to consider Austria as a conquered country, but the local population was treating them as liberators. It was bewildering to see German soldiers wearing armbands produced by O5 and to see civilians carrying guns. The History of Seventh Army described the Austrian underground in the following way:

'. . . *heavily armed Austrians swarming all over the place and the whole set-up looked like a Class C Hollywood movie . . . Some were in German uniform some in civilian clothing, all wearing the red and white arm-band of the resistance movement . . . They all seemed excited and keyed up . . . their attitude was very friendly . . . the halls were stacked with cases of MG and SA ammunition and there were long rows of Panzerfaust laid out. The men were loaded with two or three weapons each and had hand-grenades stuck in their belts . . . all seemed very excited and apprehensive that SS troops were coming in . . .*'

Although some SS elements entered the city and released General Boeheims, they were a spent force and outside the city their formations dissolved leaving only small groups, sometimes only single individual Wehrwolves, to maintain the unequal fight. Innsbruck, capital of the Tyrol, which had been thought of as the headquarters town of the Alpine Redoubt, was soon firmly in American hands and while the bulk of 409th regiment formed a strong front to the east of the city, VI Corps sent the 411th Regiment out to undertake Seventh Army's last combat mission in Europe. The Regiment was ordered to strike southwards through the Brenner Pass to link up with the regiment from 88th Division coming up out of Italy.

Above: abandoned German
transport vehicles at the entrance
to the town of Brenner. **Left:** the
US armies make contact.
American forces in southern
Germany link up with men of Fifth
Army advancing from Italy.

This operation was not without a great element of risk. Certainly the capitulation of Army Group 'C' in Italy had brought the war there to an end, but who could be certain that there would be no last-ditch resistance to the troops of Seventh Army during the link-up drive. It was a calculated risk. One hundred and seventy-five vehicles formed the column which drove southwards out of Austria with headlights full on, cutting through the dark Alpine night. This, too, was a risk. It illuminated the target beautifully, but with full lights on the column could move fast. And it did. Less than two hours into 4 May and touch had been gained between the US Fifth and Seventh Armies.

Back in Innsbruck arrangements were being made for the surrender of the German Forces in the Tyrol and the Vorarlberg. In point of fact the only officer with the authority to do this was General Boeheims, but he was unavailable to attend the surrender ceremony, so General Brandenberger, commanding Nineteenth Army, was directed to substitute for him. He was ordered to report at midday on 5 May. Despite the little time there had been for the Americans to prepare for the ceremony, VI Corps arranged a splendid parade. A motor escort was laid on and a guard of honour was mounted, complete with Colours.

The protocol was exact and detailed, from the seating allotted to the German delegation right down to the drill movements which the guard of honour would make. Everything was ready. The guards were positioned and the Colours paraded – only the Germans were missing. Eighty minutes late, General Brandenberger finally arrived at the Landsrat building in Innsbruck. There were neither salutes nor handshakes for the Germans. The terms of surrender were read out to them, there was some discussion and then, at 15.00 hrs, came the signing; twelve copies in all. The war for VI Corps and French First Army was over. Brandenberger left. Again there were neither salutes nor handshakes. Then the victorious Allied commanders stepped out of the Landsrat building and were greeted with a present arms from the guard of honour and the playing of the United States and French national anthems.

Meanwhile, the war on the other sectors of Seventh Army front had been continuing. The city of Salzburg and its surrounding area, which had been set out as an objective of Patton's Third Army, became the responsibility of Patch's Seventh. His XV and XXI Corps drove through Berchtesgaden towards Salzburg, accepting en route the surrender of 9th Hungarian Infantry Division. This ceremony had all the elements of a comic opera. The Division was drawn up on parade. The Magyar General made an impassioned speech and then rode to the rear of his Division. A series of sharp commands was given, the whole formation turned about, thereby, symbolically, allying themselves with the Allies. There were sword salutes and frisky horses, Regimental Colours and all the courtesies and pomps of a bygone age. Outside Berchtesgaden only sporadic sniper fire from diehard SS men met the US columns which then drove through the little Alpine town, burning as a result of air raids and deliberate arson by the SS. A halt was made for the

Left: tanks of the US 20th Armored Division ford a river en route to Salzburg. **Below left:** Salzburg liberated, 4 May 1945. **Right:** at Innsbruck, the German commander, General Brandenburger, arrives to surrender Nineteenth Army to the US VI Corps on 5 May 1945. **Below:** German troops coming in to lay down their arms.

night and 5 May was spent removing all traces of Nazi influence from the streets and houses.

The surrender which had been signed in Innsbruck did not, as it should have done, bring an end to the fighting in the provinces of Tyrol and Vorarlberg. In this latter province there was an outbreak of hostilities between the French and Germans on 6 May. The reason for this was due to the lack of communication which existed between German units. Many headquarters were out of touch with their subordinate formations and could pass no messages except by the slow method of dispatch-rider or runner.

General Schmidt, commanding German 24th Army, had asked the French for an armistice but had failed to appear at the rendezvous. By a tragedy one of the few messages that Schmidt did receive was that which placed his Army under the command of 19th Army; and 19th Army had already surrendered to the Americans. So far as Schmidt was concerned he had no need to go to the rendezvous; the war was over, but he forgot to tell the French. They thereupon resumed hostilities against an enemy which they believed was still operational and which had not surrendered. The fighting lasted only one more day, for a new ceasefire, this time including Schmidt's Army, was ordered for 7 May. The war in Vorarlberg was finally over.

Kesselring, the Supreme Commander South, put out feelers regarding the surrender of those forces under his control. They were, by now, few indeed. The capitulation in Italy on 2 May had ripped open his South-Western Front and the imminent capitulation of Army Group 'E' in Jugoslavia would soon take out the whole of the south-eastern theatre of operations. There remained still Army Group 'G' and Allied Supreme Headquarters ordered General Devers to prepare for its surrender, for this could not now be long delayed. From Sixth Army Group Headquarters instructions were sent out to Seventh Army and during the night of 4/5 May the white-flagged cars holding the German plenipotentaries rolled into the positions held by 3rd US Infantry Division. General Foertsch, commanding First German Army, and acting on behalf of General Schulz, General Commanding Army Group 'G', was taken with his aides to the Thorak estate outside Munich where the terms of the capitulation were read out.

Once again, the History of Seventh Army, sets the scene of this major event:

'At noon General Foertsch mounted the few, polished, black marble steps and stood in the open door. He was dressed in the polished black boots and the field grey uniform of the German Army. Around his neck was the Knight's Cross . . . He was followed by the officers of his party . . .

General Foertsch began to speak, taking up the paragraphs of the surrender document one by one. He spoke in a clear deep voice, very slowly and distinctly so that every word could be understood by anyone having even a smattering of German. He never argued. He knew, of course, that he was beaten. He would often begin his statements with the sentence "I deem it my duty to point out . . ." and then would show, for example, that the German troops were so scattered that it

Above and **below:** Lieutenant-General Foertsch surrenders Army Group 'G' to Lieutenant-General Devers, commander of 6th Army Group, at Haar on 5 May 1945.

*would take more than the contemplated number of hours to get the news to them . . .
His suggestions were all of that type. He stressed the number of refugees and the lack
of food in his area.*

*General Devers would respond, asking questions and giving his views. After brief
discussions, each point in turn was taken up . . . General Devers was insistent that
there be no misunderstanding on the big points; there was to be no armistice. This
was unconditional surrender . . .*

*The point had to be made quite clear. At the will of the Allies all commissioned
and enlisted personnel of Army Group 'G', including General Foertsch and General
Schulz, would become prisoners of war. Foertsch sat stiffly at attention. It was a full
minute before he said anything. The man was manifestly suffering from the impact
of emotion of the most violent character. Finally he bowed his head slightly, flushing
a little and replied, "I understand it. I have no choice. I have no power to do
otherwise" . . .'*

The meeting was adjourned and then reconvened for the signing of the
surrender document. This was to take effect from 12.00 hrs on 6 May. The
proceedings had been formal and military, but were not without some
confusion. As we have seen, VI Corps was accomplishing the surrender of the
German forces in the Tyrol and in Vorarlberg and, in fact, the surrender of
Nineteenth Army, was signed after the entire Army Group 'G' had
surrendered.

The chaotic state of the front-line units meant that neither side was in
contact with all its subordinate formations and as a consequence some of
Seventh Army's forces were involved in local surrenders, quite unaware that
these were now unnecessary. Although the German Army was prepared to
acknowledge its defeat, the SS had its own ideas on how to treat those who
surrendered to the enemy and forced the cars containing the German
delegation to return to the American lines. Only Foertsch was able to go on
to his own forces.

Conditions in the front line continued to be chaotic and while some units
came in to surrender other groups continued to fight on. This was
particularly true of the situation around Schloss Itter, a twelfth-century castle,
set on a hill, which was being used as a prison for many famous Frenchmen.
Word had come to 142nd Infantry Regiment, 36th Division, that there were
'prominent' prisoners held in the castle. Captain John Lee, a tank commander
in the 12th US Armoured Division, together with his crew and four
infantrymen from 36th Division, drove through Wörgl and climbed the hill
towards the Schloss, passing a number of parked German vehicles. The
German commander of the VIP prison-camp offered to surrender, but other
soldiers, chiefly from the SS, noting how few Americans had gone into the
castle, attacked strongly in an attempt to retake it and to kill the former
prisoners. This German battle group advanced under a barrage of shells fired
by an 88mm gun, which not only blew gaping holes in the fabric of the old
castle, but also knocked out the American tank. Captain Lee organized his
men for the defence of Schloss Itter assisted by the German major who put

his men at the disposal of the Americans. If the SS took the castle their lives were forfeit, in any case. The French VIPs, many of them Army commanders, also played their part and one 'prominent' person, Jean Borota, a famous tennis player, disguised himself and set out to contact men of the 2nd Battalion of 142nd Regiment, which was already on a rescue mission.

Late in the afternoon of the siege, the 2nd Battalion arrived and opened the road. The unit arrived in the nick of time, the defenders having run out of ammunition. This group of French Generals and politicians was only one of the groups of 'prominent' persons who were being released all over Austria, and it is interesting to note that the Schloss Itter group included, Daladier and Reynaud, both of them former Prime Ministers of France. Among the military leaders were General Weygand and General Gamelin, the former Commander-in-Chief of the French Army.

In an attempt to bring news of the capitulation to scattered German units, the Americans sent out trucks fitted with loudspeakers and also scattered leaflets from the air. It did not stop the violent little skirmishes which blew up or the isolated attacks upon American detachments. Although the war against 6th Army Group was to go into effect at midday on 6 May, late in the evening of that day three men of 101st Airborne Division were taken prisoner by a German patrol and there was still firing in the hills.

As an example of the SS attitude towards surrenders, two German officers were shot by snipers as they tried to bring in American plenipotentiaries and there were other similar incidents. But on 8 May an American patrol met an SS officer holding a white flag who pointed out that the SS was not bound by the terms of the surrender signed with Army Group 'G' but that its units wished to make their own arrangements. From discussion with that officer it was clear that Obergruppenführer Berger wished to surrender the forces under his command, included among which was the 13th SS Corps, with 17th Division and 35th Division on establishment. Berger and his SS formations surrendered to the US 101st Airborne Division. The last German unit of major size had capitulated.

The first weeks of May were those in which the 'big fish' were netted. Not the first to surrender but certainly the most important, and the best known, was Hermann Goering who had once been seen as Hitler's successor. On 8 May, Oberst von Brauchitsch, Goering's aide-de-camp, was escorted into the headquarters building of 36th Division where he presented two letters from the Reichsmarschall to Eisenhower and to General Devers. These read in part:

'I request of you to grant me free passage . . . and to place my entourage and my family under American protection. I make it, remembering the time when the aged Marshal of France, Pétain, in a situation equally difficult for his country, asked me for a similar interview which then actually took place . . . Your Excellency will understand how I feel in this my most difficult hour and how much I have suffered through my disability, due to my arrest, to do everything possible a long time ago to prevent further bloodshed in a hopeless situation . . .'

Brigadier Stack was sent out with von Brauchitsch's driver to bring the Reischmarschall into the American lines. Goering's convoy of cars was found at Radstadt in the Steiermark, to the south-east of Salzburg. In his car were his wife and daughter and a small escort group.

It was late in the afternoon when Stack found the Marshal and by the time that Goering had agreed to accompany the American officer the evening was near and, because it would have been dangerous to cover the whole distance by night, the group was quartered in a castle which had been seized from Goering's SS guards earlier that day. Goering had had many castles in the Reich and in one of them a young wife had had to work. Anni Lendl was 26 when she was evacuated and ended up as a scullion in Goering's kitchen.

I had been evacuated from the Ost-Steier when the Ivans came in during February, first to Feldbach and then from Feldbach to Graz. As a result of the air raids our refugee group was sent to a village in Kärnten. I was given work by the Labour Exchange. They told me to report to a castle owned by Reichsmarschall Goering. My job was to be a kitchen maid.

What I saw there sickened me. My man and my brothers had all been taken for front-line duty. Even an uncle of mine – my Mother's youngest brother – who had a deformity in the arm was taken for the army and put on active service. While they were away fighting in Goering's place he had an SS guard unit of about 800 men. You have never seen men like it. Tall, young, handsome, very fit and not a war medal among them – no medals at all except for Party badges.

I knew that things were bad for the Reich. There were food queues even in Feldbach, which is only a little market town out in the country. Yes, things were bad for the civilians. Those SS swine in Goering's castle, they had never heard of rationing. In the kitchens we prepared food for them that I had never even heard of. Things like fillet steak, Châteaubriand, steak tartare. They ate plenty of meat. We had the left-overs unless we could steal and eat some titbit before we served it. Some of those swine fed their dogs on steak – we got soup. I have seen whole pigs roasted in the kitchens and cut up for men who were too drunk to know what they were eating.

When a man is in drink – I mean when he really has been on a drinking bout, then unpleasant things happen to him physically. He will vomit all over his clothes and while one end of him is vomiting the other end is – well – shit is coming out of the other end. And we, the skivvies had to clean all that sort of stuff up. There was one terrible night when the whole unit sat down to dinner fully armed. This would have been just before Hitler died. They all had weapons and the floor was littered with the anti-tank rockets. They all seemed to be waiting for something to happen, but by late in the evening whatever it was they were waiting for had not happened, so thay all got stinking drunk again.

One morning I got up and it was very quiet. There was nobody about. We kitchen staff started looking. All we found were discarded uniforms, some weapons, lots of mess to clear up and two dead bodies. They had committed suicide, so I was told. All that time I worked in the castle I never saw Goering. For all I know he may not have been in the place at all. In all that time there was no pay, no kindness, no thanks. Nothing. Only the usual Pifke (Prussian) arrogance. The SS spent a great deal of time shouting and slapping the staff. Very free with their insults and face slapping were the Pifke. It made me realize that there are two worlds – theirs and ours. Ours was misery during the war and hunger in the years after it. They had lived like princes and then vanished. I bet they were well off after the war, while we were hungry. When I used to read about the Nazi bosses in the Argentine I used to wonder how many other SS, like those in Goering's bodyguard unit, had also reached there.'

When Goering's party and the American officers arrived next morning in the Grand Hotel in Kitzbuh, the headquarters of 36th Division, Goering was wearing a simple Luftwaffe tunic with Reichsmarschall's shoulder-boards and the most important of his many decorations. One unusual piece of decoration was the white cloth armband on his left arm, worn as a sign that he had surrendered. Goering, the 36th Division's Commander and General Stack met for a champagne discussion in the hotel, a discussion which brought massive and immediate condemnation from every quarter and the direct order from Eisenhower that Goering was to be treated like any other prisoner. The Reichsmarschall made one more public appearance when he was shown to the international Press and claimed that he, too, had been a victim of Adolf Hitler.

The Head of the Gestapo, Kaltenbrunner, was caught hiding in an Alpine hut near Altaussee waiting, like so many others, for the dust of defeat to settle so that, with excellently forged papers and a large sum in foreign currency, he could once again take up the threads of a new life.

Then in came Kesselring, the Supreme Commander South, accompanied by a long column of cars, all bearing white flags. Charmingly, but firmly, 'smiling Albert' refused to deal with anybody from 101st Airborne Division, for they were all junior in rank to him. That the power he had once held was gone seemed not to have been realized. To his small personal staff his was still the voice of God, but this was not an opinion shared by many. Among those who were still prepared to treat Kesselring as if he commanded huge armies and wielded enormous executive power, were Doenitz and Jodl. They requested that he be flown to the German 'enclave' in Flensburg, but the request was turned down. The Allied authorities had priorities greater than that of reuniting the former commanders of a discredited regime.

Kesselring's removal from command of the southern armies a few days later was a hollow formality and at the end of a short period of idleness and speculation, he was formally taken prisoner and held as a war criminal to answer charges brought against him by the Italian government.

Another of the most prominent military commanders captured at that time by American troops was von Rundstedt, who was taking the waters of Bad Tölz. The first remark he made when US troops entered his room in the sanatorium was, 'It is a disgraceful situation for a soldier to give himself up without offering resistance.'

That the greatest number of prominent Nazi leaders and German military commanders were caught in Bavaria and Austria is evidence of their belief in

the existence of the Alpine Redoubt. In addition to those already mentioned the following were apprehended: Hans Frank, the Governor General of Poland; Max Amman, the third man to join the Nazi Party – Hitler was only Number 7; Sepp Dietrich, General of the Waffen SS and commander of Hitler's bodyguard; the Luftwaffe Marshals, von Greim and Sperrle. One other captive, less exalted in rank, but an airman who had made his mark in the history of German military aviation, was Galland, the celebrated fighter ace. While he was explaining his spectacular success in aerial combat to his captors another German airman, Hartmann, the most successful fighter pilot of the war, was shooting down his last victim over Brunn in Czechoslovakia. Another famous, notorious is the *mot juste*, 'fish' was Eichmann, who had taken leave of Kaltenbrunner only a few days earlier.

Many of the 'big fish' who came in to surrender were men who until a few days earlier had demanded the harshest sentences upon common soldiers

Left: released VIPs at Brunico, 5 May 1945. Local partisans stormed the prison at nearby Lago di Braies shortly before the arrival of Allied troops. The ex-prisoners included high ranking ministers from the governments of Hungary and Czechoslovakia, as well as British and Russian officers.

who attempted to do what they themselves were now doing – going over to the enemy. It was all a far cry from those distant days when Hitler had declared – mistakenly as it turned out – that German Field Marshals did not surrender. In May 1945 many of them did and although a great many senior commanders committed suicide and others were executed as war criminals, a great many survived to live to ripe old ages in a new Germany.

Among the other important people to whom the advance of the US armies gave hope were the 'Prominenten', who had been moved around Germany and were by now in the Salzburg region. The most distinguished was King Leopold of the Belgians, who was released from internment at Strobl, on the Wolfgangsee. Less 'prominent' were politicians, including the former Chancellor of Austria, Schuschnigg, and a number of Trades Union officials. They had all believed that they would be killed before the Reich died. The swift advance of Seventh Army rescued them from that probable fate and released them from an imprisonment which was certainly not as hard as that suffered in the camps, but which was still a nerve-racking experience.

It was in the areas overrun by the Americans that the hidden hoards of gold, jewellery and banknotes were chiefly found. In some caves were discovered world-famous paintings and sculptures, carpets of indescribable value and the Crown Jewels of a number of kingdoms and empires. Among the prizes to which no positive, identifying tag can be given were the technicians and scientists who had left the dangers of Peenemunde and the Baltic coast and who had been evacuated to Austria where they worked on special projects. When the Americans came the intellectuals were 'encouraged' to choose the United States as the country in which they wished to continue their work. Werner von Braun, the rocket expert, was only one of a large group of top-ranking men who left for the United States. The Germans thought that they had been found by accident. What they did not know was that the US government agents had been briefed to search them out, that their meeting with the Americans was no coincidence, but the result of combined Allied Intelligence work.

The Allies had made careful plans. Germany at the war's end would be dead but those scientists who were valuable could be persuaded to work on in the States. Not all of them were in the western zones and one group who were sought but not found by US agents were the engineers who had developed a circular flying machine around whose edges jet engines were fitted. The scanty information available indicated that in tests carried out during the first months of 1945, the machine reached a speed of 1,800mph and that it, together with the engineers who designed and built it, were last seen on the aerodrome at Prague waiting to be rescued, only hours before the Red Army arrived. This jet-powered disc was, if the stories are to be believed, the first flying saucer. Nothing more has ever been learned of the machine or the men since that morning in May 1945.

10
REICHS PRESIDENT DOENITZ

It will be recalled that Hitler had ordered, in the event of Germany being bisected, that command of the southern area should be exercised by Kesselring and that the authority in the northern sector should be held by Grand Admiral Doenitz. In Hitler's last directive he made the Admiral President of the Reich.

Thus, at the war's end there was a German government that had been set up by Hitler. That it was a government without any authority seemed not to have been grasped by its ministers. The Allies, however, realized that it was impotent as an executive body, but that it could still be used as a vehicle for administration. The most important administrative problems were those of processing the armed forces and caring for the hundreds of thousands of refugees who had come in, and who were still coming in, from the eastern provinces. Because Doenitz's government and the OKW Departments which were at its disposal were of use to the Allied conquerors, they were allowed to exercise their brief authority. The flood of messages which passed in and out of the German 'enclave' included such trivia as whether Double British Summer Time was in advance or lagged behind German Summer Time. Some messages were, however, vitally important. That of 5 May which ordered the end of the U-boat war and the surrender of the 'grey wolves' was one of vital importance to the Allies.

Courier planes still flew to and from the embattled armies, such as Schoerner's in Czechoslovakia and Loehr's in Jugoslavia. In fact, so far as the Doenitz government and the OKW were concerned, it was very much business as usual and one junior minister, Ohlendorff, forwarded to the Reichs Foreign Minister, von Krosigk, a paper on the need to establish an 'Internal Economic Intelligence Service'.

With the Allies' conquering armies, and following them closely, came groups of men and women, experts in their fields, who set about the great task of restoring some semblance of normal life, and whose duty it was to establish how Germany had been run, economically, socially and militarily. Those teams did not come unprepared. For years there had been the most assiduous collecting of newspaper reports and radio intercepts as well as information gained from the usual Intelligence sources. Some of the information collected, collated and produced by the Ministry of Economic Warfare, can be found in the Department of Printed Books of the Imperial War Museum and it will show how thorough was the organization that sent those teams of experts into defeated Germany.

The interrogation of military leaders began almost immediately and most interviews were conducted aboard a German yacht, the *Patria*. In some instances the Red Army sent its representatives to the *Patria*, in others,

Above: outside the town hall at Luneburg, as the announcement of the surrender is broadcast.
Left: Field Marshal Busch, commander of the German armies in north-west Europe, reports to Field Marshal Montgomery on 11 May 1945, to receive details of the work that German troops must undertake in order to fulfill the surrender terms.

German staff officers were ordered to report to the Russian Kommandantura in Berlin. Lieutenant-Colonel de la Maizière was one who was flown to Zhukov's Headquarters in Berlin to be interrogated on the organization of the OKW. His report, written after his return, confirms how thorough was the Allied training for although he did not know the identity of the General who carried out the interrogation, that Soviet officer knew not only the names of the officers at OKW, but also their functions and how these were integrated into the whole Command apparatus.

To simplify the huge task of administering the surrendered German forces, German officers were ordered to the *Patria* and were given orders to produce the information and the details upon which the Allies could plan their strategy. As May advanced and the operations to imprison the servicemen and to resettle the civilians began to show results, it was time to reduce the authority of Doenitz's government. There had been flickers of disobedience from the very first days when Lindemann, the German Supreme Commander in Denmark, ordered that his troops were to refuse any orders to lay down their arms and were to resist with force, any attempt to disarm them. Then there was the flurry of signals stressing that the surrender of the German armies in the West had no relevance to the Eastern Front where the fighting was to continue, as it did until 9 May.

Above: A British bren-gunner guards Speer, Doenitz and Jodl as they go into captivity.

The Allied screw turned a little tighter when a report – one can almost hear the shock in the voice of the German officer as he dictated it – that there had been a parade on board the *Patria* during which the White Ensign had been hoisted and that the German officers and crew of the ship had been ordered to take part in the parade. A further clamp-down came with the order which forbad the wearing of any device which carried the swastika emblem of the Nazi Party. The national eagle, worn by all ranks in each of the services, carried the device. The removal of the swastika was insulting enough, according to the German officers, but worse was to come. Medals or awards from 1935, all carried the swastika and had, therefore, to be taken down. Thus, all of those who had won Germany's highest honours for bravery or who could show on their tunic the evidence of their wounds or their specialist skills, had to take them down. Medals from the First World War or Service Crosses awarded before Hitler came to power were acceptable.

One by one, piece by piece, layer by layer, the fabric of authority was peeled away from the Doenitz government until it was clear that it no longer had a function to fulfill. On 22 May, the Grand Admiral was directed to go to the *Patria* accompanied by Jodl and von Friedeburg. When the trio arrived at the dockside the following morning they noticed that the German sentries were no longer posted and that the officer of the watch was not on duty. There were, however, a number of photographers present on the quayside. The German leaders and the Allied delegates sat at a long table. In a short, five minute speech, the German commanders were informed that they were now under arrest. In reply to an invitation to speak, Doenitz replied coldly that in such a situation words were superfluous.

It is with Doenitz's words that we end this story. Von Friedeburg, who could not accept the shame, joined those to whom suicide was the only alternative to humiliation. Jodl was hanged as a war criminal. Doenitz himself, was tried at Nuremberg and was sentenced to a term of imprisonment.

Above: one of the prisoner-of-war camps overrun during the last weeks of the war. While they wait to go home, the prisoners here at Badenstadt leave their own comment on the accommodation. **Below:** VE Day celebrations in Rome.

Above: Marshal Koniev and General Omar Bradley toast each other in a victory salute at a banquet during their meeting on 5 May 1945.

EPILOGUE

Armageddon had passed and left a destroyed Germany in its wake. Her principal cities lay in ruins and beneath their shattered buildings lay the corrupting dead in unnumbered thousands. Some were the victims of the Allied bombing which had scourged those cities and others had been killed in the fighting. Among these were boys of the Hitler Youth buried under the rubble of houses from which they had attempted to halt the Allied tank armadas. Some of the dead were the victims of personal outrage; a girl raped, murdered and then thrust untidily into a hole in a shattered pile of bricks, or else the victim of an SS flying court-martial, shot and flung into the crumbling cellar of a bombed house.

Germany's armies were shattered and her surviving soldiers were the captives of nations which hated them. For some of those nations, summary execution and sickening brutality had been the norm, whereas the Anglo-Americans believed the average German soldier to have been a conscript who ought to be returned home to rebuild his shattered Fatherland. The Anglo-Americans could afford to be humane. They had not had their countries occupied. Humanity towards the Germans was an emotion which the other Allies could not share and under them the captive Germans were treated as slave labour.

If the defeat had enslaved the German men, it humiliated German women. Those in the east and in the south-east suffered terribly in the excesses of those first weeks, but by the end of May the worst was over. Rapes still occurred, but within weeks the officers of the Red Army had gained control of their men and were prepared to act with brutal severity. One Breslau housewife who had been violated staggered from the house ruins upon whose rubble she had been despoiled and fell into the arms of a Soviet officer. He listened to her accusation, walked towards her attacker and shot him dead. Although rape was most frequent in the Slav lands it was by no means unique there. In the French Zone of Austria such attacks by drunken Moroccan soldiers were not infrequent. The French, with typical *savoir-faire*, converted a quiet and secluded Vorarlberg nunnery into a maternity hospital where the rape victims could choose to retain the child or hand it over for adoption. Rape was not a common British crime and was rare among the regiments. American soldiers committed every type of excess and in one period during the fighting in Normandy there were five hundred cases of rape reported. The High Command was severe with those convicted and seventy-seven US soldiers were shot to death. In May 1945, with the war over, the troops would again be firmly under the control of their officers, but there were likely to be difficulties with the soldiers for they had no sexual outlets.

In Germany immediately after the war's end, no fraternization was allowed between soldiers of the Western armies and the German people. Loaded with men of the Eighth Army departing on their first leave to the UK after years of overseas service, this truck passes a sign on the border of Germany and Luxembourg ordering 'No Fraternization'.

Anglo-American armies did not run military brothels and in both Germany and Austria there was, to begin with, a total ban on any fraternization with the civilians. It was a court-martial charge to talk to any German other than to issue an order, but such a law was completely unworkable. The 'non-frat' ban was lifted in July after which it became possible for Allied fighting men to meet Germans on fields other than those of combat. In the hot summer of 1945, in the Western Zones, the well-endowed German girls displayed themselves by lakes and in swimming-pools to the only available men, the Allied soldiers. The girls were lithe, lovely and very willing to exchange the joys of their bodies, their only possessions, for those things which the soldiers had in abundance: food, chocolate, soap and cigarettes. The cigarette had been recognized currency in wartime Germany and gained in commercial value in the time of post-war shortages. There were stories of houses and villas changing hands for astronomical numbers of 'Lucky Strikes', 'Camels' or 'Senior Service' and indeed there was little that the cigarette could not buy. Germany became a cashless economy where money was not used except to pay for the most trivial things. For important purchases, for goods available only on the black market, which had existed from the first days of the war, there was barter. How to supplement the meagre official ration was an important preoccupation. Those who had anything of value exchanged it, while those with access to food – the farmers – lived well and obtained for their homes the treasured heirlooms which other families had been forced to surrender to keep themselves alive.

Armageddon, which had destroyed Germany economically, also smashed her politically and it was accepted that permanent Allied Four-Power control would remove her, as an independent nation, from the political scene. The differences in national policy and the administration of the individual zones of the defeated nation led to that suspicion and hostility between the Allies which Dr Goebbels had forecast. Those differences led, in time, to today's two Germanys. For ordinary Germans the question of Four-Power control and economic problems were of little consequence, initially. There were more immediate priorities. It was fortunate that the summer of 1945 was long and hot and dry, because tens of thousands were homeless. In addition to those whose houses had been destroyed by the bombing and street fighting, there were millions who had fled or who had been deported. They, too, were without shelter. The immediate priority for all those without a roof over their heads was to build a shelter. Food was a problem, but at least a rationing system had been introduced and was working, even if the amounts received were small. All over Germany the search for supplementary food occupied most minds. Those employed by the Western Occupation Forces were fortunate. They received a midday meal of bread and soup and did not have to surrender precious food coupons.

In the Russian Zone teams of women, who were recruited to clear the rubble-choked streets, were marched to a communal meal at midday. Formed into human chains, these women passed whole bricks from the cluttered roads to a point where they were piled up to be re-used as building material for the reconstruction programmes. Half-bricks were used to fill the craters and to remake the broken road surfaces. Little was wasted. In Vienna brick clearing was a condition of entry to the University and the students worked with a will. The Berlin work gangs were not always employed locally. There is an account of a group of women who were taken one May morning from their Berlin site and who did not return for two years. They had been taken first to a Polish factory where they had dismantled machinery and had gone from there to a series of factories, until at last in Kaunus in Lithuania they worked as farm labourers. The discharge and return of that group was as casual as had been their abduction. They were ordered to board a train and eventually arrived in Berlin, a vastly different city from the one which they had left in the spring of 1945. Then there had been destruction and hopelessness. Now the ruins had been cleared and there was hope of a better life.

After food and housing the third hunger was for news; news of the outside world, and when the first newspapers came onto the streets queues formed to buy them. Copies were sold, returned and then resold, so great was the hunger for news of a world away from the battlefield. The next hunger to be stilled was the cultural one. The radio was useful in this context but, in the minds of many, was associated with propaganda. Live entertainment was a better distraction from the harshness of contemporary life. The Russians understood this spiritual hunger better than the Western allies and were prepared to subsidize massively, this 'hearts and minds' operation. They provided first-class artistes and orchestras to give symphony concerts and gave to those performers preferential treatment and a higher ration scale. It was not as if western Germany were a cultural desert; the Western Allies did their best, but were not really aware of the emotional needs of the German people. German and Austrian singers, instrumentalists; actors and painters grouped in small Collectives to revitalize the Arts and to find employment for their talents. One group of Austria's most celebrated actors and actresses evacuated themselves to Bad Ischl where they set up a very active workshop. In Vienna, the cast of the Opera House went into rehearsal for its first post-War production – Mozart's *Figaro*; of course. Slowly, the cultural life of Germany and Austria was returning.

Austria is stressed here because this was another German-speaking country with which the Allies had to deal. Allied intentions towards Germany had been clear-cut. As an aggressor she had to be defeated and held in subjection so that there would be no third world war. Towards Austria, however, there was an ambivalence which is reflected in the attitude of the invading armies. Some claimed to have come as liberators; others stated that they were conquerors. If it was difficult for the Austrians to know how to greet the incoming soldiers it was equally hard for the fighting men who were being shot at to appreciate the subtle difference between his being shot at in an enemy country and being fired upon in a friendly one. At combat level there was suspicion and watchfulness and a quick burst of fire when in doubt and to hell with what the top brass said about being a liberator.

Above: Red Army field kitchens help to feed the people of Berlin in the difficult days at the end of the war.
Below: displaced persons. A civilian 'trek', having fled from the advancing Red Army and reached the British zone of Germany, waits for permission to cross into the West.

Behind the crumbling German front-lines Nazi officials from Bavaria had scrambled back into the Salzkammergut, one of the last remaining bits of the Third Reich. In eastern Styria the Red Army's advance had compelled the Germans to march prisoners of war and political detainees westwards, while Jugoslav pressure in the south together with growing partisan activity in Austria's southern provinces had forced the Nazi bosses to move into the Salzburg region. That part of Austria became, in those last days of the war, a pocket filled with an assortment of peoples, including an entire Hungarian army which had remained loyal to its German comrades in arms. According to John Brightman, formerly a member of that army, but now a respected member of a Yorkshire council, one of its élite units, the Saint Laszlo Division, was not disbanded by the British, but was held intact in case it should be needed to fight the Jugoslavs. Its soldiers were given special status by the Americans and British and its men were not deported. Ferenc Szalasi, the Hungarian Prime Minister, was one of the few exceptions to this non-repatriation order. He fled from Hungary with the Magyar objects of legitimacy; that country's most sacred relics including the mummified right hand of King Stephen, his crown, sceptre and orb. These historical pieces of treasure which, to the Magyars, were the objects of government, underwent a series of adventures before they were handed over to the US authorities by Colonel Patjas, Commander of the Hungarian Crown Guard. They were flown immediately to Fort Knox. Szalasi was returned to Hungary and condemned by the Communist regime which, according to ancient custom, had him garrotted to death.

In addition to the Hungarian Government, the leaders of Roumania, of Bulgaria, of the Croat nation and of the Serbs all ended up, in greater or lesser degrees of comfort, as refugees in the Salzburg area of Austria. But not all those who fled there were European. Other exotic creatures living out the Reich's last days included the Mufti of Jerusalem and Raschid Ali, who had fomented a revolt against the British in 1941. There were also officers of the Indian Legion, a small band of traitors to the King-Emperor.

Austria is a small country with a small population; eight million in 1938 according to official figures. In May 1945 that number had increased by three million non-Austrians. Those among this sudden influx who were soldiers would leave the country and pass into prison camps. But even when the military had gone there would still be more than a million people who would be absorbed into the population. Austria has always had a record of Christian generosity and, in accepting refugees numbering more than one eighth of her population, she demonstrated her compassion to the world. Sweden, which had avoided the bloody war and would not be too seriously affected by the post-war shortages, could have set an example. She did not, but instead handed back many German soldiers who had landed on her shores seeking sanctuary, to the revenge of the Soviet system.

The problem of the refugee was the great issue in the post-Armageddon world, but it was one that was so easy to overlook. By the end of May 1945, the guns had fallen silent and under the high summer skies it seemed as if

there were, once again, peace and quiet in Europe. But those who listened
with their souls could hear the sound of weeping. This could be heard if you
wanted to hear it. That was the criterion – if you wanted to. And few did.
The soldiers of the occupation armies did not listen because they were
enjoying a time of ease and of luxury; the fruits of victory. In any case few of
them understood German and, thus, had no appreciation of the problems
facing the members of the defeated race. Why should they worry about the
Jerries and the refugees? The Army was being fed. It stood to reason that the
German civilians must be getting their rations, too. So the soldiers did not
listen to the weeping.

The ordinary German civilians, among whom the Displaced Persons lived,
did not hear. Not because they did not want to, but because they had the
pressures of everyday life to contend with. These occupied their minds and
left them no time to listen to the cries of brothers and sisters worse off than
they, who were existing in camps all round Germany. Into the Displaced
Persons' camps, those dustbins of misery, were flung the powerless and weak
and they were condemned to live there, in some cases for decades, despised
and rejected because of an accident of birth.

But there were some who listened and there were some who helped. It was
the inspiration of one American soldier to introduce the policy of aid for
Europe and the debt which the nations of the continent owe to George
Marshall, is incalculable. Insufficient acknowledgement has been given to the
architect of that most unselfish campaign of help which enabled there to be
life again after Armageddon. Voices in the British Parliament spoke of the
terror which had been unleashed against the Volksdeutsch in the Sudetenland and in Jugoslavia. Newspaper leaders condemned the atrocities, but the
British people were still at war, sending their young men off to the Far East
and the people were, in any case, unsympathetic to the Nazis – the blanket
term for all Germans. Not until Victor Gollancz went to Germany and
published his *German Diary*, was there, at last, an awareness of the evils that
had been committed in the name of Democracy and a determination to
support the Marshall plan for Europe; for all of Europe. For, although much
of the carnage and destruction produced by Armageddon had been on
German soil, the war and its aftermath had affected every country on the
continent. We cannot, therefore, end this narrative abruptly in Germany, for
some reference must be made to post-war political developments in those
countries which have been mentioned in this book.

The people of Czechoslovakia who had welcomed the Red Army as
liberators soon found them to be no liberators but jailers. Czech Socialist
politicians who thought naively that they would rule their newly independent
country, soon found that they had no power. When they had served their
purpose they were removed. Masaryk, for example, fell out of a convenient
window. A hard-line, Soviet-supporting regime runs Czechoslovakia now,
and I think of lovely, golden Prague as the most unhappy city I have visited in
the years since the end of the War. The SS General whom we met in the
chapter on Prague – Karl Hermann Frank – went to the gallows.

Jugoslavia is the most surprising development in post-war Europe. She broke away from Soviet influence, renounced all territorial claims and, under the inspired leadership of Marshal Tito, was converted from an impoverished Balkan backwater into one of the great holiday areas of Europe. But before she broke with Moscow, Jugoslavia was a loyal satellite and had taken revenge upon the Germans in standard, Communist fashion. A great number of German senior commanders, headed by Field Marshal Loehr, were shot or hanged. The native enemies, such as Mihailovitch, whose only crime had been to demand freedom for their peoples, were tried and executed – judicially.

In Italy the post-war situation was dominated by the danger of the vast, Communist-led, partisan army, well-equipped and conscious of its power. Across the eastern border was Tito's partisan force and across the western frontier was a powerful Left-controlled guerrilla force in France. The whole of southern Europe was endangered. Those who recalled political history remembered the events of the 1930s in Austria, where the armed and revolutionary Left had sought to overthrow the elected government. Europe faced, in the summer of 1945, a repetition of that bitter struggle, but this time in Italy. In long and hard discussion the Italian guerrilla leaders were persuaded of the need to disarm. To placate their injured pride great ceremonial parades were held at each of which flamboyant speeches were made and the partisan units were lauded and saluted by the most senior Allied military commanders. The attempt by the Italian Left to gain power through the gun had been foiled and they turned instead to the voting urn where in one election after another they gained strong representation and a powerful voice in the new Republic.

Austria remained occupied by the Four Powers for years. Then, convinced by a guarantee of Austria's total neutrality, the Soviet leaders signed a State Treaty. Ninety days later and the evidences of Four-Power administration were gone. Austria as a nation and the Austrians as individuals, have since that time led the sheltered life of dedicated neutrals, while all around them were political changes, almost revolutionary in their scope. The chief of these was the re-emergence of Germany as the chief ally in both the Western and the Eastern camps. Germany today enjoys a status and a prestige that would have been unimaginable four decades ago. Then, forty years away, the Reich was dead, Armageddon had been fought and those Germans who survived, the little men, were seeking to re-establish themselves by taking up again those jobs which they had once done and living again the life they had enjoyed before the war began. For many it was difficult to adjust. Once they had fought with conquering armies; now they were the vanquished. Their pride could not come to terms with the condition in which they now found themselves. For others it was less a question of personal feelings than of possessions. They had lost everything and had to begin all over again, in a new province, a new city, a new country. There were, however, others for whom the transition from war to peace was no difficult passage. The story of Artur Schoster is just such a case of an easy transition. In his case the only

Above: among the final groups of German soldiers who came in to surrender were these Galician SS cavalrymen, who surrendered on 11 May in the St Veit area of the British V Corps. **Right:** in the weeks following the end of the war, patrols from the British Army went out to round up SS, Wehrwolves and others who had not obeyed the order to surrender. This picture shows a patrol from the London Irish Rifles of 78th Division at a farmhouse in Austria.

thing that changed was the colour of the uniform of his superiors, the rank badges they wore and the language they spoke, for he exchanged the Nazi police organization for that of the American Provost Corps. In his case it really was a case of *plus ça change*.

Schoster was a Criminal Commissioner in the police force of South Tyrol, and he pursued, under the Americans, a gang that he had first accused when Himmler ran the German police force. There is in the Department of Documents in the Imperial War Museum a file dealing with Schoster's case. It is a thin file, but it is interesting for what Schoster claims in his report. The criminal acts of what he calls 'The Wendig Group' of criminals were carried out 'through a network of informers and the area of their operations comprised the entire territory of Europe which was under the control of the German Armed Forces'. The group was guilty, so Schoster claims, 'of the illegal purchase of machinery, of works of art and of property'.

In his report to the Americans, Schoster stated that he had been obstructed in his investigations during the Nazi period because the 'Wendig Gang' drew its authority direct from Himmler whose protection shielded them, SS officers and civilians alike, despite the fact that their acts 'involved breaches of monetary, economic or other legal regulations'. The report mentions crates being brought into a castle which had been purchased by Schwendt, one of the SS officers of the gang. The same man is also accused of bigamy, currency deals, transactions in forged English banknotes, blackmail and murder. The impression left by Schoster's report is that the SS were either preparing safe houses en route to Switzerland, as part of an SS escape route, or else that, as early as April 1944, the more far-seeing officers of that organization had begun to ensure that if the outcome of the war went against Germany they, at least, would be financially protected.

The relish with which Police Commissioner Schoster continued his investigations under the Americans and the gusto with which he wrote his reports are all very evident. Nothing could be permitted to obstruct him in his determination to put the criminals of the 'Wendig Gang' behind bars. The end of the story is, unfortunately, not known. The file contains only his report, but it would be nice to think that the American officers to whom Schoster made his report did do something about the blackmailing, sexually athletic, murdering and black-marketing SS Major Schwendt. To Schoster it mattered little who formed the government. If a crime had been committed the culprit had to be caught and brought to trial. Schoster had opened his file under the Nazis, showing great courage in treading on such dangerous ground in accusing those under the protection of Heinrich Himmler. He closed the file under the Americans, not out of pleasure in denouncing the criminals of the SS to the occupying power, but because he was a simple copper who believed that crime should not be allowed to pay. His transition from war to peace was an easy one and I see Schoster as a representative of optimism and, despite every adverse thing, that first summer of peace since 1939, was a time of optimism and of hope. At the end of the second major war in a quarter of a century, the people of Europe had a new hope that out of the ashes of war a better means of managing international affairs might be produced. Already the structure of the United Nations had been formed. Already the principles of the Atlantic Charter had been expressed so that all might enjoy 'Freedom of thought, freedom of speech, freedom from want, and freedom from fear.' Inspired by such noble sentiments Europe would, it was hoped, unite and work towards those expressed ideals.

The summer of 1945 was a time of hope and courageous optimism. For the Germans Armageddon had come and gone and now the survivors of that slaughter could rebuild upon the ruins of a discredited Reich a new nation which would be based on the principles expressed in the national anthem; 'Unity and Right and Freedom for the German Fatherland'.

Four decades after Armageddon there are Germans still waiting for their hopes to be realized.

APPENDIX 1
CHRONOLOGY OF EVENTS

March

18/23   The Red Army tries unsuccessfully to break the front of Eighteenth German Army during the sixth battle for Kurland.

19   Hitler orders the implementing of his scorched earth policy. Factories, industries and sources of supply are to be destroyed as the Germans retreat.

20   The Jugoslav forces open an offensive in Dalmatia.

23   The offensive by 2nd Ukrainian Front splits Second German Army into three groups: that on Hela, on Gotenhofen and in Danzig.

23/24   The British and Canadian Armies cross the Rhine.

23   Colonel General Loehr becomes Supreme Commander South-East.

26   Seven Allied armies which have crossed the Rhine advance eastwards against diminishing German resistance.

26   Montgomery issues the order forbidding fraternization between British troops and German civilians.

27   The last V2s fall on London.
The leading members of the Polish Underground organization are invited to meet Marshal Zhukov. They are all arrested, charged with treasonable activities in the rear of the Red Army and are imprisoned.

28   General Eisenhower, the Supreme Commander of the Allied Expeditionary Forces, advises Marshal Stalin that the objective of the Allied armies is 'to advance along the Erfurt–Leipzig line and to reach the upper Elbe. His forces will stand along the line of the Elbe and await the arrival of the Red Army.' Eisenhower further assures Stalin that the Allied forces will then take out the 'Alpine Redoubt'.

29   The Red Army crosses the Austrian frontier.

30   The city of Danzig is captured by the Red Army. The defenders retreat to an area around the lower Vistula which they hold to the end of the war.

31   General Eisenhower gives orders to Field Marshal Montgomery that 21st Army Group is not to advance upon Berlin.

April

1   With the joining of First and Ninth US Armies at Lippstadt, German Army Group 'B', is encircled in the 'Ruhr pocket'.

1/15   During this period the evacuation by sea from the Hela peninsula rescues 96,000 wounded, 81,000 refugees and 66,000 soldiers.

5   The Red Army opens its assault upon Vienna.
The end of the V2 operations. The last rockets were aimed at Brussels, Antwerp and Liège.

6   The offensive by the Red Army in East Prussia leads to the surrender of Königsberg on 9 April.

7   'Operation Wehrwolf' takes place. Over Western Germany 183 German pilots attempt to ram the Fortresses and Superforts of the 8th USAAF. More than 130 German aircraft are lost for the destruction of 23 American machines.

9   The British Eighth Army opens its offensive on the Adriatic coast of Italy.

11   The US Ninth Army establishes a bridgehead on the River Elbe to the south of Magdeburg.

12   Keitel, Himmler and Bormann sign an order which demands that German cities will be defended 'to the utmost'.

13   Vienna falls to the Red Army.
      A second bridgehead is established on the Elbe by US Ninth Army.

14   The US Fifth Army opens its offensive in Italy.
      The British capture Arnhem.

15   The 9th Soviet Guards Army captures St Poelten in Austria and halts its westward advance.
      Hitler issues a preliminary order that in the event of Germany being divided into two parts, Field Marshal Busch is to be the military commander of the north-west.

16   The last organized opposition in the Ruhr pocket is destroyed. Field Marshal Model, Commander of Army Group 'B', commits suicide.
      The Ninth Army's bridgeheads on the east bank of the Elbe are smashed by the German Twelfth Army.
      The 1st Ukrainian and 1st White Russian Fronts open the attack upon Berlin.

18   The US Ninth Army captures Magdeburg.
      Operations by Canadian First Army are halted when the Germans blow the dykes and flood western Holland.
      The US Third Army under Patton, crosses the Czech frontier and advances into western Bohemia.

18/19   The last British air raid on Berlin.
      The British Second Army reaches the Elbe at Lauenberg.

20   Hitler's 50th birthday.
      The US First Army captures Leipzig.
      Hitler divides the Reich territory into a 'northern area' under Grand Admiral Doenitz and a 'southern area' under Field Marshal Kesselring.
      During the afternoon of 20 April Red Army artillery begins to bombard the centre of Berlin.

21   Polish troops fighting with the British Eighth Army capture Bologna.

22   Hitler decides to remain in Berlin.

23   Hitler discharges Field Marshal Goering from all his offices and promotes Field Marshal Ritter von Greim to command the Luftwaffe.
      British Second Army reaches the suburbs of Hamburg.

24   The German Ninth Army is surrounded west of Frankfurt. Some of
        its units escape the encirclement and link with Twelfth Army.
        Together they withdraw to the Elbe.
        Keitel and Jodl leave Berlin for Rheinsberg where they co-ordinate
        the attempts to raise the siege of Berlin.
        British Eighth Army captures Ferrara. The US Fifth Army enters La
        Spezia and reaches the Po north-west of Bologna.
25   Berlin now surrounded and cut off.
        Under pressure from the Red Army the defenders of Pillau carry out
        a fighting retreat down the Hela peninsula.
        Elements of US First Army link with 5th Guards Army at Torgau.
        Germany is now bisected.
        The Fifth and Eighth Armies in Italy cross the Po and capture
        Mantua, Reggio and Parma.
        The news reaches London that Himmler has asked Count Bernadotte
        to approach the Allies with the offer of a capitulation.
        The San Francisco Conference proclaims the Charter of the United
        Nations.
26   Bruenn in Czechoslovakia is captured by the Red Army.
        British Second Army captures Bremen.
        The US 5th Army takes Verona.
27   A provisional government is formed in Vienna under Karl Renner.
        The US Fifth Army reaches Genoa.
28   The offensive to relieve Berlin by German Twelfth Army fails.
29   Mussolini and Clara Petacci shot by Communist partisans.
        In Italy the instrument of surrender of German Army Group 'C' is
        signed, but the capitulation is not announced until 2 May.
        British Second Army crosses the Elbe at Lauenberg.
        An agreement between the British and the Germans allows aircraft of
        Bomber Command to carry out airdrops of food and clothing to the
        Dutch civil population in the areas still held by the Germans.
        The British 56th Division captures Venice.
        Hitler marries Eva Braun. He then signs his private and political testa-
        ments and names Doenitz as President of the Reich.
30   Hitler commits suicide and is cremated.
        The Red Army hoists the Soviet banner over the Reichstag at
        14.30 hrs.
        The 'Ulbricht Group' flies from Moscow to set up a Communist
        government in the Soviet zone of occupation.
        The US Seventh Army captures Munich.
        The US Fifth Army takes Turin.
        Jugoslav units reach the suburbs of Trieste.

May
1   Doenitz advised by Bormann of Hitler's death. This news is broadcast
        to the German people at 22.30 hrs.

Goebbels commits suicide in Berlin and his body is cremated.

The 2nd New Zealand Division of Eighth Army links up with the Jugoslav Army of Liberation in Trieste.

Other units of the partisan forces occupy Gorizia and the Istrian peninsula.

2   The fall of Berlin.

Doenitz moves his headquarters to Flensburg. Schwerin von Krosignk replaces von Ribbentrop as Foreign Minister.

Elements of 6th Airborne Division meet the Red Army at Wismar.

The last RAF raids by Bomber Command. Kiel is attacked from the air and in the raid upon Lübeck a number of ships loaded with refugees from the east and with concentration camp inmates are hit. In one ship, the *Arcona*, 7,000 prisoners from north German concentration camps are killed.

3   The US Seventh Army occupies Innsbruck and part of VI Corps is sent southwards through the Brenner to meet a group from US Fifth Army coming out of Italy.

The British Second Army enters Hamburg.

4   The surrender of all German forces in Holland and north-west Germany and Denmark is signed at Field Marshal Montgomery's Headquarters on Luneburg Heath.

German Army Group 'Vistula' seeks to break through so as to be taken prisoner by the British.

German Army Group 'G' surrenders to General Devers and this ends the fighting in Bavaria and western Austria.

5   A Government for 'carry on the Reich business' is formed under the leadership of Count von Krosignk.

The Americans capture Linz.

In Jugoslavia, German Army Group 'E', moves northwards towards the Austrian border.

The people of Prague rise against the Germans.

6   The final convoy leaves from German ports for Hela where it will rescue 43,000 people in this operation.

The Red Army opens its final operation against Schoerner's Army Group in Czechoslovakia.

The 'fortress' city of Breslau falls to the Red Army.

Patton's V Corps takes Pilsen.

Eisenhower orders Third Army to halt its advance into Czechoslovakia.

The US Fifth Army enters Austria from the south.

Doenitz discharges Himmler from all his offices.

7   The surrender document covering all German forces signed in Eisenhower's Headquarters in Reims. The capitulation to take effect from 00.01 hrs on 9 May.

German Twelfth Army surrenders to the Americans.

The Red Army reaches the line Wismar–Schwerin–Wittenberge.

Other Soviet forces reach the Elbe.

In Jugoslavia, the 220,000-strong Croatian Army tries to fight its way through to Austria but its advance is checked by Eighth Army and Tito's forces. Eighth Army enters Klagenfurt ahead of Tito's forces.

9   The surrender of German forces takes effect after the surrender document is signed at Soviet Headquarters in Berlin.

The Channel islands liberated.

10   With the surrender of Army Group Kurland, 208,000 men pass into Soviet captivity.

Prague captured by the Red Army.

Dunkirk surrenders.

11   The British and American members of the 'Control Commission of the OKW', make contact with the Doenitz government and the OKW officers.

The Czech government in exile returns to Prague.

12   The Serbian regiments which fought for Germany surrender to Eighth Army, but are handed over to the Jugoslavs and, together with the Slovenes, are murdered.

13   Field Marshal Keitel arrested. Colonel Jodl takes over as Chief of OKW.

14   The German Army Group in East Prussia surrenders and more than 150,000 men pass into Soviet captivity.

15   Between Bleiburg and Marburg a major part of the Croatian Army, some 80,000 soldiers and 30,000 civilians, chiefly women and children, are murdered by the partisan army.

17   The Soviet Press criticizes the Doenitz government in Flensburg.

23   The arrest of the members of the Doenitz government brings the Third Reich to an end.

Himmler commits suicide in Luneburg.

25   Jugoslav forces, which have been occupying parts of Carinthia since the middle of May, pull back out of Klagenfurt.

APPENDIX 2
THE LAST COMMUNIQUÉ
ISSUED BY THE GERMAN ARMED FORCES
DURING THE SECOND WORLD WAR

9th May, 1945. From the headquarters of the Grand Admiral the High Command reports:

In East Prussia yesterday German divisions were still defending the mouth of the River Vistula and the western sector of the Frische Nehrung. The 7th Division in particular distinguished itself. Panzer General von Saucken, the Supreme Commander, was awarded the Diamonds and Swords to the Knights Cross of the Iron Cross in recognition of the exemplary behaviour of his soldiers.

Forming an advanced bulwark, Colonel General Hilpert's armies in Kurland covered themselves with untarnishable honour throughout the months of bitter fighting against vastly superior Soviet infantry and tank forces. They rejected a premature surrender. Aircraft first transported wounded and then children were evacuated to the west. Commanders and officers remained with their men. At midnight all movement and fighting ceased on the German side in accordance with the conditions laid down.

The defenders of Breslau, having resisted the attacks of the Soviets for two months, bowed to the enemy superiority.

On the south-eastern and eastern Fronts, from Bruenn to the Elbe near Dresden, the orders to cease fighting were obeyed. A Czech uprising covering the whole of Bohemia and Moravia may affect the implementing of the capitulation in that area. To date no reports have been received by OKW from the Loehr, Rendulic or Schoerner Army Groups.

The garrisons of the Atlantic fortresses, our troops in northern Norway and the Occupation forces in the Aegean islands, through their obedience and discipline have demonstrated German military honour.

From midnight the guns have been silent on all Fronts. The Grand Admiral has ordered the armed forces to cease a struggle which was hopeless. The honourable struggle which has lasted almost six years is, therefore, at an end. It has brought us not only great victories but also heavy defeats. The German armed forces have been overcome, finally, by a superior force. The German soldier, loyal to the oath he had sworn, has achieved imperishable things in this struggle for his people. To the end the homeland supported him with all its strength, despite its own suffering. History will one day judge objectively this unique effort of the front and of the homeland. The achievements and sacrifices of German soldiers at sea, on the land and in the air cannot be denied by our opponents. Every soldier can, therefore, lay down his weapon with pride and in this, the bitterest hour of our history, begin to work bravely and honourably for our people.

In this bitter hour the armed forces remember those comrades who fell facing the enemy. Those dead compel us to work loyally, obediently and with discipline on behalf of our fatherland which is bleeding from innumerable wounds.

BIBLIOGRAPHY

AHLFEN, H. VON, *So kämpfte Breslau*. Munich, 1959
BARBARASCHIN, *Die Wieder Operation*
BUSSE, T., *Die letzte Schlacht der 9. Armee*
DOENITZ, K. *10 Jahre und 20 Tage*. Bonn, 1958
HALDER, F. *Kriegstagebuch*
KEILIG, *Das deutsche Heer. 1939–1945*. Bad Nauheim, 1955
KEMPKA, *Ich habe Hitler verbrannt*. Murburg Verlag, 1957
KLIETMANN, *Die Waffen SS. Eine Dokumentation*
KORKODINOV, *The Pager Operation*
LASCH, O. *So fiel Königsberg*. Munich, 1958
MABIRE, J. *Berlin in Todeskampfe*. Oldendorff, 1977
MAJENOSKA AND SOZANSKA, *Die Schlacht von Breslau*. Union, 1977
MONTGOMERY, B. *From Normandy to the Baltic*
PATTON, G. *War as I knew it*
RAUCHENSTEINER, M. *1945: Entscheidung für Oesterreich*. Graz, 1976
RENDULIC, L. *Gakaempft, gesiegt, geschlagen*
SCHEIBERT, H. *Panzergrenadier Division 'GD'*. 1970
SCHMIDT-RICHBERG, *Der Endkampf auf dem Balkan*. 1955
SCHULZ-NAUMANN, *Die letzten dreissig Tage*. Universitas, Munich
TELPUKOVSKY, B. *Die Geschichte des Grossen*
— *Vaterländischen Krieges. 1941–1945*. 1981
ZIENSONE, *Die Kaempfe um die Befreiung von Lausitz*. Bautzen, 1975

Unpublished sources
GEYER. OBERST i.G: Kaempfe bei Heeresgruppe 'H' 10/3 – 8/5/45
OKW: Kapitulationsverhandlungen 4–22 Mai. 1945
OKW: Events leading to the German capitulation April 1945
OKW: DETAILS: Details of the German surrender 7–12 May 1945
OHLENDORF: Proposal for an internal economic Intelligence service.
SEEGER, LIEUTENANT-GENERAL W. Bericht uber die Taetigkeit des Divisions 405, von Sommer 1944 bis Frühjahr 1945
WESTPHAL, General. Orders referring to the Armistice of Army Group 'G'. 6 May 1945

In addition to the above, the war histories of British, German and American units, war diaries, military journals and individual papers. To complete the personal background to the purely military events interviews were conducted with civilians and former soldiers.

INDEX